CONSERVATION, TOURISM, AND IDENTITY OF CONTEMPORARY COMMUNITY ART

A Case Study of Felipe Seade's Mural
"Allegory to Work"

CONSERVATION, TOURISM, AND IDENTITY OF CONTEMPORARY COMMUNITY ART

A Case Study of Felipe Seade's Mural
"Allegory to Work"

Edited by

Virginia Santamarina-Campos, PhD
María Ángeles Carabal-Montagud, PhD
María De Miguel-Molina, PhD
Blanca De Miguel-Molina, PhD

APPLE ACADEMIC PRESS

Apple Academic Press Inc.
3333 Mistwell Crescent
Oakville, ON L6L 0A2 Canada

Apple Academic Press Inc.
9 Spinnaker Way
Waretown, NJ 08758 USA

© 2018 by Apple Academic Press, Inc.
Exclusive worldwide distribution by CRC Press, a member of Taylor & Francis Group
No claim to original U.S. Government works
Printed in the United States of America on acid-free paper
International Standard Book Number-13: 978-1-77188-401-3 (Hardcover)
International Standard Book Number-13: 978-1-315-20958-6 (eBook)

All rights reserved. No part of this work may be reprinted or reproduced or utilized in any form or by any electric, mechanical or other means, now known or hereafter invented, including photocopying and recording, or in any information storage or retrieval system, without permission in writing from the publisher or its distributor, except in the case of brief excerpts or quotations for use in reviews or critical articles.

This book contains information obtained from authentic and highly regarded sources. Reprinted material is quoted with permission and sources are indicated. Copyright for individual articles remains with the authors as indicated. A wide variety of references are listed. Reasonable efforts have been made to publish reliable data and information, but the authors, editors, and the publisher cannot assume responsibility for the validity of all materials or the consequences of their use. The authors, editors, and the publisher have attempted to trace the copyright holders of all material reproduced in this publication and apologize to copyright holders if permission to publish in this form has not been obtained. If any copyright material has not been acknowledged, please write and let us know so we may rectify in any future reprint.

Trademark Notice: Registered trademark of products or corporate names are used only for explanation and identification without intent to infringe.

Library and Archives Canada Cataloguing in Publication

Conservation, tourism, and identity of contemporary community art : a case study of Felipe Seade's mural "Allegory to work" / edited by Virginia Santamarina Campos, PhD, María Ángeles Carabal Montagud, PhD, María de Miguel Molina, PhD, Blanca De Miguel Molina, PhD.
Includes bibliographical references and index.
Issued in print and electronic formats.
ISBN 978-1-77188-401-3 (hardcover).--ISBN 978-1-315-20958-6 (PDF)
1. Seade, Felipe, 1912-1969. Alegoría al trabajo. 2. Mural painting and decoration--Conservation and restoration--Uruguay--Case studies. 3. Cultural property--Conservation and restoration--Uruguay--Case studies. 4. Social realism--Uruguay--Case studies. 5. Art and society--Uruguay--Case studies. 6. Art and globalization--Uruguay--Case studies. 7. Sustainable tourism--Uruguay--Case studies. 8. Hospitality industry--Uruguay--Case studies. I. Carabal Montagud, María Ángeles, editor II. Santamarina Campos, Virginia, editor III. Miguel Molina, María de, editor IV. Miguel Molina, Blanca de, editor
ND429.S43A44 2017   759.9895   C2017-905556-9   C2017-905557-7

Library of Congress Cataloging-in-Publication Data

Names: Santamarina Campos, Virginia, editor. | Uruguay. Comisiân del Patrimonio Cultural de la Naciân. | Universidad Politêcnica de Valencia.
Title: Conservation, tourism, and identity of contemporary community art : a case study of Felipe Seade's mural "Allegory to work" / editors: Virginia Santamarina Campos, María Ángeles Carabal Montagud, María de Miguel Molina, Blanca De Miguel Molina.
Description: Toronto; Waretown, NJ : Apple Academic Press, 2018. | Includes bibliographical references and index.
Identifiers: LCCN 2017037302 (print) | LCCN 2017042123 (ebook) | ISBN 9781315209586 (ebook) | ISBN 9781771884013 (hardcover : alk. paper)
Subjects: LCSH: Art and society--Uruguay--Case studies. | Heritage tourism--Uruguay--Case studies. | Mural painting and decoration, Uruguayan--Conservation and restoration--Uruguay--Colonia del Sacramento. | Seade, Felipe, 1912-1969. Alegorâi al trabajo.
Classification: LCC N72.S6 (ebook) | LCC N72.S6 C5924 2018 (print) | DDC 701/.03--dc23
LC record available at https://lccn.loc.gov/2017037302

Apple Academic Press also publishes its books in a variety of electronic formats. Some content that appears in print may not be available in electronic format. For information about Apple Academic Press products, visit our website at **www.appleacademicpress.com** and the CRC Press website at **www.crcpress.com**

CONTENTS

About the Editors .... *ix*
List of Contributors .... *xiii*
List of Abbreviations .... *xv*
Acknowledgments .... *xvii*

Introduction 1
V. Santamarina-Campos, M. Á. Carabal-Montagud,
M. De Miguel-Molina, and S. Kröner

PART I: CONTEMPORARY MURAL AND FELIPE SEADE 21

1. **Contemporary Uruguayan Mural Painting, Tradition, and Relevance** 23
   A. E. Sánchez-Guillén and A. A. Berriel-Benvenuto

2. **Social Realism in Contemporary Mural Painting** 49
   V. Santamarina-Campos

3. **Felipe Seade as the Main Figure of the Uruguayan Social Realism** 65
   M. Fernández-Oscar, V. Santamarina-Campos,
   M. Á. Carabal-Montagud, and M. J. Guirado-Ruano

4. **The Contemporary Mural Painting "Allegory to Work"** 79
   M. Á. Carabal-Montagud, V. Santamarina-Campos,
   M. Fernández-Oscar, and M. J. Guirado-Ruano

PART II: ETHNOGRAPHIC RESEARCH OF THE PAINTING "ALLEGORY TO WORK" 93

5. **"On the Face of It": Wall-to-Wall Home Ethnography** 95
   J. Skinner

6. Participatory Action Research (PAR) in Contemporary
   Community Art 105
   V. Santamarina-Campos, E. M. Martínez-Carazo,
   M. Á. Carabal-Montagud, and M. De-Miguel-Molina

PART III: SCIENTIFIC RESEARCH OF THE PAINTING
"ALLEGORY TO WORK" 137

7. Physical Identification and Digital Record of Painting 139
   J. C. Valcárcel-Andrés, M. Fernández-Oscar, E. M. Martínez-Carazo,
   and M. Sánchez-Pons

8. Colorimetric Characterization 163
   M. L. Martínez-Bazán, M. Fernández-Oscar, D. J. Yusá-Marco,
   and E. M. Martínez-Carazo

9. Study of the Chemical Composition Through Cross Sections:
   Optical Microscopy, Scanning Electron Microscopy, and
   X-Ray Microanalysis 181
   D. J. Yusá-Marco, X. Mas-i-Barberà, M. Fernández-Óscar,
   and M. J. Guirado-Ruano

10. Technical Documentation Sheet of Painting:
    Scientific Cataloging 195
    M. Sánchez-Pons, M. Fernández-Oscar, J. C. Valcárcel-Andrés,
    and M. L. Martínez-Bazán

PART IV: INTERVENTION PROCESS OF THE PAINTING
"ALLEGORY TO WORK" 209

11. State of Conservation 211
    J. L. Regidor-Ros, M. A. Zalbidea-Muñoz, and M. Fernández-Oscar

12. Restoration Process 225
    M. A. Zalbidea-Muñoz, J. L. Regidor-Ros, V. Muhvich Meirelles,
    and A. R. Benítez Alcieri

PART V: MUSEOGRAPHIC AREA AND SUSTAINABLE
TOURISM OF THE PAINTING "ALLEGORY TO WORK" 255

13. The Use and Social Enjoyment of Murals: 'The People's Art,'
    Its Publics and Cultural Heritage 257
    S. Carden

14. **Preventive Conservation Policies** 271

    X. Mas-i-Barberà, M. Sánchez-Pons, and J. Osca-Pons

15. **Guidelines to Stimulate Use and Social Enjoyment** 283

    M. De-Miguel-Molina, B. De-Miguel-Molina, and
M. V. Segarra-Oña

Conclusions: Management, Touristic Promotion, and Social Enjoyment of Contemporary Mural Painting 301

    V. Santamarina-Campos, M. Á. Carabal-Montagud,
M. De-Miguel-Molina, and B. De-Miguel-Molina

Index *317*

ABOUT THE EDITORS

Virginia Santamarina-Campos, PhD
Associate Professor, Department of Conservation and Restoration of Cultural Heritage, Universitat Politècnica de València (UPV), Spain

Virginia Santamarina Campos, PhD, is currently an Associate Professor at the Department of Conservation and Restoration of Cultural Heritage at the Universitat Politècnica de València (UPV), Spain. She is also the coordinator of the research micro-cluster VLC/CAMPUS International "Globalization, tourism, and heritage," and of the research group "Sustainable management of the cultural and natural heritage" at the Faculty of Fine Arts, UPV, Spain. She has been a visiting researcher at Italy and Mexico. Her specialization is related to conservation and Restoration of Mural Art. She received a national award for her final dissertation by the Ministry of Education, Culture and Sports in Spain.

She completed her master degree in internet–intranet programming (2001); and PhD on conservation and restoration of the historic-artistic heritage (2003) at Universitat Politècnica de València (UPV), which resulted as a platform for self-learning and research of mural art in many Latin American universities. She also holds a Drone/UAV Pilot Training Certificate awarded by the Flyschool Air Academy (Spain) in the year 2015.

In the last five years, she has conducted eight international R&D projects supported by competitive calls and five R&D international contracts supported by public and private organizations. The results have been disseminated through several scientific journals and contributions to national and international congress. Currently, she is the coordinator of a European Project (Proposal: 732433 – AiRT) H2020-ICT-2016-2017.

María Ángeles Carabal-Montagud, PhD
Professor, Department of Conservation and Restoration of Cultural Heritage, Universitat Politècnica de Valencia (UPV), Spain

María Ángeles Carabal- Montagud, PhD, is a Professor at the Department of Conservation and Restoration of Cultural Heritage at the Universitat Politècnica de Valencia (UPV), Spain. She is a member of the research micro-cluster VLC/CAMPUS "Globalization, tourism, and heritage" and of the research group "Sustainable management of the cultural and natural heritage" at the Faculty of Fine Arts, UPV. In addition, she has supervised several PhD theses and Master and degree dissertations.

María De Miguel-Molina, PhD
Associate Professor, Management Department and Head of Studies at the Management School, Universitat Politècnica de Valencia (UPV), Spain

María De Miguel-Molina, PhD, is an Associate Professor at the Management Department and Head of Studies at the Management School at the Universitat Politècnica de Valencia (UPV), Spain. She is member of the research micro-cluster VLC/CAMPUS "Globalization, tourism, and heritage." Her main research focus is on the public sector, public policies, public management, and inclusive policies. She has participated in several international and national R&D projects (competitive calls). In addition, she has been at the Lakehead University in Canada and the UC Berkeley in the USA as Visiting Professor in order to research muralism public policies. She supervised several PhD and Master theses and has published more than 35 papers.

Blanca De Miguel-Molina, PhD
Associate Professor, Management Department, Universitat Politècnica de Valencia (UPV), Spain

Blanca De Miguel-Molina, PhD, is an Associate Professor at the Management Department of the Universitat Politècnica de Valencia (UPV),

About the Editors

Spain. She teaches courses mainly in strategic management and business models. Her main research involves innovation in creative and cultural industries, corporate community involvement, and bibliometrics. She is the supervisor of various PhD and Master theses, and she has published her research results in several indexed journals on creative and cultural industries, among other fields.

LIST OF CONTRIBUTORS

A. R. Benítez-Alcieri
Department of Restoration of Cultural Heritage, Commission of the Nation, ECM of Uruguay. Canelones 968-111000, Montevideo, Uruguay, Tel.: +598-2900-7415, E-mail: alberto.benitez.al@gmail.com

A. A. Berriel-Benvenuto
Institute National School of Fine Arts, University of the Republic. José Martí, 3328, 11300 Montevideo, Uruguay, Tel.: +598-2708-7606/27080764, E-mail: alejandraberrielbenvenuto@hotmail.com

M. Á. Carabal-Montagud
Department of Conservation and Restoration of Cultural Heritage, UPV, Camino de Vera s/n, 46022 Valencia, Spain, Tel.: +34-963877000, E-mail: macamon@crbc.upv.es

S. Carden
School of Planning, Architecture and Civil Engineering, Queen's University Belfast. Room 0G/036, Belfast, United Kingdom, Tel.: +44 (0)28-9097-4151, E-mail: s.carden@qub.ac.uk

B. De Miguel-Molina
Department of Management, UPV, Camino de Vera, s/n, 46022, Valencia, Spain, Tel.: +0034963877680/76843, Ext. 76844, E-mail: bdemigu@gmail.com

M. De Miguel-Molina
Department of Management, UPV, Camino de Vera, s/n, 46022, Valencia, Spain, Tel.: +0034963877680/76821, Ext. 76844, E-mail: mademi@omp.upv.es

M. Fernández-Oscar
Department of Conservation and Restoration of Cultural Heritage, UPV, Camino de Vera s/n, 46022 Valencia, Spain, Tel.: +34-661685561, E-mail: mirferoscr@gmail.com

M. J. Guirado-Ruano
Department of Conservation and Restoration of Cultural Heritage, UPV, Camino de Vera s/n, 46022 Valencia, Spain, Tel.: +34-635814197, E-mail: mariajguirado@gmail.com

R. Koster
School of Outdoor Recreation, Parks and Tourism, Lakehead University. 955 Oliver Road Thunder Bay, ON Canada P7B 5E1, Tel.: 807-343-8440, E-mail: rkoster@lakeheadu.ca

S. Kröner
Department of Conservation and Restoration of Cultural Heritage, Polytechnic University of Valencia. Camino de Vera s/n, 46022 Valencia, Spain, Tel.: +34-664711624, E-mail: stephan.kroner2013@gmail.com

M. L. Martínez-Bazán
Department of Conservation and Restoration of Cultural Heritage, UPV, Camino de Vera s/n, 46022 Valencia, Spain, Tel.: +34-963877000, E-mail: lmartine@crbc.upv.es

E. M. Martínez-Carazo
Department of Conservation and Restoration of Cultural Heritage, UPV, Camino de Vera s/n, 46022 Valencia, Spain, Tel.: +346-55868675, E-mail: evmarca2@posgrado.upv.es

X. Mas-i-Barberà
Department of Conservation and Restoration of Cultural Heritage, UPV, Camino de Vera s/n, 46022 Valencia, Spain, Tel.: + 34963873128, E-mail: jamasbar@upvnet.upv.es

V. Muhvich-Meirelles
Department of Restoration of Cultural Heritage, Commission of the Nation, ECM of Uruguay. Canelones 968–111000, Montevideo, Uruguay, Tel.: +598-2900-7415, E-mail: vladimirmuhvich@gmail.com

J. Osca-Pons
Department of Conservation and Restoration of Cultural Heritage, UPV, Camino de Vera s/n, 46022 Valencia, Spain, Tel.: +34963877312/73120, E-mail: juosca@crbc.upv.es

J. L. Regidor-Ros
Department of Conservation and Restoration of Cultural Heritage, UPV, Camino de Vera s/n, 46022 Valencia, Spain, Tel.: + 34656887931/79419, E-mail: jregidor@crbc.upv.es

A. E. Sánchez-Guillén
Institute National School of Fine Arts, University of the Republic. José Martí, 3328, 11300 Montevideo, Uruguay, Tel.: +598-2708-7606/27080764, E-mail: asanchez@enba.edu.uy

M. Sánchez-Pons
Department of Conservation and Restoration of Cultural Heritage, UPV, Camino de Vera s/n, 46022 Valencia, Spain, Tel.: + 34963877221/72215, E-mail: mersanpo@crbc.upv.es

V. Santamarina-Campos
Department of Conservation and Restoration of Cultural Heritage, UPV, Camino de Vera s/n, 46022 Valencia, Spain, Tel.: +34-963879314/79414, E-mail: virsanca@upv.es

M. V. Segarra-Oña
Department of Management, UPV, Camino de Vera, s/n, 46022, Valencia, Spain, Tel.: +0034963877000, Ext. 76844, E-mail: maseo@omp.upv.es

J. Skinner
Department of Life Sciences, University of Roehampton. Holybourne Avenue SW15–4JD London, United Kingdom, Tel.: +44-208-392/4895, E-mail: jonathan.skinner@roehampton.ac.uk

J. C. Valcárcel-Andrés
Department of Conservation and Restoration of Cultural Heritage, UPV, Camino de Vera s/n, 46022 Valencia, Spain, Tel.: +34963877312/73120, E-mail: jvalcara@crbc.upv.es

D. J. Yusá-Marco
Department of Conservation and Restoration of Cultural Heritage, UPV, Camino de Vera s/n, 46022 Valencia, Spain, Tel.: +34-963877000/79129, E-mail: doyumar@crbc.upv.es

M. A. Zalbidea-Muñoz
Department of Conservation and Restoration of Cultural Heritage, UPV, Camino de Vera s/n, 46022 Valencia, Spain, Tel.: +34-963877000/73126, E-mail: manzalmu@crbc.upv.es

LIST OF ABBREVIATIONS

ANCAP	General Administration of Fuels, Alcohol, and Portland
CBR	community-based research
CBT	community-based tourism
CCHN	Commission of Cultural Heritage of the Nation
CSL	community service learning
ECM	Education and Culture Ministry
EDX	x-ray microanalysis
FTIR	Fourier transform infrared
IENBA	National Institute of Fine Arts
IR	infrared
MAS NMR	magic angle spinning (MAS) NMR
MIC	Municipal Intendancy of Colonia
NMR	nuclear magnetic resonance spectroscopy
OM	optical microscopy
PAR	participatory action-research
PUCM	Project Uruguayan Contemporary Muralism
R&D	Research and Development
RH	relative humidity
SCE	specular component excluded
SCI	specular component included
SEM	scanning electron microscope
SEM-EDX	scanning electron microscopy – energy dispersive X-ray spectrometry
UDA	Ulster Defence Association
UDELAR	Republic's University
UFF	Ulster freedom fighters
UNESCO	United Nations Educational, Scientific and Cultural Organization
UPV	Polytechnic University of Valencia
UV	ultraviolet

ACKNOWLEDGMENTS

To Adriana Ramos Capeci—precursor, heart and soul of this project

To Miriam Fernández Oscar and Eva María Martínez Carazo—for your infinite generosity

To Nelsys Fusco Zambetogliris—for her support at the beginning of the project

To Javier Royer Rezzano—for his collaboration

To Vladimir Muhvich Meirelles—for being always there

To our kids—born during this project, for lost time

To the team—for having believed and made this project possible

INTRODUCTION

V. SANTAMARINA-CAMPOS[1], M. Á. CARABAL-MONTAGUD[2], M. DE MIGUEL-MOLINA,[3] and S. KRÖNER[4]

[1]*Associate Professor, Research Micro-Cluster Globalization, Tourism and Heritage, Department of Conservation and Restoration of Cultural Heritage, UPV, 3N Building, Camino de Vera s/n, 46022 Valencia, Spain, Tel.: +34-963879314/79414, E-mail: virsanca@upv.es*

[2]*Associate Professor, Research Micro-Cluster Globalization, Tourism and Heritage, Department of Conservation and Restoration of Cultural Heritage, UPV, 3N Building, Camino de Vera S/N, 46022 Valencia, Spain, Tel.: +34-963877000/73132, E-mail: macamon@crbc.upv.es*

[3]*Associate Professor, Research Micro-Cluster Globalization, Tourism and Heritage, Department of Management, UPV, Camino de Vera, S/N, 46022, Valencia, Spain, Tel.: +0034963877680/76821, Ext. 76844, E-mail: mademi@omp.upv.es*

[4]*External Staff, Department of Conservation and Restoration of Cultural Heritage, Polytechnic University of Valencia. Camino de Vera S/N, 46022 Valencia, Spain, Tel.: +34-664711624, E-mail: stephan.kroner2013@gmail.com*

After the Mexican Revolution of the twentieth century, a new concept of nation was created, which therefore required a new identity. In this democratizing movement, the participation of the artists played a key role, redefining a new concept of art, using the murals as a communication channel with the population. This movement crosses the Mexican boundaries through the muralist Siqueiros (Informant 1), who called the new American generation of artists, inviting them to construct a monumental, human, public, and identitarian art.

As a result, in the Southern Cone we find a huge muralist production along the twentieth century that reflects a subversion to the international art conceptions and shows local contents, favoring an esthetics based on a nationalism with equalitarian tendencies and interpreting reliably their cultural origins. It leads to murals with artistic and historic qualities related to social realism, constructivism, and formal tradition, painted by an exclusive minority of artists, and located in indoor and centralized places, linked to the 'high culture' (Figures 1–6). This nonconformist character can be reflected not only at the concept level, but also at a technological one with an experimentation period where traditional techniques are substituted by new procedures and commercial products (Figure 7).

FIGURE 1 Demetrio Urruchúa, Amalia Polleri, Carmen Garayalde and María Rosa de Ferrari. The man's partner, 1941 (detail) library from the Artiga Professors Institute, Montevideo. Social Realism. *Source:* Graphical record of the R&D Project PUCM, 2010.

Introduction 3

FIGURE 2 Norberto Berdía. San Rafael Casino-Hotel.1948. Punta del Este. Social realism. *Source:* Graphical record of the R&D Project PUCM, 2010.

FIGURE 3 Norberto Berdía. Press Freedom, 1953. El Pais, Montevideo. Social realism. *Source:* Graphical record of the R&D Project PUCM, 2013.

FIGURE 4 Luis Mazzey and Carlos González. Works of ANCAP, 1949. ANCAP Building. Montevideo. Social Realism. *Source:* Graphical record of the R&D Project PUCM, 2011.

Nowadays, in Uruguay there is a lack of resources and training in heritage management, whose consequence is the loss of conscience about the symbolic dimension of these murals, forgetting their social purpose, and increasing their deterioration due to the absence of social interest as their values being manifestations of cultural practices are unknown. As Bulanti (2008:57), one of the principal researchers on these topics, points out 'our country should analyze in profound the esthetic significance of these murals.' Moreover, following this idea, Hugo Achúgar (2001:73), in relation to the mural artists who started their activity with the encouragement of Siqueiros, wrote:

'What happened with all of them? They are dead, forgotten. It is not worth to remember their names. The people who will read this autobiography would not have any idea about who they were. They would not know if they were painters or poets. They would not know that those days they were fundamental actors of the Uruguayan art or at least they thought it.'

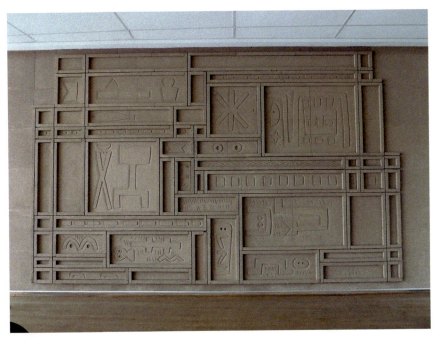

FIGURE 5 Augusto Torres. Constructivism in sand stone, 1964. Montevideo. Constructivism. *Source:* Graphical record of the R&D Project PUCM, 2013.

To this complexity, we have to add the difficulty of facing the conservation of these works, as many of them were painted with experimental materials that have generated complex problems difficult to manage. Finally, the lack of restoration specialists and the nonexistence of a regulation for this profession, have allowed professional intrusiveness and, therefore, inadequate interventions. This fact can be contrasted in the following transcript found at the National General Archive:

Issue: The Assistance Centre of the Medical Union of Uruguay (CASMU) requests to the National Cultural Heritage Committee of the Education and Culture Ministry of the Oriental Republic of Uruguay the restoration of the mural painted by Augusto Torres that was declared as National Historic Monument (decision no. 128/998), and located at the CASMU Sanitarium no. 1, Floor 2, Arenal Grande and Colonia Street. Signed by Raúl Germán Rodríguez (Accountant of the

FIGURE 6 Edwin Studer. Sand Stone Mural with surface for a building in Juan María Pérez and Ellauri, 1956. Montevideo, Uruguay. Constructivism. *Source:* Graphical record of the R&D Project PUCM, 2010.

Board of Directors), 23th June, 2008. The transcript includes the report of Miguel Umpiérrez, Head of the Restoration Department at CCHN-ECM, explaining the impossibility of succeed to the restoration due to the reduced staff that have and the tasks priorities pending and recommending the request to a private company, but taking into account some guidelines:

1. to control if the damage zone is dried, to consolidate the existing paint and to repair the missing areas.
2. to consolidate the crackles since they will become firmed.
3. to clean totally the mural from all the existing dirties, especially oil, as it has to be cleaned carefully.
4. to use varnish retouching in the entire surface to separate the new reintegration of color.
5. final protective varnish.

FIGURE 7 Miguel Ángel Battegazzore, Entropy II, 1988. Located in the outdoor facade of the firemen building, in Magallanes street, Montevideo. Synthetic vinyl painting, on synthetic preparation. Highly deteriorate. *Source:* Graphical record of the R&D Project PUCM, 2010.

In addition, they request that the company that will conduct the restoration send a descriptive report of the works to be done, so that the department could audit them, as it is a National Historical Monument (Transcript no. 2008.11.008–316/08, 24 June, 2008).

The last document includes the decision from the CCHN-ECM, signed by the Director Alberto Quintela and the Architect Renée Fernández, approving the report from the Restoration Atelier and giving permission to the work from a private company if it follows the mentioned guidelines by the Restoration Department of the CCHN-ECM.

The heritage enjoyment in Uruguay, enhanced with the inclusion in 1995 of the Historical Neighborhood of Colonia del Sacramento into the world heritage list, attracts a cultural tourism more and more exigent, and these murals spaces become highly vulnerable. The triad tourism, heritage, and market presents in the present Uruguay new 'glocalizated' maps (glocalization: from local to global and vice versa). In addition, in this context, it is necessary to enhance researchers about new models of sustainable management that will guarantee the required resources for this social art.

The recent declaration of new heritage elements has generated a wider and spreader perception of the cultural assets, being observed as a tool to offer essential goods for the human welfare, so that their accurate management is essential to construct a process of social, economic and environmental sustainable development. Tourism, globalization, and heritagization of new cultural assets, require the revision and proposal of new management models that will include sociocultural aspects, their use, formal and symbolic/identitarial value. That is, the restoration should bear in mind the actors' perspective and contain it in the intervention process. It will be necessary for the involvement and interaction of the different stakeholders to develop a sustainable conservation.

In this framework, the research project 'social function of the Uruguayan muralism of the twentieth century as a tool and model of sustainable heritage activation' has been developed, with the participation of the Polytechnic University of Valencia, University of Valencia (participated in the first stage of the research project, dealing with the area of ethnographic research), University of the Republic Uruguay, the Unit of Restoration of the Cultural Heritage Commission and the National Cultural Board of the ECM of Uruguay. The main objective was to use Colonia del Sacramento as a strategic location in Uruguay, to create a management program that could be re-created in other heritage places of the country, with the main objective of being sustainable by employing the tool of activation of the social function of the Uruguayan muralism of the twentieth century.

One of the specific objectives of the project was to give urgently a periodic support to a complex process of intervention; in this case the "Allegory to work" by Felipe Seade (Figure 8), by developing a sustainable model of restoration-management, while at the same time covering the three principal problems of the Uruguayan muralism. This goal could be achieved through three interconnected national subprograms financed by the Spanish government and the UPV. These included intervened works that experienced a complete process of illusionist chromatic reintegration; murals that, for different reasons, had to be moved as the only measure

Introduction

FIGURE 8. Detail of the artwork "Allegory to work" by Felipe Seade, located in the conference room of the culture house (old High School of Colonia del Sacramento), before the intervention process. *Source:* Graphical record of the R&D Project PUCM, 2010.

to preserve the work of art; works painted in schools that have experienced a heritage deactivation and a lack of management; paintings from the twentieth century with problems of conservation, as a consequence of the period of experimentation when they were created; murals created in the twenty-first century with problems of instability due to the lack of technical knowledge regarding the methodology for outdoor paintings.

The first program of research-intervention included, on the one hand, the statement and heritage activation of the mural "Allegory to work" in its wider and extended vision through the scientific record of it, and, on the other hand, the analysis of the problems of mural intervention, developing a sustainable model of restoration-management, replicable in other murals located throughout the country, from an economic, cultural and locally participative perspective. The second program (training), had the

objective of creating step-by-step of a decentralized project to implement a University teaching area of heritage intervention. The approach was, in a first step, to train the human resources using the work of Felipe Seade as an object for practice in order to gain access to information, which could help those people work independently. Moreover, this will at the same time promote the protection of artworks in general, and also the cultural expression as a tool. Finally, the program of sensibilization and diffusion was focused on:
   a. promoting a program of social sensibilization to favor the synergies with the cultural and development policies; and
   b. helping to conduct ethnographic researches in the framework of the mural "Allegory to work," in order to contextualize the reasons for its heritage deactivation and to understand the mechanisms of its deterioration.

Enhancing the value of the cultural heritage 'contemporary muralism' and, in particular, the object of study, special attention is paid to integrate the local community and the most vulnerable groups, focusing each action to a concrete public by using the participatory action research (PAR) method. Moreover, diffusion of the results is done in the academic area to promote the sensibilization of interculturalism values and to improve the research methodologies to manage sustainably the contemporary muralism.

The mural "Allegory to work," located in the Cultural House of Colonia del Sacramento has been selected due to its different damages, including problems of heritage deactivation and conservation, and previous interventions that had modified totally the original work.

In addition, Felipe Seade was a key artist in the Uruguayan contemporary muralism of the twentieth century. He was follower of the Mexican and the political-social movement (Informant 24) and one of the top examples of the artistic Social realism movement (Informant 32), which is opposed to the Constructive Universalism of Torres-García's Attelier that had a huge improvement in the Uruguayan artistic panorama since the 30s, when it started to be defined the social function of the artist and its plastic application. The mural "Allegory to work" is one of the most significant paintings of this artist (Informant 32).

With this background, one can understand that the commitment of preserving the heritage is a shared responsibility, not only of the government but also of the different stakeholders (social groups, educational organizations and NGOs). For this reason, it is necessary to benefit from the synergies that a heritage intervention project in local areas is able to generate: sharing knowledge and experience. Following this idea, the participation and collaboration of four stakeholders was targeted: (i) public institutions, (ii) academics, (iii) NGOs, and (iv) local community.

With these stakeholders, a horizontal structured team with capacity of decision making by consensus, based on communication and active and continuous participation of the different Uruguayan institutions was formed. A process of co-training was started to help them to design new projects based on the experience acquired of this project, correcting detected problems. Those institutions are aware of the complexity of the work to be intervened and the ways to enjoy the Uruguayan heritage.

Furthermore, the local community defined the symbolic dimension of this mural, and redefined its social function and its capacity of proposing fantastic discourses. They demonstrated us the knowledge of its values as significant expressions of a cultural tradition. To incorporate them and have an effective feedback, the cooperation actors and the local associations played a key role.

The methodology used had as objective to consider the mural by Felipe Seade as a whole and with its intrinsic finality. During the heuristic (preparatory) phase the inventory process of the mural was developed, adding the principal data for later extend the information at the scientific cataloguing process during the analytical phase, with the objective to obtain a wider knowledge of the mural, considering its background, significance, and value.

Filling in the scientific cataloguing form at the mural's place, was a fundamental step and it became a coherent report of the critical research about the mural in its identity. It was a tool to cover all the morphological, historical-critical, technical, administrative, and legal information in an organic synthesis.

After the analytical phase, all the information was processed in Valencia (synthesis phase). The materials and the possible interactions with the conservation and restoration processes of the work were studied and, together with this information, a final catalogue, a proposal for the mural intervention and the design of the museographic program was created.

The activities for that program were:

1. **Analysis of Secondary Source**
   Archives' research. Search of documents in the principal public and private archives that could have information about the conceptions, uses and functions of the cultural heritage, and specially referred to contemporary Uruguayan muralism and the mural "Allegory to work" by Felipe Seade.
   Study of bibliography. Books, journals, monographs, official documents, autobiographies, experts' reports, films, video records, and documentary films about Uruguayan contemporary muralism and its intervention, focusing the research in the object of study.
   The work plan for the analysis of the secondary source was:
   a. Find, collect, and manage public and private archives.
   b. Scan and record the documents.
   c. Organize and register the information.
2. **Ethnographic Study**
   The ethnographic fieldwork was mainly developed in two locations, the city of Montevideo and the town of Colonia del Sacramento. In each of these urban locations, we used the same analytic methodologies (semistructured interviews with people from different backgrounds to have a first impression of the perception and valuation of the Uruguayan muralism and, secondly of Felipe Seade's work), focusing on the valuation and social uses of the contemporary Uruguayan muralism, but adapting them to the specific objectives in each location.
   In the city of Montevideo, the study was oriented to analyze the Uruguayan muralism of the twentieth century. The main objective, from the ethnographic point of view, was to observe the way the cultural manifestations transcend the historic-artistic value to become important identitarian symbols for the community. Moreover, the quantitative (because of the huge amount of murals in Latin America and, particularly in Uruguay) and qualitative (because their recognized technical quality) importance of the muralism, it appends new dimensions regarding its symbolic value and its capacity to strengthen identity. For this reason, it was fundamental to under-

stand the perception, comprehension, use and social function of the contemporary Uruguayan muralism. From this point of view, the need to reassess the mural art and highlighting its influence in society was studied.

Particularly, in Montevideo 19semi-structured interviews were conducted, using a previous planned set of questions, with the aim to focus them on main research objectives. The informants have been interviewed from different professional profiles to elaborate a complete framework of the comprehension and valuation of the Uruguayan muralism and the works of Felipe Seade. The informants were selected based on a set of criteria (age, professional career related to the intervention of mural works, relevance of their work, and so on) and grouped together, according to their professional characteristics, as follows:

a. Relevant plastic artists in the Uruguayan environment (muralists and family members of muralists of the twentieth century), with technical knowledge of contemporary muralism. For example, an interview with Miguel Ángel Battegazzore, one of the prestigious artists (and muralists) in Uruguay, who has written many books, and is one of the inheritors of the Felipe Seade's Atelier (Informant 24), was included. This interview, and one by Seade's sons, were relevant testimonials to collect the information regarding the life and work of this renowned artist of the first term of the twentieth century.

b. Technical and research institutional staff (universities, institutional centers), with observed experience in intervention, manage and research of the muralism works. From them, it special relevance to the results of the staff from the National Cultural Heritage Committee of the Education and Cultural Ministry was attributed; and above all, the restorers (active or retired) who have worked in the conservation and restoration of murals, as a public service or working for private organizations. Many of them had a wide experience in the senior management of a restoration atelier, as well as in the interventions of murals made from them. The most important intervention could be the

one of the murals in the Saint Bois Hospital, executed by the Torres-García Atelier.
c. Civil society (cultural associations). In particular, the Saint Bois Association, that leads the movement for recuperation and return to their original context of the murals of the Saint Bois Hospital that were removed from there and then located in Antel Tower, where they are at present.
d. Relevant critics and art historians in the study of Uruguayan art (and, specially, muralism).

The work plan includes:
a. Digital record of the interview (audiovisual record).
b. Transcription of the interview.
c. Analysis of the most relevant documents to categorize analytically them and then analyze the information in order to extract conclusions.

The information was processed following the ethical guidelines of anthropology, with the informants' consent for using the materials for research and diffusion purposes.

3. **Sensibilization Program**

The workshop 'heritage, participation, and collective action'; and 'dialogues on Colonia del Sacramento heritage town,' using the methodology participatory action research (PAR) was held. The topics of the activities were related to the heritage applications and the intervention-management of murals, focusing each activity on a specific public, depending on their age, and grouping them in adolescents, teenagers, adults and elderly people.

Work teams should:
- 'draw your heritage' and 'treasure search' (8–16 years).
- 'from participation to action: sustainable heritage action plan for Colonia del Sacramento' (18–55 years).
- 'before and after: alive memories of Colonia' (over 55 years).

The sensibilization workshops were developed in the conference room, where the mural "Allegory to work" by Seade is located, as it was not only the key object of the project but also a muralist icon of the Colonienses. To generate more sensibilization with the mural and the intervention of the work, as well as with the performed activities, the professional staffs were working on the record and proposal steps, encouraging interaction of the restores with the participants so that they could know directly some of the processes that conform a mural intervention project.

At this research phase, the work plan was:
a. Preparation and performance of the workshops.
b. Photographic and video-graphic record.
c. Information digitalization.
d. Analysis and interpretation of the information.
e. Conclusions.

4. **Training Program**
Development of the teaching program of a specific learning module in the Republic University of Uruguay, through the postgraduate course 'Sustainable management of the Latino-American cultural heritage,' which practical part was made about the mural "Allegory to work," to give a real and close vision. The course lasted 72 h (40 h of theory and 32 h of practice), divided into five independent modules:
- *Module 1:* Cultural heritage.
- *Module 2:* Tools for cataloguing and inventorying the cultural heritage.
- *Module 3:* Photography applied to the analysis of art works.
- *Module 4:* Research of nondestructive methods in heritage intervention. Characterization and colorimetric monitoring.
- *Module 5:* Design of the technical project on mural intervention.

5. **Graphical Record and Physical-Chemical Analysis of the Work**
a. Physical identification, localization, and description of the work for the inventory process. Record of the principal data of the mural: author, title, technique, measures, support, year of creation, intervention, conservation status, and so on, using a standard form.
Work plan:
i. Compelling data,
ii. Database development, and
iii. Reports.
b. Scientific cataloguing based on the inventory data of the mural and enhanced with specific record devices: video-endoscopy,

laser distance-metric, temperature and humidity measurer, lux-metric, GPS, and contact video-microscopy. The technical data were inserted in an excel database to be processed later and added to the designed cataloguing forms.
Work plan:
i. Compelling data,
ii. Database development, and
iii. Reports.
c. Scientific cataloguing based on chemical analyses. Compilation of microsamples of the pictorial film, esplanades, and support, following a patron related with the rest of records and the information needed. The analysis were:
- Stratigraphic study: morphological and chemical analysis MO and SEM/EDX.
- Identification of pictorial binders: through FT-IR and Pyr-GC/MS.
- Chemical-mineralogical characterization of mortars: through FT-IR.
- Compelling of microsamples of external elements from the pictorial film (dirtiness, repainting, and so on). One part was made in situ with the conduct-meter and analysis strips for the semiquantitative determinations.

Work plan:
i. Compelling samples.
ii. Laboratory analyzes.
iii. Reports.
d. Scientific cataloguing based on physical analyses, including colometric characterization and digital photographic documentation.
- Colorimetric characterization through visible spectrophotometric.

Work plan:
i. Colorimetric measurements with contact techniques by selection of sample points.
ii. Data processing.
iii. Results of the analyzes.

- Digital photographic documentation of the mural.

    Work plan:
    i. Photos with visible radiation of the original status of the painting, including photos with raking light, macrophotos and reflected light with incident angle of 90°.
    ii. Photography with nonvisible light. Red reflectography for the study of internal paint layers and ultraviolet photography of fluorescence to detect the presence of repainting and identify materials.
    iii. Laboratory analyzes.
    iv. Reports.

  e. Creation context based scientific cataloguing. Precise biographic data from the author and the work was collected, as well as more specific aspects according to their particularities.

6. **Restoration Process of the Mural "Allegory to Work" by Felipe Seade**

    Intervention for conservation (consolidation processes) and restoration (cleaning process and volumetric and pictorial reintegration) was executed directly on the artwork. During the whole process, the different steps have been monitored/evaluated with photography with visible and invisible radiations and colorimetric measurement, using contact techniques by selecting samples points, in order to compare results (values) from the different conservation/restoration processes.

    Work plan:
    i. Direct intervention for conservation,
    ii. Direct intervention for restoration, and
    iii. Reports.

7. **Design of a New Use and Social Enjoyment Scheme of the Mural "Allegory to Work" by Felipe Seade**

    After the intervention project, we defined the policies for preventive conservation (minimize the deterioration, create maintenance routines, manage guidelines for the staff and users, development of security measures and contingency plans in case of disaster, design of protective measures to reduce deterioration processes, presentation and photography processes, and so on) and the guidelines to

enhance the use and social enjoyment of the mural (routines for guided visits, new activities, and so on).
Work plan:
i. Definition of policies for preventive conservation.
ii. Design of guidelines to enhance the uses and social enjoyment.
iii. Reports.

KEYWORDS

- contemporary muralism
- heritage activation
- PAR
- participatory action research
- scientific cataloguing
- sensibilization program
- social sensibilization
- Uruguayan muralism

REFERENCES AND BIBLIOGRAPHY

Achúgar, H. (2001). *"Falsas memorias: Blanca Luz Brum."* Montevideo: Ediciones Trilce. ISBN: 9974-32-219-7.
Bulanti, M. L. (2008). *"El taller Torres-García y los murales del hospital Saint Bois."* Montevideo: Ediciones Tradinco. ISBN: 978-9974-675-17-9.
Expedte. no. 2008.11.008-316/08, con fecha de 24 de junio de, 2008. Archivo General de la Nación, Uruguay.
Santamarina, V., & Carabal, M. A. (2013). *Informe Final del proyecto Función social del muralismo uruguayo del siglo XX como vehículo y modelo de activación patrimonial sustentable. Descentralización, identidad y memoria.* Ministerio de Asuntos Exteriores y de Cooperación.
Santamarina, V., & Carabal, M. A. (2014). *Informe Final del proyecto Función social del muralismo uruguayo del siglo XX como vehículo y modelo de activación patrimonial sustentable.* Universitat Politècnica de València.
Santamarina, V., & Carabal, M. A. (2016). *Informe finaldel proyecto Diseño e implementación de políticas culturales inclusivas: el muralismo uruguayo contemporáneo como herramienta de activación patrimonial sustentable.* Ministerio de Economía y Competitividad, Dirección General de Investigación Científica y Técnica.

Introduction

INTERVIEWS

- **Informant 1.** Didier Calvar. Profile: Lecturer of Arts History, Faculty of Humanities and Education Science (RU) and Professor of the University ORT, Montevideo. Date of Interview: 28–09–2010.
- **Informant 24.** Miguel Angel Battegazzore. Profile: Artist and lecturer. Date of Interview: 02–04–2011.
- **Informant 32.** Carolina and Juan Felipe Seade. Profile: Artists of recognized prestige in Uruguay. Descendants of muralist Felipe Seade. Date of Interview: 14–04–2011.

PART I

CONTEMPORARY MURAL AND FELIPE SEADE

CHAPTER 1

CONTEMPORARY URUGUAYAN MURAL PAINTING: TRADITION AND RELEVANCE

A. E. SÁNCHEZ-GUILLÉN[1] and A. A. BERRIEL-BENVENUTO[2]

[1]*Associate Professor, Institute National School of Fine Arts, University of the Republic, 3328, 11300 Montevideo, Uruguay, Tel.: +598-2708-7606/27080764, E-mail: asanchez@enba.edu.uy*

[2]*Grade 2 Teacher, Institute National School of Fine Arts, University of the Republic, 3328, 11300 Montevideo, Uruguay, Tel.: +598-2708-7606/27080764, E-mail: alejandraberrielbenvenuto@hotmail.com*

CONTENTS

1.1	Introduction	24
1.2	Objectives	26
1.3	Methodology	26
1.4	Development	26
1.5	Conclusions	46
	Keywords	46
	References and Bibliography	46

1.1 INTRODUCTION

This chapter is based on a study about the practice and research on mural painting "National Mural Painting: 1930 to 1970" (Sánchez, 2002, unpublished). Since then, students, alumni, and faculty of the IENBA (National School of Fine Arts Institute) continue to work, creating an area of production and research in mural painting, through the professional practice of visual arts. Since 2013, the School of Fine Arts participates in the research projects like "The social role of 20th-century Uruguayan muralism as a vehicle and model for the sustainable activation of heritage," Decentralization, identity, and memory." Most of the photos that accompany the text are photos of murals in which the authors themselves participated, either in their design or execution. Other photos were taken from the research project "National Mural Painting: 1930 to 1970." Except for Figure 1.15, all photos were taken by the authors (Figure 1.1).

The objective of the research project "National Mural Painting: 1930 to 1970" was to present in an organized fashion the mural art in Uruguay, and its authors, in the context of modernity. Within this framework,

FIGURE 1.1 Mural painting in Barros Blancos, Canelones, Uruguay.

researchers surveyed, ordered and systematized the existing documentation in the stated period and studied the link between mural painting, architecture, and urban planning, in the cultural-historical context of its time. The research included an inquiry into the world of the different artists and their motivations, as historical memory largely determines the relationship of the individuals with their environment; learning about the history and making sense of it requires awareness of the conditions under which the individual acts.

The experience of mural painting relates to sharing experiences and reflections about the "why" and the "what for" of creating art and recognizing the transcendent axis of holistic training, which includes teaching, research and community outreach.

The concern about heritage is one of the driving forces behind initiatives at the national and institutional level. The state of our heritage demands proposals that contribute to its recovery, valuation, and critical appropriation, and that are presented in a participatory manner, so that the majority of stakeholders become involved.

As artists and professors at the IENBA, we see mural painting as a useful tool for educational processes, since our teaching objectives are to promote supportive spaces of creation and to generate critical awareness of the market, by promoting egalitarian connections in our practice.

Therefore, we propose an elective course, delivered partly online, for 2016. This course aims to give students an overview of contemporary Uruguayan mural painting and to generate awareness about the importance of the state of conservation of these murals, the criteria used for their restoration, and the ethical issues associated with restoration practices.

In this course, we will share the results of two studies on the subject: "National Mural Painting, 1930 to 1970," by Ariel Sánchez, and "The social role of 20th-century Uruguayan muralism as a vehicle and model of the sustainable activation of heritage: Decentralization, identity, and memory."

The proposal for this course is based on the interest to rescue the rich pictorial mural heritage of Uruguay, which goes hand in hand with the concern for its preservation, dissemination, and appropriation.

At the IENBA there is a strong tradition of teaching mural painting; it is an important part of the institution's engagement with the community. However, it does not offer training in conservation and restoration of works of art. It is therefore essential to design a pedagogical program to meet this demand and to explore possible links between the creation of knowledge in this field, instruction, and community outreach.

1.2 OBJECTIVES

The general objective is to research aspects of the production of mural painting in Uruguay in relation to the educational, historical, social, and artistic context.

The specific objectives are:
1. To explore identity traditions that form the basis of the research on mural art.
2. To contribute to the preservation, dissemination, and appropriation of the pictorial mural heritage.
3. To contribute to the promotion and social awareness on the issue, and the development of actions aimed at the sustainable management of the cultural heritage.

1.3 METHODOLOGY

To achieve these objectives two strategies have been devised:
1. Begin the systematization of some experiences and makes the results available to the public.
2. Create a network of pedagogical and educational experiences that follow the same direction as the research project in order to strengthen links and interactions among participants.

In this scenario, this report attempts only a synthetic approach to some of the key issues related to the topic (Figure 1.2).

1.4 DEVELOPMENT

Art is a phenomenon of such importance and social value that its access should not be limited to certain social groups. The creation of murals, as well as the research into their historical background, makes it possible for

Contemporary Uruguayan Mural Painting

FIGURE 1.2 Mural at Colonia Etchepare, a psychiatric institution in Santa Lucía, Canelones, Uruguay.

new generations to share the values these works embody. The attitudes adopted in their creation express a complex system of statements about reality and about the ethical and social commitment of artists. Hence, the interest in rescuing this intangible cultural heritage drives the research into the visual arts and goes hand in hand with the concern for the preservation, dissemination, and appropriation of a rich pictorial mural heritage (Figure 1.3).

1.4.1 CONTEMPORARY MURAL PAINTING IN URUGUAY

In Uruguay, even the most remote precedent in painting goes back to Western art: its origins are determined by the development, structures, representations, and teachings of Western art. This origin does not inhibit the fact that, in the history of Uruguayan art, we find different positions or trends that marked our identity and determined a particular model in the field of visual arts. Identifying those defining traditions and proposing

FIGURE 1.3 Mural painting at the Asociación Civil Villa Centauro, Villa García, Montevideo.

typologies complicates the categorization of each artist, as different influences often mix and we observed a large number of hybrid creations. The trajectories of different artists illustrate the different directions that mural art can take.

In Uruguay, formal education in the visual arts began with the Circle of Fine Arts (Círculo de Bellas Artes), an organization founded in 1905. Until then, the only way to access arts education was through scholarships to travel and study at academies in Rome, Florence, and Madrid. That is how the academy determined the ideological aspects that formed structures and market relations; its influences are still felt today as an undercurrent that flows beneath the art world. Uruguayan architect and art historian Peluffo Linari (2009:53) stated that while the Circle of Fine Arts "postulated a painting in facets, of Luminist roots, associated with late expressions of 'Art Deco,' both in graphic art and advertizing," which was also applied to sets and mural decoration, on the margins, a type of painting that placed an increasing importance to the order of the formal elements, the structure, and the tone of the painting slowly began to bear down on the art scene.

In the 30s, artists got together and worked in a climate that was very distant from the previous decade. The threat of war loomed and the utopia of social redemption through art appeared; all this is lived with a deep ethical commitment, albeit from a relatively contemplative situation (Peluffo Linari, 2009:54). "Let's say it like it is—painter Felipe Seade used to say—our generation has to dive into the human drama because […] we were born at a time of bombs and cannon shots and we can't deceive the public with illuminated photography and landscapes…" (Peluffo Linari, 2009:66).

Between 1930 and 1950, in Uruguay, as in the rest of the Americas, social realism erupted. Direct influences of social realism arrived mainly through Mexican muralist David Siqueiros, who visited Uruguay and Argentina. When Siqueiros arrived to Buenos Aires, Botana, the editor of the newspaper Crítica, handed over his country house in Don Torcuato for Siqueiros to do his mural along with Castagnino, Spilimbergo and the Uruguayan Lázaro. Siqueiros was against painting on easels and almost the first thing he shouted after stepping out of the plane was: "Down with easel painting!" He aspired to translate the experience of murals to South American countries. On this point he clashed with Berni, because Berni thought the situation in Argentina differed from the situation in Mexico and they had to search for different solutions. While the revolution was going on, the Mexican government commissioned political murals, but in Buenos Aires, according to Berni, that was impossible, as it was impossible in any country where the bourgeoisie dominated. But to do murals without social content didn't make sense to those who advocated for an art for the masses. Berni wrote at that time: "To take as an excuse the willingness to have a technical experience does not justify the absence of content. In order to do a mural painting, Siqueiros had to accept the first life line the bourgeoisie threw at him" (Haber, 1975:30).

David Siqueiros, when visited Uruguay and Argentina and through Norberto Berdía, who, thanks to a scholarship, traveled to study fresco with Diego Rivera. Brazilian influences came mainly through Candido Portinari. But the most important contribution came from across the Río de la Plata, from Argentina. Perhaps because it was a region in development in which social struggles were taking place, and also because of the influence that the Spanish Civil War had, Argentina became a major focus of social realism, with artists such as Berni, Urruchúa and Spilimbergo, among others. There, intellectuals had split into two groups, Boedo and Florida, fueling controversy about what constituted the cutting edge of art—"The group of Florida and the group of Boedo" Pettoruti's art is a necessary precedent to explain the emergence of abstract, concrete, and geometric art in Argentina. Pettoruti was supported by the Florida group. Young writers had agreed about the need to shake up the apathy that ruled the literary world. They were struggling to introduce new trends that had transformed literature and had no respect for the academic writers who were victims of their epigrams, epitaphs, and derisive notes in the periodical publication Martin Fierro, where they expressed themselves. Among the artists whose art matched the literary impulse of the Florida group and the Martín Fierro publication were Xul Solar, Pettoruti, Gómez Cornet and Figari. The group from Paris also found support in the writers of Florida. But there were those who opposed Florida, the Boedo group, which consisted of writers for whom the concern about the content prevailed over the

FIGURE 1.4 Fresco painted by Urruchúa in 1939 at the library of the ex-IBO (Batlle and Ordóñez Institute), Montevideo.

concern of form. For them, art should be a medium for political and social action and has to operate on the masses to awaken their consciousness and incite the struggle (Haber, 1975:30). Those who followed Boedo's line accused their opponents of formalism and creating art that did not reach the people and which evaded the most important problems of society. They claimed that they distanced the public from reality and left the field open for reactionary policies. In Uruguay, there was no such radicalization.

The 30s was a turbulent decade for Uruguayan art. In the early 30s, the concept of Uruguay as a "model country" was consolidated, shaping a corresponding discourse in the art world. Important Spanish intellectuals and David Siqueiros visited the country; also, in 1934, Joaquín Torres García returned to Uruguay (Peluffo Linari, 2009:51).

In this context, often seeking to find new funding sources, independent artists and intellectuals formed various distinct groups. Thus, from 1932 to 1937, the Workshop-School of Visual Arts (Escuela Taller de Artes Plásticas) was formed, and in 1937, the first National Exhibition of Fine Arts was convened. Later, internal cracks in the Circle of Fine Arts led to the

FIGURE 1.5 Fresco by Norberto Berdía at the premises of the daily newspaper El País, Montevideo.

creation of the group "Paul Cezanne." During that time, a subsidiary of the Association of Intellectuals, Artists, Professionals and Writers (AIAPE), a network of antifascist intellectuals, was created. At the end of the decade, on the one hand was the AIAPE group, and on the other, there was an official art, based on a patrimonialist and neo-academic approach.

However, in general terms, the dominant imaginary among the politicized painters of this period, particularly among the followers of social realism, was burdened by the Romantic tradition from the Río de la Plata region. The works of art derived from it failed to reach the combative temperament of the Mexican paradigm; rather, the art produced at that time in Uruguay was akin to a melancholic look at the regional human landscape. The traditional intimate tone prevailed, even in those cases that included the most explicit social criticism.

Under these circumstances, Uruguayan artists traveling to Europe did not have much influence on Uruguayan arts upon their return. Joaquín Torres García was the exception: his arrival meant a significant contribution to national art, particularly if we consider what his ideas brought to the Montevideo of that time. Torres rocked the national art scene by presenting a third option to the visual arts of the time. Because of his position as one of the important figures of modernity, and due to his personality and militant advocacy, he gave a new direction to Uruguayan art and greatly influenced constructivism in Latin America.

We believe that no Uruguayan art, to a greater or lesser extent, can escape the influence of Torres; it was through his teachings that generations of artists gained access to modern art traditions and the particular worldview from which our modern Western culture sees traditional societies.

Torres' teachings align with the epistemic conception that defines them. Without denying its artistic values, the value of information and of rational knowledge, Torres recognized that there is a truth in the artistic creation that goes beyond all this.

He questioned modern art and yet was part of it. While for the avant-garde movements primitive art had a formalist perspective, Torres aspired to a different type of art; his gaze was directed to classical antiquity, the traditional art that aspired to the monumental, to be popular and metaphysical, with celebratory and ritual meanings and an identification with a universal order.

Contemporary Uruguayan Mural Painting

FIGURE 1.6 Taller Torres García Mural when it was extracted from the wall of the Ex-Saint Bois Hospital, Montevideo.

For Torres, truth was not linked to the fractures of knowledge nor did it experience crisis, it was about the eternal. That is why he criticized positivism for forgetting the values and the morals in favor of the utilitarian.

Torres outlined its opposition to descriptive art that was focused on a theme (as does social realism), but also to the more formalist avant-garde movements. In this regard, Torres stated that "those who philosophized about art, separated the work, the base (that is, the subject) from the form (that is, its artistic creation) and the misunderstanding that originated then and continues today is the result of that separation. And, since then, it has been said that art should serve a theme; or art serves itself because the form is the base. The first ones would be the academics; the second ones, the modernists. The first ones made naturalist, descriptive and imitative or literary art. The others, in search of geometry and specific values, mutilated and distorted reality or they simply eliminated it from their work. Neither group achieved balance, the balance we admire in Greek sculpture" (Torres, 1965:73).

Later on, other, more superficial contributions to Uruguayan art were identified; they were associated with new directions and brought new

FIGURE 1.7 Mural by D'Andres in Thirty-Three city, Uruguay.

energy to mural production in our country. The rise and fall of mural art creation in Uruguay is not only related to specific social and economic situations, but also to the interests of the artists of those times, such as their concern about the values of matter through research in mosaic, tapestry, brick, stained glass, etc.

The building boom in our country and the interest in the possibilities of matter took visual artists towards the creation of murals. In addition, there was the influence exerted by the research done by avant-garde movements in Europe, which, after World War II, worked to rebuild the continent, consolidating new values.

From this period, we can cite research done by the Taller Torres García, which aimed to create art integrated to architecture and as part of everyday life. This posed particular technical challenges. Like the architects close to Torres, the artists from the Taller Torres García began to use bricks in the creation of murals, not only because they were inexpensive

Contemporary Uruguayan Mural Painting

FIGURE 1.8 Studer Mural, Parque Batlle and Ordoñez (Batlle and Ordoñez Park), Montevideo.

and locally produced, but also because traditionally they had been used in Uruguay.

Another example of the use of new materials is Francisco Matto's use of Plastiglas for the stained glass projects in the Archdiocesan Seminary in Toledo, because of how expensive the application of colored glass was.

In the 50s, several Uruguayan artists traveled to Europe to specialize in different techniques. For example, in 1954, Miguel Ángel Pareja went to study mosaic in Ravenna; Amalia Nieto also went to study mosaic; in 1957, José Pedro Costigliolo traveled to study stained glass; and Oscar García Reino traveled to study tapestry.

Though the discussion about the involvement of artists in architectural projects began in the 1940s, only in 1958 and 1959 did the issue make it into the agenda and was debated by professors of the School of Architecture and the National School of Fine Arts, which had just been incorporated into the university. The discussion was centered about the design of handicrafts and household items, as well as mural paintings. The horizontal property

FIGURE 1.9 Malvín School, mural created in the context of the Law of Schools.

FIGURE 1.10 Capurro School, mural created in the context of the Law of Schools.

Contemporary Uruguayan Mural Painting

FIGURE 1.11 Fresco by Jorge Paez Vilaró, at an apartment building in the Rambla of Montevideo, 1967.

law had caused a boom in the construction of buildings, a field in common for designers, architects, and artists.

In 1960, the legacy of the first modern avant-garde movements was in crisis and the questioning became even more radicalized. We witnessed a period in which many artists distanced themselves from the art market institutions. In Latin America, the revolutionary climate in the political context heralded the advent of dictatorships: "From the theory of the avant-garde movement, the rationale behind the avant-garde as an opponent of the museum became clear. One might think that the radical confrontation of the avant-garde movements of the interwar period against art institutions led to its adaptation into new artistic trends through new ways of incorporating novelty. That process would be expressed, in the postwar era, in the emergence of certain 'updated' institutions in big capital cities: the modern museums of contemporary art, the biennials, and the cultural centers" (Longoni and Mestman, 2000:32).

On the one hand, some leftist intellectuals dug deeper into the "realist" side (a case in point was the foundation of the Club del Grabado, a printmaking organization, in 1953). Others, with more formalist concerns that would have an application in everyday life, did research in pictorial work in the field of geometric abstraction or did research in design, aiming to bring art back to the widest possible sectors of society (Peluffo Linari, 2009:109).

In this context, a certain art production sector operated outside the traditional circuits of the art market.

The avant-garde art movements of that moment were attempts to break the isolation to which art was condemned in society and to bring it back to the lives of the average person, an attitude that we see even today among different creators.

The stretching of the boundaries of art, the new relationship between the work and the viewer—which did not put the viewer in a place of observer—, the collective creation, the search for inclusion outside the art markets, were all characteristic of this era.

The mural was (and is) a medium particularly well suited for this. The common thread of most murals in Latin America during this period was the social commitment that inspired them.

In Argentina, the Spartacus Group (Ricardo Carpani) attempted a response that went back to a social realism without political party affiliations, painting murals in unions and social organizations. In Chile, brigades of Salvador Allende's Popular Front recruited artists to paint murals.

In Uruguay, art followed similar paths: the artists sought to find their place beyond traditional art circuits and to maintain a strong social commitment. These characteristics can be attributed to the experiences of the National School of Fine Arts (IENBA) at the beginning of the 60s, in the context of a particular experience.

The IENBA represented a pluralistic sector of the culture of the country, which attempted a radical response of commitment to the working classes, but not affiliated to any political sector. Before its curriculum was subject to reform, the school supported mural art research through the mosaic workshop led by Miguel Ángel Pareja. Through the university's outreach program, that knowledge was expanded and developed.

Murals were painted at the Maritime School of Malvín, the Nicaragua School (encaustic) the Compte and Riqué School, the Textile Workers Cooperative (mosaic), a building at the corner of Colonia Street and Joaquín Requena Street (mosaic), another building on Uruguay Street

Contemporary Uruguayan Mural Painting

FIGURE 1.12 Mural by Miguel Ángel Pareja, Hospital de Clínicas (photography by José Brin).

FIGURE 1.13 Mosaic by Miguel Ángel Pareja, apartment building on Colonia Street, Montevideo.

(mosaic), the Hospital de Clínicas, etc. Entire neighborhoods were painted, moving beyond the framework determined by architectural structures.

Mural painting campaigns were carried out in the Barrio Sur and the city of Dolores, in "Neighborhoods in which more than 16,000 square meters of color were left, fighting against the all-enveloping gray of the city and its inhabitants. The IENBA underwent its clearest formative process through the thousand human stories that these paintings told, from the food that was prepared to the artwork itself. The assumption was that the strengthening of the people's languages was the seed of their strength, and therefore, of their emancipation process." (IENBA, 1963:45).

The strategy was to have an impact through the sudden appearance of artwork in an urban space: "In terms of color, what was interesting

FIGURE 1.14 Painting of the Reus Neighborhood, IENBA, 1990.

Contemporary Uruguayan Mural Painting

FIGURE 1.15 Mural at Marne Sport Club, Montevideo.

FIGURE 1.16 Mural at the Villa Dolores Zoo, Montevideo, 2000.

FIGURE 1.17 Panel of the Carmelo City Mural, IENBA outreach activity.

was its sudden appearance on a large scale and then its absence in those places where it had irrupted, confirming in a short period its strengths and impact. This way, we raised awareness among passers-by." (IENBA, 1963:46). Also, modules printed on silkscreen were pasted in different combinations, to explore the impact of shape and color in the urban space.

When in 1973 the IENBA was shut down by the dictatorship, students and professors had to find work in other areas within and beyond national borders. With this purpose, small cooperatives and production groups were created and they navigated those years more or less successfully. Such was the case of the "El Carrito" and "KO" pottery workshops, among others.

After the reopening of the IENBA, contact with the rest of the community was resumed through awareness campaigns, popular sales, and mural paintings. When the Reus neighborhood was painted, there was a debate about architecture and color, and whether this type of painting respected the original architecture.

1.4.2 TRADITION AND RELEVANCE

Culture is a factor of inequality and exclusion but also of equity and integration. Argentinean anthropologist Néstor García Canclini says: "There are no sectors of society devoted exclusively to building hegemony, nor others dedicated exclusively to consumerism, or others who live only for resistance and the development of a popular alternative existence." (Canclini, 1984:6).

This picture that we describe is not far from what Miguel Ángel Pareja proposed as director of the IENBA: "Everything that is done in an attempt to connect people with artistic expressions, we support. When these things are made because of personal interest, based on the interest of promoting the individual creator, then, we do not approve. In this sense, the school is not interested in promoting any individual artist but in carrying out effective cultural events as a group within society." And he added: "Meanwhile, the people have lived for centuries deprived of the work of artists. These artists, in a traditional sense, have a single possible field of action, called

FIGURE 1.18 Mural by Alinda Núñez, across from the school in San Gregorio de Polanco.

the elite. There, one can be conservative, reactionary, and even revolutionary. Being revolutionary within the elite means to bring something new, unparalleled, the more surprising and groundbreaking, the better. That is to say that the elites act as real concentration camps of culture ..." (Pareja, 1971:27).

This extensive quotation reveals the spirit and critical awareness of a pedagogical stance committed to social change, which has inspired the educational experience of the School of Fine Arts since its inception.

Among the attempts to link artistic creation to social life—without which this overview would not be complete, we must highlight the project carried out in San Gregorio de Polanco. There, with the support of artists, culture in general and mural art in particular were used as tools to energize the local tourism industry. Since its beginnings and for the past 20 years, the local community and many artists have shared a particular experience, the Open Museum of Visual Arts of San

FIGURE 1.19 Mural on the wall of the Banco República (Bank of the Republic), San Gregorio de Polanco.

Contemporary Uruguayan Mural Painting

FIGURE 1.20 Mural by Tola Invernizzi, bar in San Gregorio de Polanco.

Gregorio de Polanco, reaping benefits that are shared across the whole community.

The importance of this museum, beyond the artworks that were created, "lies in the active participation of the population, their perception of the events, the change in the way of thinking, the development of citizen participation as a heritage shared with the community, the process of taking ownership of the collective phenomenon of art, its enjoyment, the communication potential and awareness generated among children and youth. The children participate in the paintings, schools have incorporated the history of murals into their curricula, and students at different educational levels visit and study the murals. The people of San Gregorio de Polanco have a collective intelligence that encourages them to be proactive and to be agents of feasible projects, always seeking the welfare of the community. It proves that it is possible and sustainable to maintain this rich intellectual and cultural heritage if people feel part of it." (Clariget et al., 2013:8).

1.5 CONCLUSIONS

From other creative fields with origins in different cultures and subcultures (such as, urban subcultures), creations emerge that involve spontaneous participation and circulate outside the art market, some of which are expressed through murals, graffiti, stenciling, etc.

The street becomes a field of ideological dispute for spaces of power and political struggle in a broad sense. On the one hand, we find the established knowledge—the official and consecrated—and on the other, the marginal, the peripheral. Between the two areas there are communicating vessels. Public art, resistance, popular culture, and academic culture are linked: artists act on the public space, and in turn, creators from the periphery access areas of the art market.

Artists and collectives of different origins explore public spaces or spaces of public appropriation, regardless of considerations of recognition or prestige. They are all contributors to social construction, energizing relations with space and people, transmitting values and participating in identity formation. By researching these issues we intend to address a critical understanding of the representations of the works and their authors in different social, cultural, and historical areas, deconstructing gazes and creating new avenues to appreciate our heritage.

KEYWORDS

- appropriation
- art
- dissemination
- identity
- mural painting
- preservation

REFERENCES AND BIBLIOGRAPHY

Clariget, L., Tarigo, L., Vázquez, M., & Amoza, M. (2013). *Asociación Civil Amigos del Arte y la Cultura de San Gregorio de Polanco.* Lic. y Mus. Raineri Guedes, E. Intendencia Departamental de Tacuarembó. El MAAIS: un espacio de apropiación del patrimonio comunitario. Exposición para Extenso. University of the Republic [Online]. Retrieved from http://formularios.extension.edu.uy/ExtensoExpositor2013/archivos/554_resumen1321.pdf (accessed Oct 25, 2015).

Errandonea, J. (1993). *El Mercado del Arte*. 1a. ed. IENBA: Montevideo, p. 153.

García Canclini, N. (1984). Cultura y organización popular. Gramsci con Bourdieu. Cuadernos Políticos. 1a. ed. No. 38., enero-marzo, 1984. Ediciones Era: México D. F., pp. 75–82.

Haber, A. (1975). La pintura argentina. Vanguardia y tradición. Pueblos, hombres y formas en el arte No. 1. Centro Editor de América Latina: Buenos Aires, p. 35.

IENBA. (1986). Escuela Nacional de Bellas Artes. Proyección de su experiencia educacional. 2nd ed. Nemgraf S. R. L.: Montevideo, p. 74.

Longoni, A., & Mestman, M. (2000). Del Di Tella a Tucumán Arde. Vanguardia artística y política en el '68 argentino. 1ª ed. Ediciones El Cielo por Asalto: Buenos Aires, p. 384.

Pareja, M. A. (1971). El yo y el nosotros. Entrevista de Gabriel Peluffo y Hugo Gilmet. Semanario Marcha No. 1573. Montevideo, December 10, 1971.

Peluffo Linari, G. (2009). *Historia de la pintura en el Uruguay*. In: *Representaciones de la modernidad, 1930–1960*. 6th ed. De la banda oriental: Uruguay, Vol. 2. ISBN: 99-7410-053-4. p. 115.

Sánchez, A. (2008). Entrevista a Silvestre Peciar para la realización de un documental con motivo de los 50 años del arte en la Universidad. [Recording] Montevideo.

Sánchez, A. (2002). La pintura mural nacional entre, 1930 y, 1970. Investigación financiada por la Comisión Sectorial de Investigación Científica, University of the Republic. Montevideo, 2002 (Unpublished).

Torres García, J. (1965). La recuperación del objeto. Tomo 1. 1a. ed. Colección Clásicos Uruguayos, Ministerio de Instrucción Pública: Montevideo, p. 227.

Umpiérrez, R., & Pastorino, M. (2006). Orígenes de la reforma del Plan de Estudios del IENBA. Informe elevado al Consejo del IENBA producto de la investigación: Proyecto de investigación sobre percepción y arte. March 7, 2006.

CHAPTER 2

SOCIAL REALISM IN CONTEMPORARY MURAL PAINTING

V. SANTAMARINA-CAMPOS

Associate Professor, Research Micro-Cluster Globalization, Tourism and Heritage, Department of Conservation and Restoration of Cultural Heritage, UPV, 3N Building, Camino de Vera s/n, 46022 Valencia, Spain, Tel.: +34-963879314/79314, E-mail: virsanca@upv.es

CONTENTS

2.1	Introduction	50
2.2	Objectives	50
2.3.	Methodology	50
2.4	Historical and Documentary Research	51
2.5	Conclusions	62
	Keywords	63
	References and Bibliography	63

2.1 INTRODUCTION

The artistic movement of social realism in Uruguay is strongly interconnected to the people and their history as it shows the great diversity of ideological nuances that narrate and represent the everyday life of early nineteenth century to the mid-twentieth society.

This chapter is intended to capture the different aspects that revolve around the study of the social realism art movement, a side movement of the twentieth century muralist production. As a case study, the historical social and artistic context that frames the mural "Allegory to work" by Felipe Seade from 1936 will be analyzed.

2.2 OBJECTIVES

The aim of this study is to contribute to the recognition and patrimonial activation of the Uruguayan muralist production of the twentieth century as an element of cultural reference. The results of the research will be disseminated to promote social awareness and the development of sustainable management methodologies for cultural heritage. In order to achieve this, firstly a bibliographic and documentary investigation about the social realism and sociopolitical context was organized and then complemented with the study of the work within its historical framework.

2.3 METHODOLOGY

The search for documentation was carried out on both public and private archives. The most important ones were searched for primary sources likely to contain relevant information for the study. The following step consisted of the analysis of bibliographical sources such as monographs, journal articles, official documents, newspaper articles, reports, and experts' testimonies, in relation to Felipe Seade's mural.

The work plan was organized as follows: location, collection and management of public and private archival documentation, scanning and document capture, organization and cataloging of information and finally, analysis and pre drawing conclusions to interpretation.

2.4 HISTORICAL AND DOCUMENTARY RESEARCH

2.4.1 STATUS OF URUGUAYAN PEOPLE IN HISTORY: FROM INDEPENDENCE TO THE FIRST DECADES OF THE TWENTIETH CENTURY

One could say that the country of Uruguay has always felt the need for independence. From the Hispanic American clashes in the nineteenth century until finally achieving independence from the Oriental Republic of Uruguay on the 25th of August 1825, the country suffered several historical events that shaped its community and created a feeling of common identity. Prior to this historic moment, we find various theories that point to a social atomization, with no common link. Hence, this event would mark a turning point in the structure of the country as such (Table 2.1).

TABLE 2.1 Overview of Uruguay Before the Spanish-American Independence

				Oriental fight against Spain	
1516	1527	1680	1726	1811	1813–1814
Spain arrives in Uruguay	First Spanish settlement at the Rio de la Plata	Portuguese domination	Founding of the Spanish Montevideo	Beginning of the Independence Oriental revolution	April congress. Proclamation of the revolutionary political principles
		Founding of Colonia del Sacramento		The ruling of José Artigas in the country begins	Spanish independence

José Gervasio Artigas, (1764–1850) Uruguayan politician and military leader, was the first head of the Orientals and first statesman during the Rio de la Plata revolution. Since the beginning of his administration in 1811 until his defeat in 1820, he managed to bring together the citizens' shared values, transforming them into symbols of the Oriental nation new collective identity that would form the future Uruguayan society. For this contribution, he is now considered a national hero (Barrán, 1995).

After the defeat of Artigas in 1820 and the resulting national independence, a new period of revolution followed known as *Revolución de los 33 Orientales*, headed by the Uruguayan politicians and military leaders Juan Antonio Lavalleja (Montevideo, 1853; Mines, 1784) Manuel Oribe (Montevideo, 1792–1857) and Fructuoso Rivera (Paysandu, 1784; Melo, 1854). Lavalleja and Uribe had an outstanding performance in the fight for the independence of Uruguay; the latter became the Leader and founder of the White Party—later known as the National party. Rivera had a special role in the emancipation of his country and in the early years of the Uruguayan independence history, becoming the first constitutional president of the Republic (1830–1834).

The process of independence of the Uruguayan people should be understood as a series of successive events that originated from different riots and social assemblies facing the continuous invasions that the country was suffering from Spanish, Portuguese and English troops among others. This might be the reason why the first decades of the nineteenth century (Table 2.2) are regarded as a symbol for the accomplished identity of a united population (Barrán, 1995).

The turn to the twentieth century brought airs of change to Uruguay that implied a process of adjustment to the established values and emerging concerns. While immersed in a period of economic, political and social crisis, far away from the stability lived in former years, a loss of confidence in its Uruguayan identity fell upon Uruguay (Table 2.3).

Uruguayan art of the twentieth century develops alongside:
- Socio-cultural changes: The arrival of new social classes that diversified the cultural space of the Bohemian artists, writers, etc.
- Issues regarding the moral and social foundations of a culture.
- The change from a traditional to modern society, embracing the war as an element of crisis and transition.

Social Realism in Contemporary Mural Painting

TABLE 2.2 The Nineteenth Century in Uruguay

Portuguese domination	Brazilian domination		Manuel Uribe	1835 Rosista regime. Buenos Aires	
1817	1824	1828	1834	1838	1852
1815	1820	1825	1830 Fructuoso Rivera	1839–1851	1867–1870
The Orientals take Montevideo back	José Artigas is defeated	National Independence	1st Constitution of the Oriental republic of Uruguay	Great War	Triple Alliance war against Paraguay

TABLE 2.3 The Twentieth Century: Uruguay Until the Military Dictatorship

Democratic consolidation	Economic development				Cultural development	Economic stagnation		
1903	1930	1931	1933	1947	1950–1952	1959	1973	1973–1985
Beginning of reforms	Economic crisis		Gabriel Terra coup d'état	Beginning of economic development	New constitution		The fall of the democratic institution	Military dictatorship

- Continuity of a utopian modernity. During the twentieth century, Uruguay sees the rise of different ideological and social conflicts that will influence the arts by capturing and treating the themes represented in realistic painting (Peluffo Linari, 2009).

The changes in the internal political structure of the country, the international, regional and national conflicts, the ideological struggle between liberal and authoritarian tendencies, American or pro-European or the clashes between political fractions created an atmosphere of drama, affecting the state arrangement of the country.

In the department of Colonia this situation occurred in a particular way. The past regional relationship with Argentina and the economic and social environment with its river resources attracted political refugees from the Rosista Regime—established in Buenos Aires by Juan Manuel de Rosas during the periods of 1829–1832 and 1835–1852. The river was also regarded as a strategic point for water management.

Traditional society was divided into superior classes and subordinates, patricians and founders who controlled the urban and rural environment due to their lineage and prestigious heritage (Orsi, 2008).

The various social sectors that characterized the Uruguayan society can be grouped as follows:

- Free Sector: Free social group, excluded from the rudimentary forms of domination.
- Intermediate Sector: Farmers and pastoralists, this group is characterized by its density and variety in social relationships.
- Patricians: Sector that included landholders, merchants, bureaucrats, military, lawyers and the church. These are the main owners of property and land.

With the beginning of the seventeenth century comes the introduction of livestock farming into this macroeconomic region. It is in the second half of the nineteenth century that this area is particularly important among the immigrant groups.

At this time smallholders and farmers use family labor to produce goods for self- consumption and trading. The poverty faced by these sectors of the population, force them to forge alliances with the social elite. Eventually as a result of these relationships, some will be victims of evictions and misappropriations during the republic (Caetano and Rilla, 2005). The feeling of a country in ruins will remain constant during the first half of the twentieth century and increases with the beginning of the *Guerra Grande—Great War* was a conflict among the states of the Rio de la Plata countries from 1838 to 1851. This happened alongside the Spanish resettlement and the devastation of the War of Independence—a war that occurred in Spain against the French invasion during 1808 to 1814.

In this context, various artistic movements develop, among which Social Realism is standing out because of its capacity to represent the conditions and situations experienced by the civilian population from the birth of Uruguay as a nation until the early twentieth century. The celebration of the centenary in Uruguay was used as a political opportunity for the affirmation of nationalist and identity standards (Orsi, 2008). At the beginning of the 1930s significant changes occurred, both in the relationship between intellectuals and the political power, and in the way of conceiving the social role of the artist and his esthetic preferences.

These political and social changes provide the artistic theoretical basis to establish themes of Americanism against the European standards. In addition to assuming this position, paintings will influence the social realism inspired by the political and cultural program of the Mexican muralist.

2.4.2 THE ANTECEDENTS OF SOCIAL REALISM IN URUGUAY: THE DIRECT INFLUENCE OF TWENTIETH CENTURY MEXICAN MURALISTS

David Alfaro Siqueiros, the greatest exponent of the Mexican muralists, played an important part in the development of a popular art movement committed to the Uruguayan society. His visit to Uruguay in 1933, and his relationship with artists like Felipe Seade significantly shaped the artistic production of the country.

The Mexican muralist, since the beginning, supported the consolidation of the idea of the painter and mural art as the basis and true representation of the many cultural changes the country was experiencing. The didactic nature and denouncing connotations of this art movement would exemplify the diversity of symbols that portray the most disadvantaged sectors of the population, its revolutions. and class struggle.

As will be seen later, the influence of David Alfaro Siqueiros on the mural work of Felipe Seade will be reflected in the representation of local people and social conflicts, using the wall as a witness of Uruguayan history.

After the Mexican Revolution of the twentieth century, a new concept of nation arose that demanded the creation of an identity. In this democratizing movement, the participation of artists that rethink and redefine the art scene using the wall as a means of communication with the people, played a fundamental role. This movement goes beyond the Mexican border, thanks to the muralist Siqueiros, who makes an appeal to the new generation of American artists inviting them to build a monumental, human, public and identitarian art.

The momentum of the development of art and culture is reflected in laws as No. 10,098 "Debt Public Buildings" published in the Official Gazette on December 31 of 1941, which stated that in addition to the construction of schools these areas should contain plastic works. Article 8 of the same law cites: "In the construction of school buildings may be invested up to five percent (5%) in artistic decoration, which will be entrusted to national painters and sculptors" (Tomeo, 2011).

As a result in the Southern Cone, there is a greater mural production which reflects the subversion of international languages to discuss their own content. These events promoted the development of an art esthetic based on a nationalism of egalitarian impulses and performing an authoritative interpretation of pre-Columbian culture roots. This nonconformist character is reflected not only conceptually, but also technologically as art techniques go through a period of experimentation where traditional ones are replaced by newer products.

2.4.3 IMPLICATIONS IN THE ARTISTIC ACTIVITY: URUGUAYAN SOCIAL REALISM

During the first decades of the twentieth century there is a transformation regarding the view of "the ideal Uruguayan country" as a result of the changes of thought, conscience and perception that take place both in Uruguay and abroad.

At the beginning of the 1930s, the social role of the artist and his artistic purposes are starting to be considered. Social realism in Uruguay takes place within a dynamic and artistic cultural context, bringing together diverse artists representing certain ideological nuances and different esthetic and plastic formations (Linari, 2009).

This way they defend a humanistic realism, disregarding the aspects of artistic language and strengthening the ethical aspects of the social role of the work. The creation responds to the artist's attitude towards reality, engaging with the problems of society, telling revolutionary historical moments, and ultimately, presenting a duality between art and life.

Social Realism in Contemporary Mural Painting

The type of art that would speak about man and history and would serve as a visual platform to project political and social demands, regards the walls the ideal space to project itself. The murals made in some cases had a didactic intention recounting the Uruguayan history. While many of the artists who promoted the murals were Communists, the most common theme in the murals they created was the allegory, based on universal values such as work and dignity (Tomeo, 2011).

2.4.4 URUGUAYAN SOCIAL REALISM'S MOST RELEVANT ARTISTS

2.4.4.1 Norberto Berdía (1900–1983) (Portyn de San Pedro, 2013)

The information about Norberto Berdía is given in Table 2.4.

Table 2.4 Norberto Berdía Information

Author details	
Name	Norberto Berdía
Birth:	Montevideo: June 6th, 1900
Death:	Montevideo: March 13th, 1983
Brief bibliography:	

1920–1924: He began his work in the Fine Arts Circle, organizing his first group show in Uruguay in 1924.

1925–1930: Moves to Buenos Aires.

1947: Wins first prize for a mural at the Faculty of Architecture.

1955: Travels to Mexico.

He traveled through Europe and America.

He painted murals in:
- School Lorenzo Rosales, Mexico.
- Hotel San Rafael in Punta del Este with the theme AMERICA.
- Guide base of the Grand Chamber, Newsroom of the country of Montevideo Journal.

Work inspired by the American themes.

Source: Graphical record of the R&D Project PUCM, 2013.

FIGURE 2.1 Mural detail Casino San Rafael (*Source:* Graphical record of the R&D Project PUCM, 2010).

FIGURE 2.2 Work of ANCAP, 1947, Fresco (*Source:* Graphical record of the R&D Project PUCM, 2013).

2.4.4.2 Luis Mazzey (1895–1983)

The information about Luis Mazzey is given in Table 2.5.

TABLE 2.5 Luis Mazzey Information

Author details	
Name	Luis Mazzey
Birth:	Montevideo; August 15th, 1895
Death:	October 3rd, 1983
Brief bibliography:	
1910–1915: began his studies at the Fine Arts Circle.	
Entered the school of arts and crafts.	
1936: Travels to Buenos Aires, returning after a few months.	
1937: Travels to Europe, France, and Italy.	
1957–1970: Professor of drawing, painting and engraving at the School of Fine Arts (Uruguay).	

(Portón de San Pedro, 2013)

2.4.4.3 Carlos González (1905–1993)

The information about Carlos González is given in Table 2.6.

TABLE 2.6 Carlos Gonzalez Information

Author details	
Name	Carlos González
Birth:	Melo: December 1st, 1905
Death:	Montevideo: April 30th, 1993
Brief bibliography:	
He created several murals in collaboration with the painter and engraver Luis Mazzey, one through tender organized by the ANCAP and another one for the Wholesalers Center.	
ANCAP industries. 1947. Fresco. ANCAP headquarters.	
Trade history in Uruguay. 1948. Fresco. 2.60 x 1.65 m. Center for traveling salesmen of Uruguay.	

Source: Graphical record of the R&D Project PUCM, 2013.

(Portón de San Pedro, 2013)

2.4.4.4 Demetrio Urruchúa (1902–1978)

The information about Demetrio Urruchúa is given in Table 2.7.

TABLE 2.7 Demetrio Urruchúa Information

Author details	
Name	Demetrio Urruchúa
Birth:	Pehuajó, Buenos Aires; April 19th, 1902
Death:	October 2nd, 1978
Brief bibliography:	
1908: Moves from the province to the capital.	
1910: Returns to the countryside, he later returned to the capital of Buenos Aires.	
1941: He paints with Amalia Nieto Carmen Garayalde and Mª Rosa Ferrari, La mujer compañera del hombre. Fresco 23 m x 3 m located in the Artigas teachers Institute Library.	

Source: Graphical record of the R&D Project PUCM, 2013.
(Urruchua, 2015)

2.4.4.5 Esteban Garino (1919–2001)

The information about Esteban Garino is given in Table 2.8.

TABLE 2.8 Esteban Garino Information

Author details	
Name	Esteban Garino
Birth:	Montevideo; 1919
Death:	2001
Brief bibliography:	
Self-taught, he specialized in painting with watercolors.	
Travels to Argentina, Brazil, Chile, Paraguay and Europe.	
Construction workers. 1964. Synthetic paint. Hall of Faculty of Social Sciences, UDELAR.	

Source: Graphical record of the R&D Project PUCM, 2013.
(Castillo, 2010)

Social Realism in Contemporary Mural Painting

FIGURE 2.3 Detail of *Women are man's companion*, 1939–1941. Fresco. 23 m x 3 m. *Source:* Graphical record of the R&D Project PUCM, 2013.

FIGURE 2.4 Detail of *Construction workers*, 1964 (*Source:* Graphical record of the R&D Project PUCM, 2013).

Finally, the role Felipe Seade (1912–1969) played in Uruguayan social realism will be extended in later chapters, with an emphasis on one of his works, "Allegory to work" carried out in 1936 and located in the No.1 room or hall of the House of Culture of Colonia del Sacramento.

2.5 CONCLUSIONS

Deprived of its identity for centuries, Uruguay was forged under foreign domination until it achieved national independence in 1925.

The different artistic movements developed in the early twentieth century are therefore included in a context of changes and ideological conflicts that directly impact the arts. The Uruguayan social realism is also affected by these vicissitudes and settles into the country due to its profound social and human message. The development of a popular art committed to society was brought to Uruguay by Mexican muralist David Alfaro Siqueiros. His visit to Uruguay in 1933, and its relationship with artists like Felipe Seade influenced significantly the artistic production of this movement.

Therefore, Uruguayan Social Realism symbolizes a humanistic realism in which the social and historical message of the work wins over the traditional language. The creative process responds to the problems faced by society, using revolutionary historical moments as a theme, and portraying the relationship between art and life.

KEYWORDS

- documentation
- historical research
- popular art
- social realism
- Uruguayan history

REFERENCES AND BIBLIOGRAPHY

Ainsa, F. (2008). *Espacios de la memoria: Lugares y paisajes de la cultura uruguaya*; Ediciones Trilce: Montevideo, p. 106. ISBN 13: 978-99-7432-484-8.

Barrán J. P. (1995). El nacimiento del Uruguay moderno en la segunda mitad del siglo XIX. Web de la Red Académica Uruguaya. [Online]. Published online: Sept, 1995. Retrieved from: http://www.rau.edu.uy/uruguay/historia/Uy.hist3.htm (accessed Dec 11, 2013).

Barrán J. P. (1995). El Uruguay indígena y español. Web de la Red Académica Uruguaya [Online]. Published online: Sept, Retrieved from: http://www.rau.edu.uy/uruguay/historia/Uy.hist1.htm (accessed Dec 11, 2013).

Barrán J. P. (1995). El Uruguay pastoril y caudillesco en la primera mitad del siglo XIX. Web de la Red Académica Uruguaya [Online]. Published online: Sept, 1995. Retrieved from: http://www.rau.edu.uy/uruguay/historia/Uy.hist2.htm (accessed Dec 11, 2013).

Barrán J. P. (1995). Historia del Uruguay en el siglo XX. Web de la Red Académica Uruguaya. [Online]. Published online: Sept, (1995).. Retrieved from: http://www.rau.edu.uy/uruguay/historia/Uy.hist4.htm (accessed Dec 11, 2013).

Benvenuto L. (1981). *Breve historia del Uruguay*; Ediciones Arca: Montevideo.

Caetano, G., & Rilla, J. P. (2005). *Historia contemporánea del Uruguay. De la colonia al Mercosur*. 3rd ed., CLAEH/Fin de Siglo: Montevideo, ISBN: 99-7461-429-5

Demetrio Urruchua's web [Online]. Retrieved from: http://www.urruchua.com.ar/biografia.html (accessed Nov 30, 2015).

Di Maggio, N. (2009). Norberto Berdía faltó a la cita. La Red 21, Cultura. [Online]. Published online: Aug, 31, 2009. Retrieved from: http://www.lr21.com.uy/cultura/378711-norberto-berdia-falto-a-la-cita (accessed Nov 30, 2015).

Fernandez Oscar, M. (2011). "Allegory to work" de Felipe Seade: Activación Patrimonial, Estudios Previos y Propuesta de Intervención. Master Thesis. Departamento de Conservación y Restauración de Bienes Culturales. UPV.

Goldman, S., Handwerg, M. J., Stein P., Faulkner, S., & Pacheco, M. (1996). *Otras rutas hacia Siqueiros*. Instituto Nacional de BBAA: México, pp. 216, 221, 222. ISBN: 96-8299-573-6.

Herner, I. (1994). Siqueiros: el lugar de la Utopía. INBA: México, p. 115.

La Independencia de la Republica Oriental del Uruguay. Sus próceres, grandes figuras y confraternidad sudamericana. Biblioteca Americana, Buenos Aires, 1950.

Orsi Meny, Z. (2008). *Liceo departamental de Colonia. Historia y proyección*. Ediciones del Sur: Montevideo, ISBN 13: 978-99-7481-492-9.

Partnoy, R. (2012). Con Urruchúa, el guiador. Diálogos-ensayos Poetas Argentinos. Washington [Online]. Published online: Jan, 2012. Retrieved from: http://rpartnoydialogos1.wordpress.com/con-urruchua-el-guiador/ (accessed Nov 30, 2015).

Peluffo Linari, G. (1992). Realismo social en el arte uruguayo, 1930–1950 [Catálogo]. Publicación del Museo municipal de BBAA. Museo Blanes. Ministerio de Educación y Cultura: Montevideo.

Peluffo Linari, G. (2009). *Historia de la pintura en el Uruguay*. In *Representaciones de la modernidad, 1930–1960*. 6th ed. De la banda oriental: Uruguay, Vol. 2. ISBN: 99-7410-053-4.

Portón de San Pedro. (2013). Currículum Norberto Berdía [Online]. Retrieved from: http://www.portondesanpedro.com/autor-curriculum.php?id=273#ixzz2 mnljP1Qx (accessed Nov 25, 2013).
Portón de San Pedro. Currículum Carlos González [Online]. Retrieved from: http://www.portondesanpedro.com/autor-curriculum.php?id=286#ixzz2 moN8AP7U (accessed Nov 25, 2013).
Portón de San Pedro. Currículum Luis Mazzey [Online]. Retrieved from: http://www.portondesanpedro.com/autor-curriculum.php?id=273#ixzz2 mnljP1Qx (accessed Nov 25, 2013).
Rela, W. Uruguay (2006). Banda de los Charrúas Colonización Española, Vol. 1. *1527–1810. Cronología histórica documentada* [Online]. Published online: 2006. Retrieved from: http://www.walterrela.com/ (accessed Nov 24, 2013).
Rela, W. Uruguay (2006). Cronología histórica documentada. Vol. 3. *1817–1830* [Online]. Published online: Retrieved from: http://www.walterrela.com/ (accessed Nov 24, 2013).
Rela, W. Uruguay (2006). Cronología histórica documentada. Vol. 5. *Part I. 1903–1930* [Online]. Published online: 2006. Retrieved from: http://www.walterrela.com/ (accessed Nov 24, 2013).
Rela, W. Uruguay (2006). Cronología histórica documentada. Vol. 6. *Part II. 1931–1967* [Online]. Published online: 2006. Retrieved from: http://www.walterrela.com (accessed Nov 24, 2013).
Rela, W. Uruguay (2006). República Oriental del Uruguay. Vol. 4. *1830–1903. Cronología histórica documentada* [Online]. Published online: 2006. Retrieved from: http://www.walterrela.com/ (accessed Nov 24, 2013).
Rela, W. Uruguay (2013). Artigas. *Vol. 2. 1811–1820.* [Online]. Published online: (2006). Retrieved from: http://www.walterrela.com/ (accessed Nov 24, 2013).
Tomeo, D. (2011). Murales en el Uruguay: La reconstrucción de un patrimonio invisible [Online]. Published online: 2011. Retrieved from: http://www.fhuce.edu.uy/jornada/2011/Ponencias%20Jornadas%202011/GT%2033/Ponencia%20GT%2033%20Tomeo.pdf (accessed Nov 18, 2013).
Carlos Castillo (2010). Eduardo Esteban Garino. 25/11/2013, de Un mar de Pintura Sitio web: http://unmardepintura.blogspot.com.es/2010/10/eduardo-esteban-garino.html

CHAPTER 3

FELIPE SEADE AS THE MAIN FIGURE OF THE URUGUAYAN SOCIAL REALISM

M. FERNÁNDEZ-OSCAR,[1] V. SANTAMARINA-CAMPOS,[2] M. Á. CARABAL-MONTAGUD,[3] and M. J. GUIRADO-RUANO[4]

[1]Phd Student, Department of Conservation and Restoration of Cultural Heritage, UPV, 3N Building, Camino de Vera s/n, 46022 Valencia, Spain, Tel.: +34-661685561, E-mail: mirferoscr@gmail.com

[2]Associate Professor, Research Micro-Cluster Globalization, Tourism and Heritage, Department of Conservation and Restoration of Cultural Heritage, UPV, 3N Building, Camino de Vera s/n, 46022 Valencia, Spain, Tel.: +34-963879314/79414, E-mail: virsanca@upv.es

[3]Associate Professor, Department of Conservation and Restoration of Cultural Heritage, UPV, 3N Building, Camino de Vera s/n, 46022 Valencia, Spain, Tel.: +34-963877000/73132, E-mail: macamon@crbc.upv.es

[4]Phd Student, Department of Conservation and Restoration of Cultural Heritage, UPV, 3N Building, Camino de Vera s/n, 46022 Valencia, Spain, Tel.: +34-635814197, E-mail: mariajguirado@gmail.com

CONTENTS

3.1 Introduction 66
3.2 Objectives 66

3.3 Methodology 66
3.4 Felipe Seade: Artist Biography and Works 67
3.5 Conclusions 76
Keywords 76
References and Bibliography 76

3.1 INTRODUCTION

This chapter focuses on the study of the figure of the artist Felipe Seade, born in Antofagasta, Republic of Chile, in 1912. The subject of his work is part of the social realism movement that denounces the daily struggles of the popular class and attempts to bring attention to the violation of their fundamental rights.

In the words of Larnaudie "The central topic was our history, the great accomplishments but also the stories of the common men, women's everyday tasks, our own history, Uruguay's, America's, the peoples' struggles" (Larnaudie, 2004).

Like many artists, the work of Felipe Seade develops concern for social issues. Issues such as the need to describe the work of the local people or the representation of everyday hardship of the marginalized were key in the development of the Uruguayan realist and were highlighted in an interview with Carolina Seade and Juan Felipe Seade. "He adopts the Uruguayan society like just another Uruguayan, as culturally he feels Uruguayan" (Informant 32).

3.2 OBJECTIVES

The study of Felipe Seade's life and work aims to record and document the authorship of the work "Allegory to work" and to study the role of the artist, his artistic development and the murals he created.

3.3 METHODOLOGY

The search for documentation about the artist and his work was carried out in both public and private archives. The most relevant ones were searched for sources likely to contain relevant information for the study such as monographs, articles periodicals, official documents, newspaper articles, reports, and expert testimony, referencing the mural painting by Felipe Seade. The work plan was organized as follows:

Location, collection and management of public and private archival documentation, scanning and document capture, organization and cataloging of information and finally, analysis and pre drawing conclusions to interpretation.

3.4 FELIPE SEADE: ARTIST BIOGRAPHY AND WORKS

As a leading figure of the Uruguayan social realism, the work of Felipe Seade dominates the idea of portraying a social archetype to picture the Uruguayan people (Figures 3.1–3.3). Therefore, he develops a social

FIGURES 3.1 AND 3.2 Felipe Seade, 1921 and 1940 (*Source:* Family photos of Alicia Seade-Delboy, with permission).

FIGURE 3.3 Felipe Seade self-portrait, *Media Cara*, 28 x 38 cm^2 (*Source*: Family photos of Alicia Seade-Delboy, with permission).

language that promotes the celebration of the anonymous characters and defines the aspects of the rural population. The commitment to the reconstruction, preservation and popularization of the collective heritage are the foundations of Felipe Seade's work.

In an interview with the artist done by a Uruguayan newspaper, he expressed his attachment to social issues:

For me, the problem is quite clear and quite simple. Actually—and I speak especially to my younger colleagues—the important thing is not how but what we paint. Let's be straight. Our generation must dig deep into the human drama, because we were born far away from operettas and tearful Italian operas and, instead we were raised in an era of bombs and guns, and we cannot mislead the public with illuminated pictures and landscapes represented like still life [...] not during any other time before, true art was based on such anemic and small standards but, on the contrary, always sided the people and expressed their human problem, with all its tragedies and joys. Therefore, give the people, their history (Mundo Uruguayo, 1940).

3.4.1 BIOGRAPHY

Felipe Seade, as mentioned previously, was born in 1932 on August 23th in the Republic of Chile. He moves to Uruguay in 1923. In 1934 the artist settles in Colonia del Sacramento after taking a position as professor of drawing of the old Liceo Departamental (Table 3.1).

According to studies conducted in this project, during the 1920s Seade begins his artistic life. In 1931 he began creating art exhibitions with a tireless work ethic, distancing himself from the academic canons held by the Circle of Fine Arts. Instead he chose the representation of the social and human scenery of the Uruguayan people. Here begins his artistic condemnation of the way society is established a thought on which he will reflect during his entire career.

In the mid-1930s Seade developed a small number of large-scale works that are a clear reflection of the artist character and his personal ideas. An example of the large paintings he made during this time of technical and material experimentation, are the murals "Allegory to work," "The head of Artigas" and "People's march to the high stone."

3.4.2 WORK

His bold, clear and straightforward style, stood out immediately within the Uruguayan social realism movement (Figure 3.4). In the words of Alvarez, the mission of the artist's paintings roots in its necessity: "In Seade there are neither descriptions nor redundancies, but an American's indispensable language that doesn't shut up when facing the power of the arts" (*Álvarez*, 1983).

TABLE 3.1 Outline to the Chronology of the Life and Work of Seade's Mural

1912	1923	1930	1934	1936	1937	1939	1969
Felipe Seade is born	Seade moves to Uruguay	He starts his artistic life in Colonia	Teaches at the Departmental Lyceum of Colonia	*Allegory to work*	*The March of the people to the High Stone*	*The head of Artigas*	Felipe Seade's death

FIGURE 3.4 *Two drunks on the street*, Charcoal on paper 34 x 24 cm². *Source:* Family photos of Alicia Seade-Delboy, with permission.

In 1936, Seade painted "Allegory to work" (Figures 3.5 and 3.6). With dimensions of 5 x 6 m², the mural is located in the drawing room of the old Lyceum, later transformed into the *House of Culture* (Casa de Cultura). In this work he represented the fields of work, science, art and industry, with the kind of clear and direct language that characterizes him.

In 1937, he paints in Colonia with students of the Lyceum, "The head of Artigas," of 5 x 6 m² (Orsi, 2008: 94), for which no data was found.

In the main hall of the Lyceum No. 2, one of the oldest buildings in Florida (Uruguay), he paints in 1939 "The march of the people of the high stone," of 20 m long and 4 m high (Orsi, 2008) (Figures 3.7 and 3.8).

In the mural the painter portrays the moment of the declaration of Uruguayan independence in 1825. The words of Professor Daniela Tomeo taken from a press release describe the scene represented by Felipe Seade in this work:

Some kind of secular procession, led by "the Patriarchs," including figures we can identify as doctors, farmers, a priest, all of them followed by members of the popular sector, led by women and children. At the end, the most vulnerable ones, including Afro-descendants and again women and

Felipe Seade as the Main Figure of the Uruguayan Social Realism 71

FIGURE 3.5 Felipe Seade's "Allegory to work" in 2012. *Source:* Graphical record of the R&D Project PUCM, 2011.

FIGURE 3.6 Felipe Seade, 1936. *Source:* Rivero, S., & Carro, L. (2002). Reprinted with permission of the authors.

FIGURE 3.7 Detail of *The March of the people to the High Stone*. 1939. Lyceum No. 2 M Trueba, Florida. *Source:* Graphical record of the R&D Project PUCM, 2011.

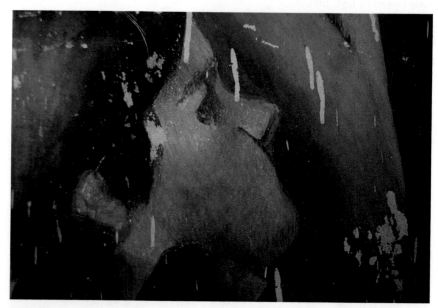

FIGURE 3.8 Detail of *The March of the people to the High Stone*. 1939. Lyceum No. 2 M Trueba, Florida. *Source:* Graphical record of the R&D Project PUCM, 2011.

children in the foreground. [...] He portrays a picture in which society is marked by its class differences. [...] The representation of the figures in profile like marching in a patriotic celebration procession (Texto de la Ley Camplementana Camplementana, 1950).

The side section of the mural shows parts of the text of the Eastern Province declaration of independence, drawn up at the Florida Assembly in 1825 August 25th, and the unification and national flag creation law. It reads:

... resuming to the eastern province its full rights, liberties and prerogatives, inherent in the other peoples of the earth, and indeed declared free and independent from the king of Portugal, the Emperor of Brazil, and from any other universe and with large and full power to follow the forms in use and exercise its sovereignty when it deems appropriate (Texto de la Ley Camplementana Camplementana, 1950).

The eastern province of Rio de la Plata is attached to the others of this name in the South American territory as is free and with an spontaneous will from the people who compose it (... In the town of San Fernando de la Florida, 25th of August of the year, 1825) (Tomeo, 2011).

In the murals already mentioned as well as in most of his artistic and muralist production, the social and documentary commitment (Figures 3.9 and 3.10) that Felipe Seade showed in his representations and the themes chosen is appreciated.

From 1941 Seade deepens his study of various techniques, preparing colors with special oils, researching the results of using resins for achieving transparencies and experimenting with the fresco technique in small formats.

His preoccupations are discussed in publications of the National School of Fine Arts: "He attempted to boost student awareness of the need to investigate materials, and reviewing the way of working" (Escuela Nacional de Bellas Artes, 1986).

His work (Figures 3.11 and 3.12) is characterized by the shape of the brush stroke, it adapts to large forms and is placing the subjects away from the light source. This feature can be seen in the making of the Lyceum mural in Florida. On the other hand, he depicts a conscious message in the wall representing the union of life experience with the treatment of visual elements.

FIGURE 3.9 Woman washing clothes in the Uruguay river. *Source:* Seade-Delboy, A. (2004). Reprinted with permission of the authors.

FIGURE 3.10 *Laundresses of the river Uruguay.* Oil on wood 118 x 80 cm^2. *Source:* Family photos of Alicia Seade-Delboy, with permission.

Felipe Seade as the Main Figure of the Uruguayan Social Realism 75

FIGURE 3.11 *Two girls*. Dora and Susanna, sisters of the painter. Oil on wood, 58 x 76 cm². *Source:* Family photos of Alicia Seade-Delboy, with permission.

FIGURE 3.12 *Susana.* Portrait of the painter's sister. Oil on plywood. 112 x 83 cm². *Source:* Family photos of Alicia Seade-Delboy, with permission.

Seade made clear in all of his works that the subject could not be separated from its living and working conditions, since it forces them into the distinctive servile attitudes of the time "he continuously insisted on the need to be bound to significant facts, in all facets of life" (Escuela Nacional de Bellas Artes, 1986).

3.5 CONCLUSIONS

Living in Uruguay since his youth, Felipe Seade developed, with direct influences of David Alfaro Siqueiros and the Mexican muralists, his pictorial work in this country. Although most of his artistic production consists of drawings and sketches on cardboard and wood, Felipe Seade, a leading exponent of Uruguayan social realism left a testimony of paintings with strong links to the people, their history and identity.

Through its two unique and now protected wall paintings, Felipe Seade makes his concern about the condition of the Uruguayan people clear. In these works he develops his own artistic language, based on the adaptation of the stroke to large spaces and to the creation volumes.

KEYWORDS

- Allegory to work
- Felipe Seade
- history
- identity
- Uruguayan Social Realism

REFERENCES AND BIBLIOGRAPHY

Ainsa, F. (2008). *Espacios de la memoria: Lugares y paisajes de la cultura uruguaya;* Ediciones Trilce: Montevideo, p. 106. ISBN 13: 978-99-7432-484-8.

Álvarez, T. (1983). Catálogo del Museo de Arte Moderno de Buenos Aires, Buenos Aires [Online]. Published online: 1983. Retrieved from: *Official Felipe Seade's web* http://felipeseade.com/blog/2004/10/tulia_alvarez.shtml (accessed Nov 1, 2013).

Arteaga, J. J. (2000). *Breve historia contemporánea del Uruguay*. Fondo de cultura Económica.
Biblioteca Nacional-Lectores de banda Oriental [Online]. Retrieved from: http://www.bibna.gub.uy/ (accessed Nov 1, 2014).
Escuela Nacional de Bellas Artes. *Texto de apertura*. In: *Folleto Exposición Homenaje* [Online]. Intendencia de Montevideo. University of the Republic y Escuela Nacional de Bellas Artes: Montevideo, 1986. Retrieved from: *Official Felipe Seade's web* http://www.felipeseade.com/blog/2004/10/escuela_naciona.shtml (accessed Nov 1, 2013).
Fernandez Oscar, M. (2011). "Allegory to work" de Felipe Seade: Activación Patrimonial, Estudios Previos y Propuesta de Intervención. Master Thesis. Departamento de Conservación y Restauración de Bienes Culturales. UPV.
Laranaudie, O. (2013). *Felipe Seade, el artista y su obra*, in *Official Felipe Seade's web*, [Online]. Retrieved from: http://www.felipeseade.com/blog/2004/10/olga_laranaudie.shtml (accessed Nov 1, 2013).
Martínez Muracciole, E. (2011). *Comisión de Patrimonio salva un mural en el Liceo de Florida*. La Red 21: 17 de junio de, 2011 [Online]. Retrieved from: http://www.lr21.com.uy/economia/458052-comision-del-patrimonio-salva-un-mural-en-liceo-de-florida (accessed Oct 25, 2013).
Orsi Meny, Z. (2008). *Liceo departamental de Colonia. Historia y proyección*. Ediciones del Sur: Montevideo, ISBN13: 978-99-7481-492-9, pág. 94.
Pini, I. (2000). *En busca de lo propio: Inicios de la modernidad en el arte de Cuba, México, Uruguay y Colombia. 1920–1930*. In *Historia y teoría del arte y la arquitectura*. Ed. Universidad Nacional de Colombia: Colombia.
Rivero, S., & Carro, L. (2002). *La construcción de la identidad: 1912–2002*. Ediciones Revista U. Liceo de Colonia: Colonia del Sacramento.
Seade, F. (1940). Entrevista concedida a *Mundo Uruguayo*: Uruguay, Retrieved from: Retrieved from: http://www.felipeseade.com/blog/criticosb.shtml (accessed Jan 10, 2014).
Seade-Delboy, A. (2004). *Official Felipe Seade's web*, [Online], Retrieved from: http://www.felipeseade.com (accessed Jan 7, 2014).
Sullivan, E. J. (1996). *Arte latinoamericano del siglo XX*. Ed. Nerea, S. A., Madrid, ISBN: 84-895-6904-5.
Tomeo, D. (2011). Murales en el Uruguay: La reconstrucción de un patrimonio invisible [Online]. Published online: 2011. Retrieved from: http://www.fhuce.edu.uy/jornada/2011/Ponencias%20Jornadas%202011/GT%2033/Ponencia%20GT%2033%20Tomeo.pdf (accessed Nov 18, 2013).
La Independencia de la República Oriental del Uruguay. Sus próceres, grandes figuras y confraternidad sudamericana. Biblioteca Americana, Buenos Aires, 1950.

INTERVIEWS

- Informant 32. (2011). Carolina and Juan Felipe Seade. Profile: Artists of recognized prestige in Uruguay. Descendants of muralist Felipe Seade. Date of Interview: April 15, 2011.

CHAPTER 4

THE CONTEMPORARY MURAL PAINTING "ALLEGORY TO WORK"

M. Á. CARABAL-MONTAGUD,[1] V. SANTAMARINA-CAMPOS,[2] M. FERNÁNDEZ-OSCAR,[3] and M. J. GUIRADO-RUANO[4]

[1]Associate Professor, Department of Conservation and Restoration of Cultural Heritage, UPV, 3N Building, Camino de Vera s/n, 46022 Valencia, Spain, Tel.: +34-963877000/73132, E-mail: macamon@crbc.upv.es

[2]Associate Professor, Research Micro-Cluster Globalization, Tourism and Heritage, Department of Conservation and Restoration of Cultural Heritage, UPV, 3N Building, Camino de Vera s/n, 46022 Valencia, Spain, Tel.: +34-963879314/79414, E-mail: virsanca@upv.es

[3]Phd Student, Department of Conservation and Restoration of Cultural Heritage, UPV, 3N Building, Camino de Vera s/n, 46022 Valencia, Spain, Tel.: +34-661685561, E-mail: mirferoscr@gmail.com

[4]Phd Student, Department of Conservation and Restoration of Cultural Heritage, UPV, 3N Building, Camino de Vera s/n, 46022 Valencia, Spain, Tel.: +34-635814197, E-mail: mariajguirado@gmail.com

CONTENTS

4.1	Introduction	80
4.2	Objectives	80
4.3	Methodology	81

4.4 Location 81
4.5 Description of the Work 82
4.6 The Passage of Time and the 1981 Intervention 88
4.7 Conclusions 90
Keywords 91
References and Bibliography 91

4.1 INTRODUCTION

The approach to document the study of the mural "Allegory to work" was instrumental in the development of this research as it allowed to gain a broader knowledge about the iconographic aspects of the mural and the historical background of the painting. In addition, it helped to acquire an insight into the artist's persona through the analysis of his work.

Considered a clear example of the Uruguayan Social Realism artistic movement, this work belongs to a time during which the concept of art in the country is redefined. It is in this moment in time and with direct influence of the Mexican muralists and its main figure David Alfaro Siqueiros that the humanist realism work of Felipe Seade develops. Ultimately, his artistic production was dominated by the idea of a social archetype that reflects the characteristics of the rural population, defending its rebuilding and promoting their collective wealth (Fernandez, 2011).

This chapter aims to translate the results of the documentation process carried out on the mural from the standpoint of the scene depicted, its history and location. The research about the circumstances surrounding the painting's attempted destruction in 1981 and the statement made by Felipe Seade's former student; Professor Dardo Ingold, are key references to understand the reasons why it was extensively over painted and the current status of the mural.

4.2 OBJECTIVES

The study about the context and the execution of the work intends to present a thorough analysis of the mural that will contribute to future investigation, its documentary recording and the intervention process.

The Contemporary Mural Painting "Allegory to Work"

4.3 METHODOLOGY

The different phases of researching the bibliographic and documentary sources about the artist and his paintings has been carried out searching on public and private archives likely to contain relevant information. The study and analysis of bibliographical sources included: monographs, articles periodicals, official documents, newspaper articles, reports, and expert testimonies referring to the mural of Felipe Seade. The working plan is structured following the activities listed below:

Location, collection and management of public and private archives, scanning and document capture, organization and cataloging of information and analysis and interpretation prior to drawing conclusions.

4.4 LOCATION

The work "Allegory to work" by Felipe Seade is located in the hall (Figure 4.1) of the current House of Culture and former drawing room of the Departmental Lyceum of Colonia del Sacramento (Figures 4.2).

Declared World Heritage Site by UNESCO in 1995 as the only place in Uruguay, Colonia Del Sacramento called originally *Nova Colonia do Santisimo Sacramento* witnessed since its founding in 1680 by Portuguese

FIGURE 4.1 Mural painting in the auditorium. House of Culture. Colonia del Sacramento (*Source:* Graphical record of the R&D Project PUCM, 2011).

FIGURE 4.2 Courtyard of the House of Culture. Colonia del Sacramento (*Source:* Graphical record of the R&D Project PUCM, 2011).

troops, the coexistence of different identities – postcolonial, Spanish and Portuguese. This defines the characteristics that currently make the city a valued cultural asset.

Colonia del Sacramento is located at 177 km from Montevideo (Uruguay) and is the provincial capital of Colonia.

The Colonia department is located south-west of Uruguay, to the North borders with Soriano, to the East with San Jose and to the South west with Argentina's capital.

4.5 DESCRIPTION OF THE WORK

The mural work represents a painting with strong links to science, art and industry.

A description of the painting can be found in a text by the teacher and codirector of the lyceum, Juan Carlos Silvestre: *The depth is treated at different levels: the choir, the rural family, the scientist with test tubes, and metal worker are placed in the foreground. The harmonic composition shows a noteworthy treatment of the figures, all of them placed in the foreground; the visual perspective or social relevance of the subjects are avoided* (Orsi, 2008).

The Contemporary Mural Painting "Allegory to Work"

FIGURE 4.3 Figure displayed in the mural painting (*Source:* Graphical record of the R&D Project PUCM, 2013).

The work depicts the social situation of the Uruguayan people in the early decades of the 1900s (Figure 4.3), closely capturing each of the existing social figures in the country and the role they played.

These subjects are located in four distinct sectors within the mural: The quadrant dedicated to the work of the land where Felipe Seade represents a household, a man next to a pregnant woman as a symbol of family prosperity. This part might relate to the bond between family and the work in agricultural lands (Figure 4.4).

To the right the subjects of art, childhood and investigation are represented. This depiction can refer to the ongoing cultural development of the country (Figure 4.5).

In the lower left quadrant is depicted the figure of a scientist portrayed in a reflective attitude surrounded by laboratory equipment and several books. This representation could allude to the intellectual part of Uruguayan society (Figure 4.6).

Finally, the lower right quadrant describes a scene about metallurgical work, another labor sector that developed in that decade in Uruguay (Figure 4.7).

FIGURE 4.4 Family: Work of the land (*Source:* Graphical record of the R&D Project PUCM, 2013).

FIGURE 4.5 Art: Children's Choir (*Source:* Graphical record of the R&D Project PUCM, 2013).

FIGURE 4.6 Science (*Source:* Graphical record of the R&D Project PUCM, 2013).

FIGURE 4.7 Industry (*Source:* Graphical record of the R&D Project PUCM, 2013).

According to the critic Fernando Garcia Esteban, it is evident that the work of Seade shows painting skills, and the creation of volumes, "[…] of sculptural quality, heavy, firm" (García Esteban, in Orsi, 2008). He applies color complementing the treatment of volume as well as glazes and subtle impasto painting with large colored areas.

Norberto Tavella in a interview (2007) described the mural as follows:

> The mural he did was wonderful, it was at the lyceum. During the dictatorship it had been painted over, because Seade was a communist. I remember that the frieze with the ants was a simple solution. It was painted with students of the Lyceum. I remember that because I was still going to school, and one day my dad took me by the hand to the lyceum … I remember they were painting the mural on the wall at the back. Seade was painting himself, helped by the pupils with better drawing skills, following the teacher's notes … It shows a scientist, a worker, a pregnant woman, the wheels, the mill's window, and then the entire wall of the large room was covered with walking ants. One of the ants carried a leaf, and the other carried a flower all along the wall. It was painted over a mold that was kept moving around (Orsi, 2008).

Seade employed a Secco technique on the original work (Figure 4.8), using the temple method with a protein binder – egg white – on a polished plaster primed ground. In written documents we find references to the painting technique used in the work." […] It was applied a pre-Renaissance art technique that hasn't been in use for a long time because of the high craftsmanship it requires" (Silvestre, in Orsi, 2008).

"He used ceramist earth pigments and an organic binder (egg white) that were previously applied on plaster, the so-called egg-encaustic technique" (Silvestre in Orsi, 2008).

In the text of Max Doerner it is possible to find some references that might be related to the egg-encaustic technique. This technique consisted in tempera painting with a saponified wax emulsion (soap wax), to which egg and water were added. The addition of a waxy material to the preparation of paint gave a greater strength and durability to the paint layer (Doerner, 2005).

The Contemporary Mural Painting "Allegory to Work"

FIGURE 4.8 Original painting of Felipe Seade. *Source:* Rivero and Carro, 2002. Reprinted with permission of the authors.

Juan Felipe Seade (Informant 32) has stated that he does not remember whether the technique his father used in the making of the mural was egg tempera or encaustic. However, he was able to describe the artist process in mural painting as follows:

The project was first drafted in a small-format paper. Afterwards the drawing was transferred to a 1 x 1 m² gridded graphite transfer paper of a larger format. Then it was fixed to the wall by adhering 1 x 1 m². frames. The drawing was transferred to the wall by means of incision marks. Finally the incision marks were connected by black thin lines followed by the application of glazes and color.

In the same interview the artist's descendants also mention some pigments used by Felipe Seade in his work that showed in the analytical test results of his paintings. "He decorated the front with parallel lines topped with a knot of red earth, ochre, sienna and ochre green colors […]" (Informant 32).

In addition to the various documentary writings confirming the use of the tempera technique for the making of Seade's original painting, it is also possible to find testimonies claiming the use of polyvinyl acetate during the repaint of the mural (Orsi, 2008).

This is a key aspect to be considered in view of the fact that the entire mural has been repainted.

4.6 THE PASSAGE OF TIME AND THE 1981 INTERVENTION

Felipe Seade's mural falls into the intellectual artistic production that develops as a result of the influence of local and Latin-American events. Ever since its making in 1938, the painting has been exposed to vandalism and defacing because of either ideological retaliations or the consequences of its location; a busy hall.

The following synopsis presents the events surrounding the work "Allegory to work" as time went by.

In 1981, the mural already was in a poor state, showing incised inscriptions, erosions, missing areas and carved scrawl in much of the wall surface. This terrible condition lead to the decision to destroy the mural, and consequently a third of the wall was chipped away.

FIGURE 4.9 Dardo Ingold and the rescued work (*Source:* Newspaper magazine "News," 1981).

A few documentary references relate an event that happened when the wall was being chipped, the process was stopped by Professor Dardo Ingold (Figure 4.9), a former student of Seade and associated to the Lyceum. He carried out an improvised restoration in order to rescue Felipe Seade's work (Orsi, 2008).

During the interview conducted on the 4th of July of 2007, Dardo Ingold stated as follows:
One day I go and see -he says- that the builders are digging on the Old Lyceum's mural. So I went to the Municipality and explained to the Colonel Mayor Orestes Apa, what kind of work they were destroying ... Although he was a person who did not have a taste for the arts, he authorized to stop the work and restore the damage. Even though the builders stopped the work, they had already taken all the plaster out up to the brick ground for replastering. So what did we do? ... the repairs took us more than two months. First we covered all cracks with a spatula and plaster, some of them had been done with a sharp point, while trying to respect all of Seade's good work left. Luckily, as he had been my Fine Arts' teacher, I knew the colors he would have worked with: cosolico red, brown, black ... and a bit of ochre. I worked along with the eldest of my students. Next, the cracks were covered and left to be aired and dry. Then the paint was prepared, I did not make it with egg white as the original, since that technique belonged to another era. I managed to make a good size with a bit of cascola (©) as binder to which the pigments were added.
Then we went into "touching-up," only where necessary, with a maximum of respect; however some of the figures had to be redone almost completely, like the scientist in the lab which had disappeared entirely. For this Miguel Angel Odriozola gave me a black and white photo as there was no color photo available, I also traveled to Carmelo to consult Professor Rogelio Ferrari, because he had been a student of Seade as well (Orsi, 2008).

In spite of Ingold's repairs, many aggressions towards the mural continue to happen until today. His effort however received at the time some criticism for being too intrusive on the original work, (Figure 4.10).

"With some of the figures repainted with brighter tonality and a few mistakes due to overlapping paint which was not present in the original" (Silvestri, 2004).

4.7 CONCLUSIONS

The investigation of the bibliography and documentation concludes that Seade's "Allegory to work" is an historic and artistic testimony of the state of Uruguayan society in the early twentieth century. It also portrays the technological and cultural development of the country. It is evident that the planning and execution of the painting on the walls of an old lyceum drawing room was conceived as a symbol of union. It was meant

FIGURE 4.10   Mural repaired, April, 1983 (*Source:* Jorge Vasallo, 1983).

to represent the Uruguayan people, tell their history and document the aspects of their identity. Thanks to the 1981 intervention by Professor Dardo Ingold the destruction of the mural was prevented. He "rescued" the painting from its complete disappearance and preserved the work of Felipe Seade to this day for the Uruguayan people who have maintained a valuable artistic piece of heritage.

This study along with the tests performed in situ on the mural contribute to support and protect a unique heritage site in Colonia del Sacramento therefore expanding the tourist and cultural offer of the city as a result.

KEYWORDS

- actual state
- Allegory to work
- documentation
- history
- painting
- Uruguayan Social Realism

REFERENCES AND BIBLIOGRAPHY

Doerner, M. *Los materiales de la pintura y su empleo en el arte.* Ed. Reverté: Barcelona, ISBN 9788429114232. pp. 249–255.

Espinola, M. (1986). *Catálogo: Felipe Seade Exposición homenaje.* Edición Escuela Nacional de BBAA: Montevideo.

Fernandez Oscar, M. (2011). "Allegory to work" de Felipe Seade: Activación Patrimonial, Estudios Previos y Propuesta de Intervención. Master Thesis. Departamento de Conservación y Restauración de Bienes Culturales. UPV.

Orsi Meny, Z. (2008). *Liceo departamental de Colonia. Historia y proyección.* Ediciones del Sur: Montevideo, ISBN13: 978-99-7481-492-9.

Rivero, S., & Carro, L. (2002). *La construcción de la identidad: 1912–2002.* Ediciones Revista U. Liceo de Colonia: Colonia del Sacrament.

Valuable Rescue. Mural from Seade. Newspaper magazine "News," Montevideo, August 19, 1981.

ARCHIVE

- Photograph of the work. "Alegoria al trabajo" from Felipe Seade, April 1983. Private archive of Jorge Vasallo.

INTERVIEWS

- Informant 32. Carolina and Juan Felipe Seade. Profile: Artists of recognized prestige in Uruguay. Descendants of muralist Felipe Seade. Date of Interview: April 15, 2011.

PART II

ETHNOGRAPHIC RESEARCH OF THE PAINTING "ALLEGORY TO WORK"

CHAPTER 5

"ON THE FACE OF IT": WALL-TO-WALL HOME ETHNOGRAPHY

J. SKINNER

Department of Life Sciences, University of Roehampton, Holybourne Avenue SW15–4JD London, United Kingdom, Tel.: +44-208-392/4895, E-mail: jonathan.skinner@roehampton.ac.uk

CONTENTS

5.1 Introduction 95
5.2 Wall-to-Wall 97
5.3 Murals and Ethnography 98
Keywords 103
References and Bibliography 103

5.1 INTRODUCTION

On the surface of it (see Figure 5.1), the walls are about 30 two bricks high along one mile of Hampton Court Road between Hampton Court Palace and Hampton Wick. That is, 30 bricks laid on top of each other in an alternating pattern of bricks side-by-side lengthwise, and bricks side-by-side widthwise, all capped by two widthwise bricks on their side. There is pattern, order, regularity and manual labor to it. It is masculine and masterly and runs for mile after mile with gentle curves and brick supports at regular intervals. It is confident, secure, esthetic for all its efforts. There is an aura to the mass produced as Benjamin and Warhol work together in symmetry. It looks an early Victorian narrative that has been accepted,

FIGURE 5.1 Hampton Court Road, near Hampton Court, London (*Source:* Skinner, 2016).

respected and repaired. It is a feature of the commute to work, bounding a busy road, each brick lost for a larger masonry that flicks by. On the other side (see Figure 5.2), lies crown land used as royal parks for the public and private crown land for paddocking horses and maintaining a stock of royal deer.

FIGURE 5.2 Bushy Park, Royal Park, Hampton near London (*Source:* Skinner, 2016).

The walls here are a feature of the landscape. They are rock stable. They guide us in our work and leisure times. They can also be read by the wall-to-wall researcher. They tell us something about their erection and their consumption: there is wealth, patience, ownership about the place. There is also an acceptance for the lines, the boundaries, the social levels on display. We fall into step with the natural world on one side neatly and crisply delineated from the charged work travel hidden on the other side. And yet we know about both of them, the other from whichever side we happen to be passing through. There, in my non-work time, I am guided by my dog along an encouraging path. The nature is laid out like an avenue before us with the trees protected from the roaming deer – deer that are human[e]ly culled twice a year. This is 'slow leisure' time. We amble along with all the other neighbors to the royal park. The Red and Fallow deer have been roaming the park since 1529.

My compatriots and I will only visit during the weekend, and my dog and I have only recently moved here.

5.2 WALL-TO-WALL

The anthropologist Eric Wolf (1966: 2) has written that 'the formal framework of [social] economic and political power exists alongside or intermingled with various other kinds of informal structures which are interstitial, supplementary or parallel to it.' Though writing about the power and politics of complex societies, his words are useful in drawing our attention to the informal, to the gaps between the brickwork, to—indeed—the mortar sustaining the social structure. Wolf (1966: 2) continues, '[t]he anthropologist has a professional license to study such interstitial, supplementary, and parallel structures in complex society and to expose their relation to the major strategic, overarching institutions.' Whilst the anthropologist might have an intellectual 'poaching license,' as Geertz picked up from Kluckhohn (Macksey, 1981; Geertz, 1988), we hardly retain a professional license to access all areas of society. Further, the informal is not just 'supplementary' to the system because it comes from it. These derivations can be critical to supporting the system just as the mortar is interstitial and supports and sustains the wall. The informal is the glue that binds and breathes. As such it should be the focus of the anthropologist.

In their work on borders and borderlands, political anthropologists Thomas Wilson and Hastings Donnan recognize Wolf's contribution to political anthropology, to drawing our attention to the informal, the margins, the space between that is symbolically, emotionally and ideologically loaded. Daphne Berdahl (1999) goes further and characterizes these frontier spaces in her ethnography of life on the former East German borderzone where the stark and immediate front-tier positionality gives an intensity and a clarity to the social and political forces on either side of the villagers. These margins are playful areas, ambiguous places for all their frontier physicalities. These borders can also be places of asymmetrical confrontation. They are 'Zwischenraum' for Berdahl (1999: 8), 'the space between the boundaries of the known in which people negotiated the limits of the possible.' Famously, it is the nature of these boundaries rather than the cultural stuff that they enclose that is of particular importance, noted Frederick Barth (1998: 15) in his game-changing comment about the study of ethnicity. We are 'canalized' and dichotomized by these structures and fissures.

When we write novels we pass through walls, metaphorically speaking. We pass through walls separating reality and the unconscious. We see what world lies on the other side of a wall, come back to our own side and describe in detail, in writing, what we saw (Murakami, 2014: 18).

Haruki Murakami makes a virtue of passing through these walls, of breaking through these obstacles, when he writes of them as a motif in his novels and takes the reader with him. He asks if it is possible to live without a system of walls, noting that for every wall that falls, another is constructed or fathomed whether mental, ethnic, religious, wall of greed or wall of fear.

5.3 MURALS AND ETHNOGRAPHY

Our usual environment is Bangor, Northern Ireland. There, the walls around us on my commute to work are covered, painted, decorated. These walls are not like the Great Wall of China or the Berlin Wall: they are not walls of division but walls of expression (like Seade's mural artwork). Some have religious slogans ('You must be born again') or cryptic references to the religious slogan (John 3:7); I once went for a walk through a local country park and every wall, gate post and tree along the path had stickers on them forcing me to read and recall this Biblical reference also found on the walls I commute past. McLuhan should visit Northern Ireland!

There is a Loyalist housing estate near my house: Kilcooley, owned by the Northern Ireland Housing Executive. It is the third largest housing estate in Northern Ireland. There, many of the walls are painted with intricate, exquisite and incontrovertible images and slogans—'Loyalist' refers to a Protestant group who support Northern Ireland being part of the United Kingdom and Northern Ireland, and so are antithetical to Republicans who want Northern Ireland to join the Republic of Ireland and are largely Catholic in religion-. They are paramilitary identifiers with pseudo-military signifiers that mark out the ethno-national living space, typically on the gable ends of houses. Here, viewed from the road (see Figure 5.3), on the left is the red hand of Ulster as a right-handed fist under a British crown as opposed to the official open palm. Around the

FIGURE 5.3 Ulster Freedom Fighters and Sir Edward Bingham murals, Kilcooley nr Bangor, Northern Ireland. *Source:* J. Skinner, 2016.

fist are 'Ulster Freedom Fighters,' and above the fist are 'Bangor Young Newton.' The Young Newtons were one of a number of 'Tartan' street gangs around East Belfast from the 1970s; young men who acted out casual violence against Catholic families, businesses and other youths. Presumably this is the Bangor local branch. These gangs became the youth wing of the Ulster Defence Association (UDA), a loyalist paramilitary group that was outlawed from 1992. Prior to that time, the UDA maintained its political credibility by using the Ulster Freedom Fighters (UFF) as the violent, illegal wing of the organization to carry out its terrorist activities ranging from intimidation and extortion to upwards of 400 murders. Had I known the depths of this inhumane history at the time, I would not have attended their annual Eleventh Night bonfires – an all-night rave with fire to commemorate Dutch Protestant Prince William of Orange arriving to fight the Scottish Catholic King James VII in 1690; an antiJacobite jump-up under a 100ft bonfire in front of the mural where the Irish tricolor and contemporary Republican or papal symbols have also been burned.

To the right of the Loyalist mural, behind 'Kyle's' graffiti, lies the peeping head in black and white of a proud man under a darkened cross. To his left runs a regimented bank of television aerials. This house gable end figures Sir Edward Bingham who was awarded the Victoria Cross during World War One. He oversees from the end of Orlock Gardens cul de sac (if you look for him on google maps, you will see his face automatically blurred). In the top of the roof apex is a rendition of the Victoria Cross: a lion above a crown above the words 'For Valour.' 'V' and 'C' are on both sides along with the curved words Messines and HMS Nestor, referencing his destroyer and one of the savage battles of World War One where Irish/Ulster Divisions suffered over 70,000 killed, wounded or missing. Below, to his left, and just out of view, are two destroyers at sea. To Bingham's right is an iconic image of British soldiers 'going over the top' of their trench into the wall of barbed wire characterizing no man's land. Uniquely, the gable wall has a small window in it below one of the soldier's helmets. The entire imagery rests on a bed of poppies and is between two supposed columns with his birth and death dates. Beneath the mural—but still a part of it—reads an explanation for the mural, as well as information for viewing Bingham's medal in the local museum:

Rear Admiral Edward Bingham VC, OBE, son of Lord Clanmorris was born in Bangor and served in the Royal Navy during the First World War. He was awarded the Victoria Cross for his actions in engaging the German fleet during the Battle of Jutland. The Bingham family name adorns various settings in the town where he is remembered with pride. Rear Admiral Bingham's Victoria Cross was purchased by North Down Borough Council and is on display at the North Down Museum.

The entire mural is painted in blacks and shades of gray with an ochre background. It smells of age, the smoke of battle, the fog of war. The military mural legitimates the paramilitary mural. It sanctions the extrajudicial activities.

As a mural, it is explanatory as well as expressive; esthetic as well nationalistic. In tourist terms, the text below Bingham is the marker for the sight. It frames the semiotic imagery. For MacCannell (1989: 45), the marking is a stage of 'enshrinement' as the tourist attraction is sacralized. Here, Bingham is made to transcend history, to justify present-day activities, to encourage future fights. He serves as a recruiting sergeant/ Rear Admiral from Bangor and for Bangor. For murals critic Bill Rolston (2010), these murals are figurative 'windows' into the community, giving us insight into loyalism – as well as the literal view into a loyalist household in this case. The mural is not a static signifier, however, for political studies critics Neil Jarman and Debbie Lisle: mural interpretations change with the contemporary swirl of politics – the murals are a backdrop for Jarman (1998); they are both products and participants in the discourses of power for Lisle (2006), the networks of production and reception and consensus as to what endures. Once the mural is finished, it is open to interpretation, mis-interpretation, over-interpretation even (Hobart, 1999); Lisle writes of reading, rereading and misreading [2006: 33]. There is authority in the presence of Bingham and the Ulster Freedom Fighters (cf. Wilson, 1983). They overlook the Bangor commuters, and they show that there is support for their perspectives.

Julian Watson (1983) asks what makes a 'homebrewed' mural such as the one on the outskirts of Bangor successful? Their appeal has to be broad, he acknowledges, but it cannot be universal we can add. Murals can be touched up, repainted, painted over, even vandalized if they are not valued. Is it fear or pride or a mixture of both that keeps the Ulster Freedom Fighters mural so prominent and so pristine? Neither the walls of Hampton Court Road, nor the walls of Kilcooley Estate have graffiti on them. There is no counter expression to their structure (park boundary) or the expression on them (political mural). They are not attacked or daubed. Perhaps they are ignored? Graffiti is the 'third force' in the Loyalist/ Republican murals mix according to Lisle (2006: 46), a form of political art in and of itself. Watson (1983: 6) writes of community art projects not appealing to the community and so suffering genital embellishment: Derry does not do Disney, so the Department of the Environment discovered at the Rossville Flats. Yet, on the corner of Strand Road leading to Queen's Quay in Derry/Londonderry, on the way to a recent self-guided walking tour of the history of the Troubles through the murals of the Bogside, I spied a gable-wide Gothic Romantic art mural of a robin sitting on an animal skull in a broken brush environment that had passed the informal community murals test (see Figure 5.4). You can see, here, stark contrast between the new mural and nearby power switch box – between what appears to be a large, sustained piece of nonpolitical art, and the shorthand staccato signatures – the tags that come and go by night. They do not seem

FIGURE 5.4 Mural and graffiti between Strand Street and Queen's Quay Road, Derry/Londonderry, Northern Ireland. *Source:* J. Skinner, 2016.

to mix. Though there are cases of hybrid wall arts, 'intertextual' (Lisle, 2006: 47), where references to those named in the covert assassination of human rights lawyer Pat Finucane were 'covered up' by paint subsequently thrown over the mural. Both the presence and absence of art and/or graffiti on walls are telling indicators in their own rights. They tell me, from wall-to-wall where I live and commute, about myself, and my neighbors. Both are walls emblazoned with meaning.

KEYWORDS

- **anthropology**
- **Bangor**
- **ethnography**
- **graffiti**
- **Hampton Court**
- **Northern Ireland**
- **walls**

REFERENCES AND BIBLIOGRAPHY

Barth, F. (1998/1969). 'Introduction,' In: Barth, F.: *Ethnic Groups and Boundaries: The Social Organization of Culture Difference*, Waveland Press Inc.: Long Grove, pp. 9–38.

Berdahl, D. (1999). *Where the World Ended: Re-Unification and Identity in the German Borderland.* University of California Press: Berkeley.

Geertz, Clifford. (1988). This Week's Citation Classic: The Interpretation of cultures. *CC*, no. 33, p. 14.

Hobart, M. (1999). 'As They Like It: Over-interpretation and Hyporeality in Bali,' In: Dilley, R.: *The Problem of Context.* Berghahn Books: Oxford, pp. 105–144.

Jarman, N. (1998). 'Painting Landscapes: The Place of Murals in the Symbolic Construction of Urban Space,' In: Buckley, A.: *Symbols in Northern Ireland.* Institute of Irish Studies and Queen's University of Belfast: Belfast, pp. 81–97.

Lisle, Debbie. (2006). Local Symbols, Global Networks: Rereading the Murals of Belfast. *Alternatives*, no. 31, pp. 27–52.

Maccannell, D. (1989). *The Tourist: A New Theory of the Leisure Class.* Schocken Books: New York.

Macksey, Richard. (1981). Introduction: Texts, Contexts, and the Rules of the Games. *Modern Language Notes*, no. 96, pp. v–vii.

Murakami, Haruki. (2014). Racing to Checkpoint Charlie – my memories of the Berlin Wall. *The Weekend Guardian*, Reviews, 22 November, p. 18.

Rolston, B. (2010). *Drawing Support: Murals in the North of Ireland*. Beyond the Pale Publications: Belfast.

Watson, Julian. (1983). Brightening the Place up. *Circa*, no. 8, pp. 4–10.

Wilson, Des. (1983). The Painted Message. *Circa*, no. 8, pp. 19–20.

Wilson, Th., & Hastings, D. (2005). 'Territory, identity and the places in-between: Culture and power in European borderlands.' In: Wilson, Th., & Hastings, D.: *Culture and Power at the Edges of the State: National Support and Subversion in European Border Regions*. LIT Verlag: Munster, pp. 1–30.

Wolf, E. (1966). 'Kinship, Friendship, and Patron-Client Relations in Complex Societies,' In: Banton, M.: *The Social Anthropology of Complex Societies*, London: Tavistock Publications, pp. 1–22.

CHAPTER 6

PARTICIPATORY ACTION RESEARCH (PAR) IN CONTEMPORARY COMMUNITY ART

V. SANTAMARINA-CAMPOS,[1] E. M. MARTÍNEZ-CARAZO,[2]
M. Á. CARABAL-MONTAGUD,[3] and M. DE-MIGUEL-MOLINA[4]

[1]*Associate Professor, Research Micro-Cluster Globalization, Tourism and Heritage, Department of Conservation and Restoration of Cultural Heritage, UPV, 3N Building, Camino de Vera s/n, 46022 Valencia, Spain, Tel.: +34-963879314/79414, E-mail: virsanca@upv.es*

[2]*Phd Student, Department of Conservation and Restoration of Cultural Heritage, UPV, 3N Building, Camino de Vera s/n, 46022 Valencia, Spain, Tel.: +34-655868675, E-mail: evatxu1893@gmail.com*

[3]*Associate Professor, Research Micro-Cluster Globalization, Tourism and Heritage, Department of Conservation and Restoration of Cultural Heritage, UPV, 3N Building, Camino de Vera s/n, 46022 Valencia, Spain, Tel.: +34-963877000/73132, E-mail: macamon@crbc.upv.es*

[4]*Associate Professor, Research Micro-Cluster Globalization, Tourism and Heritage, Department of Management, UPV, Camino de Vera, s/n, 46022, Valencia, Spain, Tel.: +0034963877680/76821, Ext. 76844, E-mail: mademi@omp.upv.es*

CONTENTS

6.1 Introduction 106
6.2 Objectives 108
6.3 Methodology 109

6.4   Development of Sensitization-Training Program 110
6.5   Conclusions.. 131
Keywords... 132
References and Bibliography... 133

6.1   INTRODUCTION

Nowadays, the conservation of cultural properties has to go hand-in-hand with heritage policies in order to achieve a social and economic balance. Heritage should consider not only the safeguard of authentic objects, but also the value of these objects as representatives of culture. Otherwise, cultural properties are reduced exclusively to objects of the past. On the contrary, we should reinterpret them. "Heritage is reformulated considering its social use, not only from a defense position, of simple rescue, but also taking into account the complex view of how a society belongs to its history and it can involve new social sectors" (García Canclini, 1993:60). These policies regarding to heritage restitution need to reach their significance during the intervention and management processes. It is necessary to include and interact with different stakeholders to carry out a sustainable intervention, where the community should take the main role. The management process should take into account the different interrelation factors of any cultural heritage site.

Other important aspect is to define which role has the community in this context. The community, as owner of their history, should protect and conserve the cultural properties because they are the testimony of their life as well as an important legacy for the present and future generations. In this context, the participatory action research (PAR) is the best option to achieve these actions, to encourage and to aware the community, by means of a collective, interactive and participatory work. History becomes a symbol of their identity and the communities have the responsibility of transmitting and keeping it.

Nowadays Colonia del Sacramento in Uruguay, has an increasingly touristic culture demand (Informant 48 and 49). It was declared as a World Heritage Site in 1995. Moreover, it is the first market access in the country. This situation let to the creation of a tourist observatory, which collects the information referent to the tourists' profile, and the Welcome, Interpretation and Tourism Centre, which is managed by the Uruguayan Ministry of Tourism since 2007 (Informant 34). Currently, Colonia del Sacramento is facing new challenges, for example how to redirect tourism to other heritage sites of the country such as Rosario's Mural Art Museum, 50 km from Colonia del Sacramento. This open-air museum was created in 1994 as a tourism attraction, inspired by the success of the San Gregorio de Polanco's mural paintings (Informant 47), to generate a local economic development as the village had a deep crisis in that time.

We observed that the heritage process in the South neighborhood (Figure 6.1) has suffered many physical and social changes, as well as a mercantilist degradation which has affected the preservation of its identity (Informant 38 and 50). The South neighborhood was "beautiful" (Informant 45) and its main feature was the neighborhood life itself. However, it was affected by the housing market converting this district into a ghost town. Furthermore, they changed its name and the color of its façades (Informant 40). Social relationships were important in the past of Colonia but no longer (Informant 42). Thus, one of the most important facts is the high gentrification process experimented in the last decade, because of the increase in the new use and value of the houses (Informant 37 and 39). The

FIGURE 6.1 Detail of the Real Street of Colonia del Sacramento's historical neighborhood. *Source:* Graphical record of the R&D Project PUCM, 2011.

heritage buildings are only conserved and preserved in their external structures, but without content for refunctionalization (Etulain and González, 2012). The local population, who lived there, have moved progressively due to new touristic and commercial interests, which are linked by the heritage as a tool of economic development (Informant 36 and 41). These risks are caused by the massive tourism. Nowadays, tourism, heritage and marketing draw the glocalization of new maps in Colonia.

6.2 OBJECTIVES

In this context, we performed a project to create synergies between culture and development by means of a sensitization-training program. The main objective of the program was to get approach to the social, political, economic and cultural reality of the community of Colonia del Sacramento. Thus, the research team and the community could discover the heritage values, to support and reactivate them, linking these values to the Uruguayan mural painting production, specifically to the Felipe Seade's artwork "Allegory to work." Within this project, the democratization construction of the community was sought out in order to gain social participation and cohesion; firstly, the integration of the local population and, in particular, of some vulnerable groups.

The topic of the different activities of the sensitization-training program was linked to the heritage use and cultural management of the Seade's mural painting. Each action was focused on one public depending on their age. They were divided into three categories: children, adults and retired people. They participated in the *"Heritage, participation and collective action Workshop. Dialogues about the heritage city Colonia del Sacramento"* (sensitization program) and the postgraduate course *"Sustainable management of Latin American cultural heritage"* (training program). The project was based on a democratic and cooperative point of view, where the local population, the institutions and the research team participated. The purpose was to get a more real view of the local issues. The Institutions that participated in the organization were UPV (including the Heritage Restoration Institute, Postgraduate Vice-Rectorate, Lifelong Learning Centre), the Colonia Intendancy and the Group "Friends of the Historical Neighborhood of Colonia del Sacramento." Other organizations that collaborated were: AECID (Spanish Ministry of Foreign Affairs and Cooperation), Forum UNESCO University and Heritage (UPV), Ministry of Education and Culture, Commission of the National Cultural Heritage, CULTÚREA, Head of Studies in Cultural Management, Provincial Deputation of Valencia and Universitat de València.

Those activities seek to ensure the community participation and responsibility, with the aim to reach a local development, encouraging social cohesion, promoting the gender equality to develop new alternatives and socializing the children from the area, using as essentials the protection of cultural right and the sustainable cultural management.

6.3 METHODOLOGY

The methodology applied in the workshop was the Participatory Action-Research (PAR). The starting point is the interaction between researchers and participants, who are the research actors, taking both part of the process. We created working groups to enhance a dialog for finding the most appropriate tools to achieve relevant and effective results, to identify issues and to reach a local sustainable development. Moreover, another intention was to give them a voice and identity (Lucas, 2013).

This method was chosen based on the idea that the community has an active role and participants are actors of the study. As the project was finished, everybody was aware of the local problems and their possible solutions. In this case, the main purpose was that they were able to identify the advantages and disadvantages in the local heritage field, in order to achieve a heritage activation, sustainable development and its cultural relation (local and global). Furthermore, the participants could recognize, by means of PAR methodology, which symbols are part of their identity. Thus, the community was able to understand the legitimate implication in these processes, empowering their identity and collective memory.

The PAR was applied in the activities of the sensitization-training program, which were focused on Colonia del Sacramento's heritage. The training project worked on some cultural heritage themes such as cataloging and inventorying of the cultural heritage, photographic analysis of the artwork and characterization and colorimetric monitoring. Moreover, the design of the technical project of the intervention in the mural painting was elaborated. The aim was to learn from these subjects and understand the different parts as a whole: mural painting intervention as a tool to preserve the heritage properties.

6.4 DEVELOPMENT OF SENSITIZATION-TRAINING PROGRAM

6.4.1 THE SENSITIZATION PROJECT: "HERITAGE, PARTICIPATION AND COLLECTIVE ACTION WORKSHOP— DIALOGUES ABOUT HERITAGE CITY OF COLONIA DEL SACRAMENTO"

Taking part of the sensitization project was free in order to obtain a high amount of local participation. The activities were performed during the Tourism Week at Easter (23, 24, 25 and 26 of April, 2011). They were designed as a competition for each group. The workshops were held in the Casa de la Cultura of Colonia del Sacramento (except to a gymkhana). We used this building for several reasons:
- This house is a symbol of the popular culture for the community.
- The Seade's mural painting "Allegory to work" is located inside this house. The artwork was a key element of the project and an icon of the Colonian muralism. The registration of the activities can demonstrate the work that took place there. The workshop participants and the researchers could interact and recognize directly the mural intervention process.

"... Seade ... became a drawing teacher who worked at the school, because the school ... this house, it was the Municipal School before ... He'd always been a very famous painter ... This mural was painted in 1938 because it isn't a usual painting ... it has a value, a high heritage value ... The fact is that he wasn't from Colonia, he settled down, his family came to live here ... Generations and generations were their students ... When the house became a school, that place was chosen to paint the mural ... It's a more representative place, indeed."

"...most of the population that went to the school has seen it because it is in the Conference hall, therefore everybody knows it."

"The mural was used as a backstage...it's a great pleasure that it was restored... because of its significance for the painter. He was

Participatory Action Research (PAR)　　　　　　　　　　　　　　　　　　　111

FIGURE 6.2   Poster of *Heritage, participation and collective action workshop. Dialogues about the heritage city of Colonia del Sacramento.' Source:* Graphical record of the R&D Project PUCM, 2011.

not Uruguayan, he settled down here but after he was more a Uruguayan. Well, he did his best for adapting to the Uruguayan culture for painting and education, this was his life" (Informant 51).

Heritage, participation and collective action workshop. Dialogues about the heritage city of Colonia del Sacramento was divided in three sessions (Figure 6.2):

SESSION 1: "Draw your heritage" and "In search of the Treasure"

Description

The activities of the session were:
1. A competition to draw what Colonia del Sacramento heritage means to them: "Draw your heritage" at Colonia del Sacramento's Culture House (Figures 6.3–6.5).

2. Cooperative gymkhana: "In search of the Treasure" Colonia del Sacramento's historical neighborhood, World Heritage (Figures 6.6–6.8).

Objectives

- Teaching by means of the participation and the importance of interacting and acknowledging the local identity, development and sustainability.
- Empathizing with the researcher environment so that the community can understand the importance of protecting and conserving their weak cultural/natural heritage.
- Helping to discover the different dimensions of Colonia del Sacramento's cultural heritage.
- Causing a collective reflection by means of a ludic and participatory-constructive dialog, in order to protect the heritage in a sustainable way.

FIGURES 6.3 The drawing process at workshop inside Colonia el Sacramento's Culture House, "Draw your heritage." *Source:* Graphical record of the R&D Project PUCM, 2011.

Participatory Action Research (PAR)

FIGURES 6.4 The drawing process at workshop inside Colonia el Sacramento's Culture House, "Draw your heritage." *Source:* Graphical record of the R&D Project PUCM, 2011.

FIGURES 6.5 The drawing process at workshop inside Colonia el Sacramento's Culture House, "Draw your heritage." *Source:* Graphical record of the R&D Project PUCM, 2011.

- Working with the Participatory Action-Research methodology to achieve planned objectives.

Topics

- Identity, development and sustainability.
- Dimensions of the cultural heritage.
- Responsibility and sustainable management of the cultural/natural heritage.

Participatory group dynamics

The first session "Draw your heritage," was offered to children to represent by drawing and painting how they understood their heritage (Figure 6.3). They described how they identified it and what encouraged both their creativity and artistic skills within the participatory-social tools. Every drawing and painting was exhibited in the Teatro Municipal Bastión in Colonia del Sacramento at the closing ceremony. This exhibition was used as a method for sensitization and education. The aim was to encourage, by means of teaching, the communities implication and participation.

With their drawings, we succeed to the participation of the children from Colonia del Sacramento. Thus, of the 26 participants, who were between 8–16 years old, 40% identified their heritage with the natural heritage, 36% with the monumental heritage, 16% with the immaterial heritage, 4% with the gastronomic heritage and 4% with the movable cultural property.

- 10 participants represented the natural heritage: seven drawings represented the Colonia's bay and five the sunset. Two of them were farms and the other was a landscape.
- 9 participants represented the monumental heritage: three of them were The Ciudadela's door (it belongs to the world heritage area), three of them the lighthouse (it belongs the world heritage area), one of them the Portuguese architecture of the XVII-XVIII century (it belongs the world heritage area) (Figure 6.4), and one of them drew Piriápolis' air view because he was born there (Piriápolis is in the Maldonado region, Uruguay).

- Four participants identified the immaterial heritage: two of them drew the tradition of taking the "mate," one of them the "Candombe" (World immaterial heritage in 2009) and the other the dance "Tango" (World immaterial heritage in 2009).
- Only one participant identified the gastronomic heritage: He drew a flag of "tortas fritas" (Uruguayan typical sweet).
- Only one participant identified the national heritage, he drew a symbiosis between the Uruguayan flag and the Uruguayan maps.

The second activity we conducted was the gymkhana "In research of the Treasure" (Figure 6.6) where we worked with the essential concepts of conservation of heritage, identity, plundering and respect. To achieve this goal the researchers and local population participated in this cooperative-interactive competition. The gymkhana was in Colonia historical neighborhood. They answered several questions about Uruguayan material and

FIGURE 6.6 Detail of cooperative gymkhana done in the workshop "In Research of the Treasure" developed in Colonia del Sacramento's historical neighborhood, which was declared world heritage in 1995. *Source:* Graphical record of the R&D Project PUCM, 2011.

immaterial heritage, taking the information from the participatory-interactive dialog with the community. For each question right, we gave them a piece of a collective puzzle, which they could make once the gymkhana finished. Besides, they had to figure out some enigmas that helped them to find the place where the answers were hidden.

All the participants were together, they do not separate at any time during the competition. Therefore, they respected each other work. Each group had the help of a researcher for the learning process, so they could enjoyed the gymkhana.

When the competition finished and they arrived to the finish line, they made the puzzle (Figure 6.7). On purpose, the organizers removed several pieces, so we could work the concepts of heritage sacking, cultural respect and the need of collective working. With the image of the puzzle we reconstructed, in a symbolical way, the process of the Uruguayan History. In this case, the image of the puzzle belonged to Carlos González's and Luis Mazzey's mural *"Las Labores del ANCAP"* (Figure 6.8) which they both

FIGURE 6.7 How we set up the puzzle of *"Las Labores del ANCAP"*'s mural. The pieces each groups ontained by proceeding the gymkhana. *Source:* Graphical record of the R&D Project PUCM, 2011.

Participatory Action Research (PAR) 117

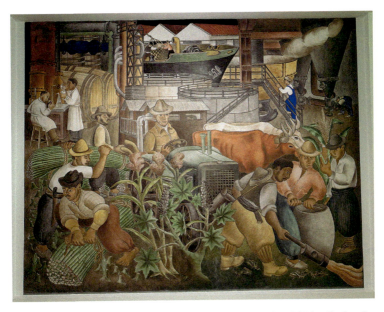

FIGURE 6.8 Mural *"Las Labores del ANCAP,"* it painted in 1947 by Carlos González and Luis Mazzey inside the ANCAP Building. *Source:* Graphical record of the R&D Project PUCM, 2011.

painted in 1947 inside the ANCAP building in Montevideo (Ministry of Education and Culture). In this painting, the artists represented the concept of social function very well, and it was the base of the project. The theme of the mural is a great expression of the Social Realism style, which portrays the fast industrial and social process that Uruguay experimented after the Second World War (1939–1945). Thus, in *"Las Labores del ANCAP"* we can see at the forefront the farm working in several labors, the harvest, the pruning time… and the beginning of Modernity, with the use of a tractor replacing the oxen. The representation of the field has a double meaning, first the farm physical features follow the times of Afro-American slaves and second, the painter represents the work in ANCAP, as for example the distilling of alcohol. On the central left, there are chemists who work on the distillation. They seem to put the alcohol into the barrel. In the central area, it is represented the mechanisation of the industry where the worker seem to supervise the production. Finally, it is represented the maritime market, so important for the economy in that age with the exportation to Europe, later destroyed during the Second World War.

Results

- Socializing the youngest in essential values such as Cultural Rights, their defense and sustainable heritage management using an integral, cooperative and plural development.
- Knowing the cultural heritage in order to identify themselves.
- The contribution of this activity is based on teaching in participatory-collective values focusing on culture, development and sustainability, working the relationship between heritage sustainability and sustainable heritagization.

SESSION 2: "From participation to action. Sustainable heritage—action program for Colonia del Sacramento"

Description

The activity performed in this session was focused on our research, taking a critical and thoughtful analysis about the current situation of Colonia del Sacramento and its heritage.

Objectives

- Opening ways of civic participation for their implementation in the activation and conservation of the heritage.
- Strengthening the ability to analyze the heritage reality, its present and future, discovering different dimensions of Colonia del Sacramento.
- Working, by means of the participatory-action methodology, in the importance of the popular culture as driver of identity, development and sustainability.
- Causing a collective reflection for a constructive dialog about heritage in Colonia del Sacramento.

Topics

- Sustainable heritage management.
- Activation and conservation of the heritage.

Participatory group dynamics

Twenty people, between 18–55 years old, participated in the activity which was divided into four groups. In the first meeting we explained the main goals of the project and the dynamics (Figure 6.9). The participants could use guide notes and make a photographic analysis about Colonial heritage (Figure 6.10). We gave them a throwaway camera to each group, so they could portray local cultural properties that they selected as the most representative (Figure 6.11).

In the second meeting, they just took photos. They did a presentation (around 90 min) using guide notes, encouraging the constructive and plural dialog between participants (Figure 6.12). The four groups explained their works with the support of their photographs (Figure 6.13).

As conclusion of this session, we can say that every group had the same standpoint, based on the point of view of the UNESCO, and the 95% talked about the historical neighborhood. As a conclusion, a

FIGURES 6.9 Work dynamics, to they had been made of analysis of Colonian's heritage by the photographic images of workshop *"From participatory to the action. Action-patrimonial sustainable program for Colonia del Sacramento."* Graphical Record of the R&D Project PUCM, 2011.

FIGURES 6.10 Work dynamics, to they had been made of analysis of Colonian's heritage by the photographic images of workshop *"From participatory to the action. Action-patrimonial sustainable program for Colonia del Sacramento."* Graphical Record of the R&D Project PUCM, 2011.

FIGURES 6.11 Work dynamics, to they had been made of analysis of Colonian's heritage by the photographic images of workshop *"From participatory to the action. Action-patrimonial sustainable program for Colonia del Sacramento."* Graphical Record of the R&D Project PUCM, 2011.

Participatory Action Research (PAR) 121

FIGURES 6.12 Work dynamics, to they had been made of analysis of Colonian's heritage by the photographic images of workshop *"From participatory to the action. Action-patrimonial sustainable program for Colonia del Sacramento."* Graphical Record of the R&D Project PUCM, 2011.

FIGURES 6.13 Work dynamics, to they had been made of analysis of Colonian's heritage by the photographic images of workshop *"From participatory to the action. Action-patrimonial sustainable program for Colonia del Sacramento."* Graphical Record of the R&D Project PUCM, 2011.

reflection was made about the current situation of the heritage exploitation that suffers Colonia due to the massive tourism, where the main heritage use is based on covering a short-term economic development.

Result

- Becoming the community closer to their heritage culture knowing the situation of their heritage and achieving a collective view to manage it.

The contribution of this activity was to teach based on the participatory-collective values. It was focused on culture, development and sustainability. We worked the concept of heritage management, which combines development, culture and sustainability.

SESSION 3: "Before and after. Colonia's alive memory. Sustainable heritage action-planning for Colonia del Sacramento"

Description

The activity of this session was focused on the participatory investigation based on the collective memory. In order to achieve a critical and thoughtful analysis around the present situation of Colonia del Sacramento heritage, a study of their identity elements was done.

Objectives

- Committing retirees of the community to be bearers of their culture.
- Reflecting about the potential of the politic, economic and communicative dimension of their culture as a strategy of sustainable development.
- Becoming closer to the heritage as economic and politic element in the sustainable development.
- Working with retirees of the community around their importance as actors in the conservation and protection of their cultural/natural heritage.

Topics

- The potential that the politic, economic and communicative dimensions have on culture as one strategic form of sustainable development.
- The heritage as politic and economic driver of sustainable development.

Participatory group dynamics

During the first meeting, we explained why we had focused the project in Colonia del Sacramento and we pointed out the importance of the community to participate as bearers and keepers of the Colonia's memory and culture. They began the activity writing an essay with the support of old newspaper cuttings. Eighteen participants, from 55 or more years old, were divided into three groups. They began with a brainstorming to create an ideal environment to develop a constructive dialog (Figures 6.14 and 6.15).

FIGURES 6.14 Group dynamics in the workshop "A before and an after. Colonia's alive memory. Patrimonial sustainable action-planning to Colonia del Sacramento." *Source:* Graphical record of the R&D Project PUCM, 2011.

FIGURES 6.15 Group dynamics in the workshop "A before and an after. Colonia's alive memory. Patrimonial sustainable action-planning to Colonia del Sacramento." *Source:* Graphical record of the R&D Project PUCM, 2011.

FIGURES 6.16 Group dynamics in the workshop "A before and an after. Colonia's alive memory. Patrimonial sustainable action-planning to Colonia del Sacramento." *Source:* Graphical record of the R&D Project PUCM, 2011.

Participatory Action Research (PAR) 125

In the second meeting, the groups wrote an essay and, afterwards, they explained the old newspaper cuttings they had chosen (Figure 6.16). Sharing several ideas and points of view was very positive. The first explanation turned around The Silver River's history and its islands, as a driver of social and economic development. In the second, they described the social structure of the South neighborhood in the 60s and a sinking of The Silver River. Finally, they talked about Colonia del Sacramento tourism development (Figure 6.17).

When the explanations were finished, a reflection was made about the photographs and old documents that the participants had brought. As the documentation was so good, it was registered and inserted in the report of the project.

Results

- Heritage sustainable responsibility by the transmission of culture as a driver of socialization.

The contribution was based on teaching the participatory community values, focusing on culture, development and sustainability. The main objective was to build a collective memory and to be conscious of their importance as actors for the conservation and identity of their culture.

FIGURE 6.17 Outline of magazine made by one of the work groups in the workshop "A before and an after. Colonia's alive memory. Patrimonial sustainable action-planning to Colonia del Sacramento." *Source:* Graphical record of the R&D Project PUCM, 2011.

The sessions concluded with a closing ceremony, which was at the Teatro Municipal Bastion del Carmen (Figure 6.18). We expressed our gratitude to the participants delivering some certificates, diplomas and prizes.

Finally, there was a roundtable: *"Talk with our heritage"* where some actors took part: a consultant of the Commission of the National Heritage of the Ministry of Education and Culture of Uruguay, a historian of Colonia, a responsible of the restoration in the Rosario Mural Art Museum and a member of the Group of Friends of the Historical Neighborhood of Colonia del Sacramento. As a conclusion of all these activities with the community, they analyzed the strengths and weaknesses detected to be included in the final study.

SPECIFIC CONCLUSIONS OF THE "HERITAGE, PARTICIPATION AND COLLECTIVE ACTION WORKSHOP. DIALOGUES ABOUT THE HERITAGE CITY OF COLONIA DEL SACRAMENTO"

- Most of the participants, who were between 8–35 years old, represented the historic neighborhood as the new suburb due to the declaration as a World Heritage Site in 1995.

FIGURE 6.18 Closing ceremony of the workshop, in the Teatro Municipal Bastion del Carmen. *Source:* Graphical record of the R&D Project PUCM, 2011.

- Most of the participants who knew it before as the South Neighborhood, complained about the breakdown of the social and cultural structure.
- Most of the participants included The Silver River like an actor for the development of the Colonian identity.
- They considered tourism as a driver of economic development. However, they criticized its standpoint, **excessively** influenced by the politic activities, which affected some private economic interests.
- Altogether, 64 participants took part in the workshop.

6.4.2 TRAINING PROJECT. POSTGRADUATE COURSE "SUSTAINABLE MANAGEMENT OF LATIN AMERICAN CULTURAL HERITAGE"

Nowadays, in Uruguay an official training or Graduate in Conservation does not exist. Besides, the absence of a deontological code has favored a careless conservation of the murals, with unqualified practice and unsuitable interventions.

In this sense, most of the professionals come from other artistic areas and their perspective is repainting the artwork, not recovering it. One example of this situation is the Seade's mural "Allegory to work." Usually the technical team delegates the conservation work to the artists. This fact reduces the price of the intervention but it does not promise good results. Besides, there is no transfer of a correct training. The absence of a specific training in this area limits and complicates the research. It gives a restrict knowledge of artworks and their conservation, because there has not been previous documentation for their possible intervention.

In the same way, technicians do not have the help of a scientific laboratory, which causes an uncertainty while processing and obtaining the results. These kind of 'intuitive' methods counteract the lack of proven data.

These circumstances have generated a strong foreign dependency. Local technicians should go abroad to learn and consolidate their knowledge in Conservation. They have to work with foreign consultants and professors, even importing equipment and material. This situation causes a negative sustainable development of technical and human resources; at the same time costs increase. Besides, local technicians often pay (partial or totally) most of the time spent there, courses, etc.

This context claims the urgent need to implement an official training or Graduate in Conservation, by the National Institute of Fine Arts (University of the Republic), in coordination with the Restoring Unit of the National Commission of the Cultural Heritage (Ministry of Education and Culture of Uruguay), and the rest of organizations involved in the heritage area.

In parallel to the sensitization community program, we decided to support and encourage the progressive implementation of the conservation training at the University, giving lectures on the cultural heritage intervention. Thus, it could allow in the future to train human resources and, in particular, local experts (with or without academic degree), in the sustainable heritage management. That could delete the dependency in foreign bodies, make easier the access of training and generate the protection and promotion of the diversity of the Uruguayan cultural expressions as driver of development.

In 2011, we offered, as a first step, the postgraduate course: *Sustainable management of Latin American cultural heritage*. It had a good acceptance and we had participants from Uruguay, Argentina and Spain. As it was the first phase of the research project, it allowed the training of the local technicians and, in the second phase, their integration in the conservation process of the mural "Allegory to work. Moreover, this program was used for a meeting point between Spanish technicians and experts of the Restoring Unit of the National Commission of the Cultural Heritage (Ministry of Education and Culture of Uruguay). A process of co-learning and exchange of knowledge was initiated, which allowed to restore together the Seade's mural painting in 2013.

Furthermore, it was developed a specific training course at the University of the Republic. It was lectured by two professors, one from the Universitat de València and other from the UPV, including a practice within the framework of the mural "Allegory to work," offering a real and close view of the work in this area. The first four modules were focused on theoretical and experimental aspects, and took place at the Faculty of Humanities (Montevideo). The last module was given into the meeting room of the Casa de la Cultura (Colonia del Sacramento), where is the Seade's mural painting, in order to show a practical and direct way of the beginning of the mural's intervention, emphasizing its social and identity role (Figure 6.19). Thus, the main objective of this course was underlining the idea of a sustainable intervention as the unique model of management of the cultural/natural heritage, as it generates profits in the long-term for the community.

The course covered 72 h, 40 with theory and 32 with practical, divided in five independent modules, which specific objectives were:
1. Module: Cultural heritage:
    • Studying the process of construction and institutionalization of the cultural/natural heritage.
    • Going deeply in the most important aspects of tourism and heritage in relation to the new globalized contexts.
    • Causing a reflection of the need of sustainable practices.
2. Module: Cultural heritage tools for cataloging and inventorying:
    • Studying the register system and cataloging for the heritage.

FIGURE 6.19 Poster of the postgraduate course "Sustainable management of Latin American cultural heritage." *Source:* Graphical record of the R&D Project PUCM, 2011.

- Checking the need to coordinate actions for fully use a systematic way with giving knowledge and dissemination of the cultural heritage.
3. Module: Apply photography to analyze the artwork:
   - Processing and documenting the artwork.
   - Analyzing the different kinds of recording images by means of visible and invisible radiation, such as the infrared and ultraviolet radiation.
4. Module: Not destructive methods of research in the intervention of the heritage. Characterization and colorimetric monitoring.
   - Becoming closer to the Colorimetry by using a nondestructive method of analysis, in the field of Conservation.
   - Showing a global view of these studies, from obtaining and processing the data.
5. Module: Design of the technical project of the intervention in mural painting. Preparatory phase (Figure 6.20):

FIGURE 6.20 Students registered the painting "Allegory to work," to the development of Module 5 *Design of the technical project of the intervention in mural painting*, inside of the meeting room of the Casa de la Cultura of the Colonia del Sacramento. *Source:* Graphical record of the R&D Project PUCM, 2011.

- Acquiring basic knowledge around the previous treatment to the Conservation process, in order to decide how to finally processing it.
- Encouraging the working team.

Objectives

- Training the experts in specific subjects of the Conservation field.
- Understanding the past and actual situation of the Uruguayan mural heritage.
- Knowing, through the collective dialog between students and the technical team, the different problems about the Uruguayan contemporary mural production.
- Knowing what types of Conservation methodologies are used in Uruguay that are reflected on the interventions already made.

Results

- Drawing issue maps so that we can understand the actual situation of the Uruguayan mural heritage.
- Knowing the needs concerning the Conservation of the Uruguayan contemporary muralism through a collective dialog.
- Being sensitive to the heritage values of the Uruguayan contemporary muralism and the need to conserve it.
- Opening doors towards an official training in the Conservation field.

6.5 CONCLUSIONS

- It is necessary to work with all sectors of the community, because each generation is influenced by different experiences in their life, as well as it is better to be open to a wide variety and plurality of thoughts to understand the community.

- It is important to listen to the community and encourage its participation, as the legitimate heritage responsible people of the site.
- The best way to train and make aware the community of their heritage is education, by means of identity and sustainable development values, causing sustainable heritage activation that represents the community.
- It is crucial the communities' participation (active and constant) in the sustainable heritagization process because they are the carriers of knowledge. Therefore, they are responsible to give a cultural value to their properties as an identification process exists between them. The heritage can be assumed and legitimized as part of their popular identity.
- In the start-up management that they are planning in Colonia del Sacramento the most important part in the short-term is the decentralization of the tourism. It would be more convenient that every participant would be involved (institutional and civil) to use a constructive dialog based on the critical thoughts to find the best solution in that situation. Thus, creating a strategy in favor of the collective interests, a sustainable heritage could be reach.
- It is necessary to implement an official training in Conservation, encouraging national training for the experts to prevent the unqualified practice, which can cause risks towards the Uruguayan contemporary mural production and its conservation.
- Through a collective dialog between communities, participants of the sensitization-training program and the technical team, we could understand the current panorama of the Uruguayan mural heritage and the need for its reactivation and conservation as a symbol of Uruguayan identity.

KEYWORDS

- **Uruguayan Contemporary Mural**
- **Uruguayan Heritage**
- **participatory action research**

- Felipe Seade
- Colonia del Sacramento World Heritage Site
- sustainability
- heritagization
- sensitization community program

REFERENCES AND BIBLIOGRAPHY

Amaro, M., & Cuadrado Laroca, A. (2006). *Usos y desusos del patrimonio cultural: hacia una gestión y consumo responsables en Colonia del Sacramento*. Ideas, Grupo Uruguay, Red Puentes: Uruguay.

Ballart, J. (1997). *El patrimonio histórico y arqueológico: valor y uso*. Ariel: Barcelona, España, *Comentarios sobre la Colonia Antigua del Cnel. Roberto González Arroyo.*

Ballart, J. (2001). *Gestión del patrimonio cultural*. Ariel: Barcelona, España.

De Miguel, B., De Miguel, M., Segarra, M., & Santamarina, V. (2015). Luxury Tourist Value Propositions through Natural Asset Protection: A Study of Small Island Developing States. Parsa, H. G. (Eds.) *Sustainability, Social, Responsibility and Innovations in the Hospitality Industry, 13.* CRC Press Taylor and Francis group. Apple Academic Press, pp. 301–318.

De Miguel, M. Santamarina, V. De Miguel, B., & Segarra, O. (2013). A content analysis to identify tourism opportunities based on mural art. De Miguel, M. *y* Santamarina, V. (Presidencia). *Sustainable tourism, cultural tourism, creative tourism, culinary tourism, heritage and tourism.* Workshop in Tourism and Creative Industry, Workshop Proceedings, Valencia, España.

De Miguel, M. Santamarina, V. De Miguel, B., & Segarra, O. (2013). A content analysis to identify tourism opportunities based on mural art. De Miguel, M. *y* Santamarina, V. (Presidencia). *Sustainable tourism, cultural tourism, creative tourism, culinary tourism, heritage and tourism.* Workshop in Workshop Tourism and Creative Industry, Valencia, España.

De Miguel, M. Santamarina, V. De Miguel, M. B., & Segarra, M. V. (2013). Creative cities and sustainable development: mural-based tourism as a local public strategy" in *Workshop on Services Innovation*, Valencia, España.

De Miguel, M., Santamarina, V., De Miguel, B., & Del Val, M. (2015). Creative cities and sustainable development: Mural-Based tourism as a local public strategy. *Dirección y Organización. Revista de Ingeniería de Organización, 50,* pp. 31–36 [Online]. Retrieved from: http://www.revistadyo.com/index.php/dyo/article/view/429/449 (accessed Dec 13, 2015).

De Miguel, M., Santamarina, V., De Miguel, M. B., & Segarra, M. V. (2013). Mural-based tourism as a driver of sustainable local development. *I International Workshopon Sustainable Operationson Tourism, Travel and Hospitality*. Valencia, España.

De Miguel, M., Santamarina, V., Segarra, M., & De Miguel, B. (2014). Marketing places: highlighting the key elements for attracting mural-based tourism. Mondéjar, J. (Eds), *Sustainable Performance and Tourism: A Collection of Tools and Best Practices, 3*. Chartridge Books Oxford: Oxford, pp. 37–47.

Etulain J. C., & González, A. (2012). Rupturas y reintegraciones socioterritoriales en la intervención de los centros históricos latinoamericanos. *AUGM*. VII Congreso de Medio Ambiente, Montevideo, Uruguay. Retrieved from: http://sedici.unlp.edu.ar/bitstream/handle/10915/26919/Documento_completo.pdf?sequence=1 (accessed Dec 13, 2015).

García, N. (1999). *La globalización imaginada*. Paidós: Barcelona.

García, N. (1999). Los usos sociales del patrimonio cultural, en DD. AA *Patrimonio Etnológico. Nuevas perspectivas de estudio*. Instituto Andaluz de Patrimonio Histórico: Granada, pp. 16–33.

Hernández, G., Santamarina, B., Moncusí A., & Albert, M. (2005). *La memoria construida. Patrimonio cultural y modernidad*. Tirant lo Blanch: Valencia.

Koster, R. L. (2013). Murals for Tourism Development: A Canadian Perspective. De Miguel, M. y Santamarina, V. (Presidencia). *Sustainable tourism, cultural tourism, creative tourism, culinary tourism, heritage and tourism*. Workshop in Tourism and Creative Industry, Workshop Proceedings, Valencia, España.

Lucas, K. (2015). Participatory Action Research. *Nursing research using Participatory Action Research. Qualitative designs and methods in nursing.* (pp. 1–11) Springer Publishing: New York, United States Company, (2015).

Martínez, E. M., & Santamarina, V. (2011). *Patrimonio, participación y acción colectiva. Diversidad, pluralidad y diálogo constructivo entre agentes y sectores de la ciudad patrimonial de Colonia del Sacramento. Uruguay*. (Master thesis). Universitat Politécnica de Válencia: Valencia, España.

Martínez, E. M., De Miguel, M., & Fernández, M. (2013). Sustainable cultural tourism: Museum program of the Uruguayan muralist production of century XX and XXI. De Miguel, M. y Santamarina, V. (Presidencia). *Sustainable tourism, cultural tourism, creative tourism, culinary tourism, heritage and tourism*. Workshop Tourism and Creative Industry, Workshop Proceedings, Valencia, España.

Prats, L. (1997). *Antropología y Patrimonio*. Ariel: Barcelona, España.

Salazar, M. C. (1992). *La Investigación-Acción Participativa. Inicios y desarrollo*. Ed. Laboratorio Popular: Madrid España.

Santamarina-Campos, V., Carabal-Montagud, M. A., & De-Miguel-Molina, M. (2013). *Design and implementation of inclusive cultural policies: contemporary uruguayan muralism as sustainable assets activation*. In: Tourism & Creative industry. Workshop Proceedings; UPV, Servicio de Publicaciones.

Santamarina, V. Carabal, M. A. De Miguel, M., & Martínez, E. M. (2015). Social actors and Contemporary Uruguayan muralism. New trends of research and Heritage Management Plan. Sánchez, M. Shank, W. y Fuster, L. (Eds.) *Conservation Issues in Modern and Contemporary Murals*. Cambridge Scholars Publishing: United Kingdom, pp. 406–430.

Santamarina, V., & Carabal, M. A. (2013). *Informe Final del proyecto Función social del muralismo uruguayo del siglo XX como vehículo y modelo de activación patrimonial sustentable. Descentralización, identidad y memoria*. Ministerio de Asuntos Exteriores y de Cooperación.

Santamarina, V., & Carabal, M. A. (2014). *Informe Final del proyecto Función social del muralismo uruguayo del siglo XX como vehículo y modelo de activación patrimonial sustentable*. Universitat Politècnica de Valéncia.

Santamarina, V., & Carabal, M. A. (2016). *Informe final del proyecto Diseño e implementación de políticas culturales inclusivas: el muralismo uruguayo contemporáneo como herramienta de activación patrimonial sustentable*. Ministerio de Economía y Competitividad, Dirección General de Investigación Científica y Técnica.

Santamarina, V., Carabal, M. A., De Miguel, M., & Martínez, M. L. (2015). Societal and environmental sustainable tourism development. New ways of activation, delivery and diffusion of the Contemporary Uruguayan muralism. M. Shank, W. y Fuster, L. (Eds) *Conservation Issues in Modern and Contemporary Murals*. Cambridge Scholars Publishing: United Kingdom, pp. 489–512.

Valcárcel, J.C; Más, X., Sánchez, M., & Yusa, D. J. (2015). Función social del muralismo uruguayo como vehículo y modelo de activación patrimonial sustentable: Catalogación técnica. M. Shank, W. y Fuster, L. (Eds.). *Conservation Issues in Modern and Contemporary Murals*. Cambridge Scholars Publishing: United Kingdom, pp. 513–524.

INTERVIEWS

- Informant 34. Susana Rebufo. Profile: Community and integrate of cultural organizations. Integrant Asociación Amigos del Museo Municipal Bautista Rebufo. Daughter of the founder of the first Colonian museum (1951). Date of Interview: 19–4–2011.
- Informant 36. Beba Sunino. Perfil: Profile: Community. Date of Interview: 19–4–2011.
- Informant 37. Nenusa Carmen Peralta. Profile: Community. Date of Interview: 19–4–2011.
- Informant 38. Rubio Raul Martinez. Profile: Community. Date of Interview: 20–4–2011.
- Informant 39. Guillermo Haregui. Profile: Community. Date of Interview: 20–4–2011.
- Informant 40. Fernando Cardani. Profile: Community. theatral actor. Date of Interview: 21–4–2011.
- Informant 41. Cholo Jorge. Profile: Community. Date of Interview: 21–4–2011.
- Informant 42 Lula Graciela Sacco. Profile: Community. Date of Interview: 21–4–2011.
- Informant 45. Luz. Profile: Professional of tourist field. Tourist guide of Colonia. Date of Interview: 23–4–2011.
- Informant 47. Mariela Zubizarreta. Professional of tourist field. Director Departmental de Turismo IMC (Anuarios del Observatorio Turístico). Date of Interview: 25–4–2011.
- Informant 48. Pablo Parodi. Profesional of tourist field. Subdirector de Turismo IMC/Founder of the ONG "Don Juan de Arola" about the cultural heritage. Date of Interview: 25–4–2011.

- Informant 49. Cristina Castillo and Lyshie Werosch. Profile: Community. Date of Interview: 25–4–2011.
- Informant 50. Martín Cuadrado. Profesional of tourist field. Tourist observatory. Date of Interview: 25–4–2011.
- Informant 51. Carlos Deganello. Expert of field of cultural management and Conservation of the heritage. Director Dpto. de Cultura IMC. Date of Interview: 26–4–2011.

PART III

SCIENTIFIC RESEARCH OF THE PAINTING "ALLEGORY TO WORK"

CHAPTER 7

PHYSICAL IDENTIFICATION AND DIGITAL RECORD OF PAINTING

J. C. VALCÁRCEL-ANDRÉS[1], M. FERNÁNDEZ-OSCA[2],
E. M. MARTÍNEZ-CARAZ[3], and M. SÁNCHEZ-PONS[4]

[1]*Associate Professor, Department of Conservation and Restoration of Cultural Heritage, UPV, 3N Building, Camino de Vera s/n, 46022 Valencia, Spain, Tel.: +34-963877000/Ext. 73136, E-mail: jvalcara@crbc.upv.es*

[2]*Phd Student, Department of Conservation and Restoration of Cultural Heritage, UPV, 3N Building, Camino de Vera s/n, 46022 Valencia, Spain, E-mail: mirferoscr@gmail.com*

[3]*Phd Student, Department of Conservation and Restoration of Cultural Heritage, UPV, 3N Building, Camino de Vera s/n, 46022 Valencia, Spain, Tel.: +34-661685561, E-mail: E-mail: evmarca2@posgrado.upv.es*

[4]*Associate Professor, Department of Conservation and Restoration of Cultural Heritage, UPV, 3N Building, Camino de Vera s/n, 46022 Valencia, Spain, Tel.: +34-963877000/Ext. 73136, E-mail: mersanpo@crbc.upv.es*

CONTENTS

7.1 Introduction 140
7.2 Objectives 140
7.3 Methodology and Employed Material 140
7.4 Development of the Study 141
7.5 Photography with Visible Light 142

7.6 Photographs Made from Non-Visible Radiation 149
7.7 Conclusions 160
Keywords 161
References and Bibliography 161

7.1 INTRODUCTION

As a first step of direct analysis of the mural, after development of the historical research, the physical study of the work started. To do this, different measurements of the work have been taken such as registration of environmental data, an organoleptic study, and the photographic record with different techniques and types of lighting.

In this chapter, some of the obtained results and the different used methods in the digital photo analyzes for documenting the mural "Allegory to work" by Felipe Seade and location of repaintings are shown. Photography is a noninvasive analysis method, necessary in scientific cataloging projects of cultural heritage, as well as any intervention process pursuing certain scientific rigor and, together with the other studies, contributes to the analysis of the conservation state of the painting.

7.2 OBJECTIVES

The main goal of this physical identification of the work is to gather specific information regarding to:
- The dimensions of the work and alterations.
- The parameters of temperature and relative humidity of the space where it is hosted, as well as varying temperatures of the wall's surface.
- Observe and record aspects of the pictorial surface, which allows extracting data on technical pictorial execution of the work, its state of conservation and previous restorations.

7.3 METHODOLOGY AND EMPLOYED MATERIAL

The study of the painting has been done using different types of analysis, always based on methods and systems that do not involve direct sampling but do provide specific information about the work, the conditions of exhibition and its state of conservation.

For accurately recording the dimensions of the painting and the space in which it is located the laser distance meter PCE-LDM 50® has been used; for recording environmental conditions the temperature humidity meter PCE-HGP® and the multifunctional environmental controller DT-2232® have been used, combined to relative humidity and temperature, both environmentally and contact.

In order to register and observe the surface a microscope with magnifier lenses, the digital PCE-MM 200®, *ReflectaDigiMicroscope USB®*, has been connected to a Tablet-PC.

The selection of the employed instruments for register and the materials used for the photographic study of the pictorial surface was conditioned by the characteristics of the research project. In the same phase cataloging of at least 10 mural paintings spread over several municipalities in Uruguay was foreseen, which led to the conclusion that the equipment needed to be easy to transport without a need of power supply, since some of the murals were located outdoor or in rooms without electrical installation. In the case of the work by Seade, the mural located in the *Casa de la Cultura* (House of Culture) and the former *Liceo de Colonia del Sacramento* (grammar school) indeed had connection to the electricity network. Additionally, there was the possibility to darken the room for UV fluorescence registration of some materials, which is essential.

The Table 7.1 puts into relation the transported equipment which was necessary to perform photographic records of mural "Allegory to work" de Seade, as well as the other selected wall paintings for cataloging in this phase of the project. As already indicated, the choice of equipment was constrained by the requirement of portability that was necessary for the project.

7.4 DEVELOPMENT OF THE STUDY

For registration of the pictorial surface characteristics of the mural, different photographic techniques applied to the conservation and restoration have been employed, for both visible and not visible radiation. At

TABLE 7.1 Instrumentation of Photographic Record

Instrumentation of the photographic record	
Camera bodies	• Camera Nikon D3X
	• Canon EOS 400D
	• Camera *Sony DSC-H9* for IR record
Objectives	• MicroNikkor 60 mm (zoom 17–35 mm, 80–400, 18–200 mm.)
	• AF-S Nikkor (55–200 mm *y* 18–55 mm).
	• Canon: EF-S18–55 mm
Filters	• UV and IR filters, polarizers
Illumination	• UV tubes with domestic tube holder
	• Halogen spotlights Mefo H650
	• Flashes Balcar Jazz 350 W
Other measuring and recording instruments	• Photometer Minolta IV F
	• Reflecta DigiMicrosccope USB

each moment, a correlation between the different analytical techniques used for cataloging has been established, promoting the observation and analysis in the study of the problems presented by work.

The choice of the different techniques used for the photographic record, detailed in the Table 7.2, was determined by the physical characteristics of the work, the state of conservation, its locations, and material we had to our disposal. In Figure 7.1, the artwork penetration capacity by some conventional radiation techniques, used in the documentation, is shown.

7.5 PHOTOGRAPHY WITH VISIBLE LIGHT

7.5.1 GENERAL AND DETAILED PHOTOGRAPHS

Registration was effected with light in the visible spectrum, starting a wide shot (Figures 7.1A and 7.2) of the whole painting and detailed shots of each of the characters (Figures 7.3–7.5) and the most obvious damages (Figures 7.6 and 7.7). Following a more detailed record of the pictorial surface through low angle photography and macro photography is exposed.

Physical Identification and Digital Record of Painting

TABLE 7.2 Employed Photographic Techniques

Employed photographic techniques		
Photographs with visible light	General photographs and details	Wall surface, characteristics of pictorial technique, deterioration, damage, etc.
	Macro photography	Macroscopic registration of the pictorial surface
	Photographs with oblique light	Registration of textures, replacement edges, cuts, bulges, etc.
	Microphotography	Microscopic registration of the surface
Photographs with not visible light	Ultraviolet fluorescence	Registration and visualization of pictorial repaint
	Infrared photography	Registration and visualization of pictorial repaint

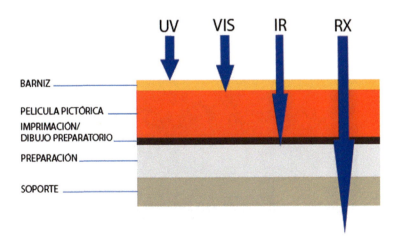

FIGURE 7.1 Penetration range of different electromagnetic radiation used in the study of artworks (ultraviolet, visible, infrared, and X-ray).

7.5.2 PHOTOGRAPHY WITH OBLIQUE LIGHT

For low angle shots (Figures 7.8–7.10) halogen lamps have been used, with an incidence angle of light on the painted surface between 5° and 10°. Information obtained with this technique is at a superficial level, recording the texture and topography of the photographed area. In this case, mainly the widespread presence of cracks, bulges, inscriptions, incisions, removal and loss of paint layer was recorded.

7.5.3 MACRO PHOTOGRAPHY AND MICROPHOTOGRAPHY

Detailed photographs with both conventional close-up objective lenses and strictly macro lenses have been made. With these a record of details of specific interest was obtained such as brush type, painting technique, zones clearly repainted which can be identified with a naked eye, and different damages which presents the work. The most obvious damages are incisions of vandalism character that become more apparent with the use of grazing lighting.

For recording details that needed closer approximation than that obtained with these accessories, USB mini microscopy has been employed

FIGURE 7.1A Overview of the whole painting space. *Source:* Graphical record of the R&D Project PUCM, 2011.

Physical Identification and Digital Record of Painting 145

FIGURE 7.2 Overiew of the conservation state in 2011. *Source:* Graphical record of the R&D Project PUCM, 2011.

FIGURE 7.3 Registration of conservation state. *Source:* Graphical record of the R&D Project PUCM, 2011.

FIGURE 7.4 Registration of the reconstruction areain 1981. Source: Graphical record of the R&D Project PUCM, 2011.

FIGURE 7.5 Registration of bulges zone. *Source:* Graphical record of the R&D Project PUCM, 2011.

Physical Identification and Digital Record of Painting 147

FIGURE 7.6 Detail of damage. *Source:* Graphical record of the R&D Project PUCM, 2011.

FIGURE 7.7 Registration of the original paint layer and repaintings. *Source:* Graphical record of the R&D Project PUCM, 2011.

FIGURE 7.8 Registration of different depths of the surficial cuts. *Source:* Graphical record of the R&D Project PUCM, 2011.

FIGURE 7.9 Registration of superficial cuts and repaintings. *Source:* Graphical record of the R&D Project PUCM, 2011.

Physical Identification and Digital Record of Painting 149

FIGURE 7.10 Visualization of cuts in the top of the mural painting. *Source*: Graphical record of the R&D Project PUCM, 2011.

which reaches 200x magnification with a resolution of 2 megapixel and includes a frontal light source of 8 LEDs with adjustable power. These shots have been directly uploaded to a *Tablet PC* (Figures 7.13–7.15.).

7.6 PHOTOGRAPHS MADE FROM NON-VISIBLE RADIATION

Photographs were taken with nonvisible radiation, and the applied techniques were ultraviolet fluorescence and gray-scale infrared photography.

7.6.1 ULTRAVIOLET FLUORESCENCE PHOTOGRAPHY

With this technique, the identification of the employed materials by the author is intended: the presence of possible repainting made after the

FIGURE 7.11 Registration of cuts by macro photography. Approach to the characteristics of incisions. *Source:* Graphical record of the R&D Project PUCM, 2011.

FIGURE 7.12 Macro photography location. *Source:* Graphical record of the R&D Project PUCM, 2011.

Physical Identification and Digital Record of Painting 151

FIGURE 7.13 View of repaint and original painting. *Source:* Graphical record of the R&D Project PUCM, 2011.

FIGURE 7.14 Microscopic view of pigments at the surface. *Source:* Graphical record of the R&D Project PUCM, 2011.

FIGURE 7.15 Registration of inner layers. *Source:* Graphical record of the R&D Project PUCM, 2011.

execution of the work or detect the presence of other materials that are not part of the original work. The quality and clarity of the results may depend on the painting and repainting technique used by the author, the conservation state of both, or the presence of varnishes – among other things. For registration it is necessary to illuminate the work with a source of long-wave ultraviolet light, visible light, to cause fluorescence of the different materials. For this, total darkness is necessary because any stray light would hide the obtained results. In the work of *Felipe Seade*, based on the fluorescence of some of the materials as a response to long-wave UV illumination it has been possible to locate large repainted areas, employed in successive repairs of the work (Figures 7.16, 7.18, and 7.20). In addition, the presence of some other materials, which do not belong to the original design, have been detected and identified at different points of the painting most superficial level (Figures 7.17, 7.19, and 7.21). The original paint layer responded with a different fluorescence within the repainted areas, allowing their exact localization and facilitating proper removal in the cleaning process of the work. Definitive identification of the materials by this photographic technique must be confirmed by the relevant physicochemical analysis.

Physical Identification and Digital Record of Painting 153

FIGURE 7.16 Increased fluorescence of the original paint layer. *Source:* Graphical record of the R&D Project PUCM, 2011.

FIGURE 7.17 Original painting and repaint remains after cleaning tests. *Source:* Graphical record of the R&D Project PUCM, 2011.

FIGURE 7.18 Fluorescence of the original painting. *Source:* Graphical record of the R&D Project PUCM, 2011.

FIGURE 7.19 Repaint. *Source:* Graphical record of the R&D Project PUCM, 2011.

Physical Identification and Digital Record of Painting 155

FIGURE 7.20 Fluorescence of the repaint. Source: Graphical record of the R&D Project PUCM, 2011

FIGURE 7.21 Figure with natural light. *Source:* Graphical record of the R&D Project PUCM, 2011.

7.6.2 INFRARED PHOTOGRAPHY

With this type of register, a more detailed painting study can be realized to make more evident the stroke of brush of the artist. Sometimes this help to identify metamerism (apparently same colors show under this radiation differences due to their different composition), providing information about the presence of repainting (Figure 7.22). In some cases, depending on the composition of the employed pigments and the layer thickness, it is possible to "see through" (cross) the upper layers of paint and detect underlying layers. This technique helps to identify lines and hidden layers of repainting, varnishes, changes made by the author himself or just over-painting of an existing work. In this case, traces or underlying forms of the external painting layer have been detected, but at the same time some pigments responded differently to others recognized as originals (Figures 7.23–7.29), identified mostly as retouching made after the execution of the work.

FIGURE 7.22 Registration of repainted zones within a detail of the work. *Source:* Graphical record of the R&D Project PUCM, 2011.

Physical Identification and Digital Record of Painting 157

FIGURE 7.23 View detail recorded with visible light. *Source:* Graphical record of the R&D Project PUCM, 2011.

FIGURE 7.24 Registration of repaint in the sleeve of the character. *Source:* Graphical record of the R&D Project PUCM, 2011.

FIGURE 7.25 View detail recorded with visible light. *Source:* Graphical record of the R&D Project PUCM, 2011.

FIGURE 7.26 Registration of repaint in the sleeve of the character. *Source:* Graphical record of the R&D Project PUCM, 2011.

Physical Identification and Digital Record of Painting 159

FIGURE 7.27 View detail recorded with visible light. *Source:* Graphical record of the R&D Project PUCM, 2011.

FIGURE 7.28 Registration of repaint. So Graphical Record of the R&D Project PUCM, 2011.

FIGURE 7.29 View detail recorded with visible light. *Source:* Graphical record of the R&D Project PUCM, 2011.

7.7 CONCLUSIONS

The photographic register of the mural painting "Allegory to work" by Felipe Seade has allowed to complete the thorough analysis that was carried out on the work, providing information that benefits the complete removal of repainting for the cleaning process.

This register has also facilitated the identification of possible sampling areas for further physicochemical analysis, depending on the response of materials, present in the work, to the different electromagnetic radiation employed.

Using photography with grazing light has been fundamental to evidence the cuts generated by human factors. Depending on their morphology, caused damage and extension, they have been classified into two types: incisions with sharp objects in order to destroy the work and inscriptions of names and dates.

By ultraviolet photography it has been found that the work has been repainted almost entirely, distinguishing different techniques and pigments depending on the fluorescence characteristic exhibited within certain areas.

Infrared photography provides information on small isolated repainting, as well as a more exhaustive knowledge of used technique and materials in the execution of the mural panting and its subsequent interventions.

KEYWORDS

- infrared photography
- non-invasive
- non-visible radiation
- photography
- register
- ultraviolet photography
- visible radiation

REFERENCES AND BIBLIOGRAPHY

Fernandez Oscar, M. (2011). "Allegory to work" de Felipe Seade: Activación Patrimonial, Estudios Previos y Propuesta de Intervención. Master Thesis. Departamento de Conservación y Restauración de Bienes Culturales. UPV.

Orsi Meny, Z. (2008). *Liceo departamental de Colonia. Historia y proyección.* Ediciones del Sur: Montevideo. ISBN13: 978-99-7481-492-9.

Valcárcel Andrés, J. C. (2005). *Estudio de la técnica empleada por Antonio Palomino en los frescos de la Real Basílica de la Virgen de los Desamparados de Valencia a partir de su análisis con radiación de diferentes longitudes de onda.* UPV. ISBN 8468877247.

Roig Picazo, P., Regidor Ros, J. L., Valcárcel Andrés, J. C., & Bosch Roig, L. (2010). *Estado de conservación actual de los murales de la Cappella Borgherini.* Nardini Editore. ISSN: 2036-1122. Italy.

CHAPTER 8

COLORIMETRIC CHARACTERIZATION

M. L. MARTHNEZ-BAZÁN,[1] M. FERNÁNDEZ-OSCAR,[2]
D. J. YUSÁ-MARCO,[3] and E. M. MARTÍNEZ-CARAZO[4]

[1]Associate Professor, Department of Conservation and Restoration of Cultural Heritage, UPV, 3N Building, Camino de Vera s/n, 46022 Valencia, Spain, Tel.: +34-963877000/79311,
E-mail: lmartine@crbc.upv.es

[2]Phd Student, Department of Conservation and Restoration of Cultural Heritage, UPV, 3N Building, Camino de Vera s/n, 46022 Valencia, Spain, Tel.: +34-661685561,
E-mail: mirferoscr@gmail.com

[3]Associate Professor, Department of Conservation and Restoration of Cultural Heritage, UPV, 3N Building, Camino de Vera s/n, 46022 Valencia, Spain, Tel.: +34-3877000/Ext. 73129,
E-mail: doyumar@crbc.upv.es

[4]Phd Student, Department of Conservation and Restoration of Cultural Heritage, UPV, 3N Building, Camino de Vera s/n, 46022 Valencia, Spain, Tel.: +34-655868675,
E-mail: evatxu1893@gmail.com

CONTENTS

8.1 Introduction 164
8.2 Instrumentation 164
8.3 Development of the Study 165

8.4 Results and Discussion 167
Keywords 178
References and Bibliography 179

8.1 INTRODUCTION

This chapter includes the methodology that was followed and the chromatic data obtained during the colorimetric studies prior to the restoration of Felipe Seade's work "Allegory to work," located in the Cultural Centre of Colonia del Sacramento.

This database of the existing colors in Seade's mural at the time of measurement (April, 2011) will allow to start the conservation process of periodic measurements, which will determine the degree of chromatic variation experienced by the piece of artwork due to the unavoidable pass of time or to any temporary reason, with the aim of warning the restorer in case it is excessively remarkable.

8.2 INSTRUMENTATION

In order to carry out this study, a Minolta CM-2600d spectrophotometer was used and the measurement conditions selected were the standard CIE type D_{65} illuminant (day light, color temperature of 6500° K) and the standard 10° observer. In this meter, a measurement area of 8 mm diameter was chosen.

Data were taken both with Specular Component Included (SCI), which minimizes the influence of the measurement surface conditions, and with Specular Component Excluded (SCE), which corresponds more closely to professional visual examination. These two measurement techniques (with and without brightness) have been included in order to assess the variations in brightness experienced by the pieces of artwork, especially after consolidation processes. To avoid repetitions, when the values obtained under both conditions (with and without brightness) are similar, only one of the aspects will be shown.

The wavelength range of the spectrophotometer is between 360 and 740 nm, every 10 nm., being its photometric range from 0 to 175% reflectance, with a 0.01% resolution. Regarding its reproducibility it presents a standard

Colorimetric Characterization

deviation of 0,1% in spectral reflectance, and 0,04 for the colorimetric values of DE^*_{ab} (CIE 76).

8.3 DEVELOPMENT OF THE STUDY

The measurement system used in this study is known as chromatic scanning and it consists of the measurement of certain key points from the piece of artwork that have been properly selected. In chromatic scanning the technique known as reflection spectrometry has been used, which, apart from the chromatic coordinates, allows obtaining the spectrum (digital print) of each one of the key points comprising the scanning.

The characteristics of the surface of the artwork allowed us to perform measurements by contact, avoiding to work in total darkness (Figures 8.1 and 8.2). The technique by contact, moreover, avoids possible sources of error associated with "the distance technique," since referencing the position of the points and instrument calibration (meter, light sources, etc.) is not that simple.

FIGURE 8.1 Measurement of the piece's key points by means of the spectrophotometer.
Source: Graphical record of the R&D Project PUCM, 2013.

FIGURE 8.2 Measurement of the piece's key points by means of the spectrophotometer.
Source: Graphical record of the R&D Project PUCM, 2013.

Therefore, to ensure the precise placement of the meter, some acetate templates are made in DIN-A4 format where, apart from the sample-points to be measured, a series of reference lines are marked in order to be able to relocate those acetates as many times as required (Figures 8.3 and 8.4).

In order to calculate the mean colorimetric values and standard deviation, the measurements of each point have been repeated three times. The physical CIE Yxy (1931) and the psychometric/ perceptive CIE(1976) L*a*b* and L*C*h° color spaces have been used. Regarding the total color differences ($DE_{ab}*$), based on the studies by Melgosa et al. (2001), significant and representative color change results are considered if DE* >2. Melgosa et al. (2001) stated that a color difference DE* between 0.38 and 0.73 CIELAB units is regarded as just perceptible (cfr. Table 8.1), while a color difference of around 1.75 CIELAB units can be classified as "supra-threshold." Above 5.0 CIELAB units, color changes are significant. From an industrial point of view, DE* between 1.1 and 2.8 is considered as tight, whereas between 2.8 and 5.6 CIELAB units, the tolerance would be called 'normal,' and above 5.6 CIELAB units "loose."

Colorimetric Characterization 167

FIGURE 8.3 Example of an acetate used in the sampling. *Source:* Graphical record of the R&D Project PUCM, 2013.

Apart from colorimetric values (chromatic coordinate and luminance factor), the spectral values of every sample-point are included.

8.4 RESULTS AND DISCUSSION

8.4.1 CHROMATIC DATA

The following two tables show the average values of the three shoots applied to each sample point, together with their standard deviation. One of them includes the values obtained from the measurements carried out with SCE (Figure 8.5) and the other shows results from SCI (Figure 8.6). These values, together with the spectral data, will comprise the database or chromatic register of the piece of artwork.

FIGURE 8.4 Location of the acetates with the measurement points used in the colorimetric measurement. *Source:* Graphical record of the R&D Project PUCM, 2013.

After the calculation of $DE_{ab}*$ for the parameters obtained with and without brightness, it may be concluded that there is practically no brightness on the pictorial surface, as could be expected from a tempera, since except for two points that reach 2 DE*, the rest is situated below the limit established as representative or visible.

The next stage in the discussion shows the graphic representation of the coordinates obtained with SCI in the diagram CIE L*a*b*. For a better analysis of the results, they have been classified into group of colors:

The blue and green colors (Figure 8.5) that were obtained, as indicated by the chemical analyzes, included in the next section, are the ultramarine and Prussian blue pigments, mixed with different quantities of white (lithopone, white lead and zinc oxide white). All these are situated very close to the achromatic center, which means they are very little chromatic colors. If we observe the lightness axis, we can notice a greater variety, in

Colorimetric Characterization

TABLE 8.1 List of Acetates, Measurement Points, and Their Apparent Color

Acetates	Points	Apparent color	Acetates	Points	Apparent color	Acetates	Points	Apparent color
1	1	Blue	4	1	Yellow	7	1	Ochre
	2	Beige		2	Pink		2	Pink
	3	Brown		3	Bright pink		3	Dark green
	4	Ochre		4	Orange		4	Bright green
2	1	Maroon	5	1	Yellowish green	8	1	Bright violet
	2	Dark green		2	Yellow		2	Very dark carmine
	3	Rose		3	Maroon		3	Violet
	4	Green		4	Green		4	Very dark carmine
	5	Yellowish green	6	1	Bluish green	9	1	Orange
	6	Black		2	White		2	Maroon
3	1	Blue		3	Dark brown		3	Orange
	2	Maroon		4	Very bright brown	10	1	Ochre
	3	Bright blue					2	Beige
	4	Green					3	Very bright green
							4	Brown

Source: Graphical record of the R&D Project PUCM, 2013.

a range that goes from dark to quite bright colors, including some mid-range lightness.

The orange, red and brown colors (Figure 8.8), obtained from lead chromates, minium, iron oxides, chrome oranges and burnt ochre, are situated in a more chromatic zone than those of the previous section

Nombre	Coordenadas Fisicas			Coordenadas Psicofisicas			
	Y	x	y	L*	a*	b*	C*	h
Ac1/1	23.16	0.4561	0.4408	55.24	9.08	48.90	49.74	79.49
δ	0.04	0.0004	0.0002	0.04	0.06	0.17	0.18	0.04
Ac1/2	30.55	0.3735	0.3616	62.13	9.76	16.09	18.81	58.76
δ	0.09	0.0004	0.0001	0.08	0.07	0.07	0.10	0.08
Ac1/3	7.94	0.3286	0.3579	33.85	-2.31	5.63	6.08	112.3
δ	0.03	0.0004	0.0004	0.06	0.02	0.08	0.07	0.4
Ac1/4	26.59	0.3402	0.3653	58.60	-1.93	11.69	11.85	99.4
δ	0.26	0.0005	0.0002	0.24	0.10	0.15	0.13	0.6
Ac2/1	29.15	0.3578	0.3493	60.91	8.644	10.46	13.57	50.4
δ	0.10	0.0002	0.0002	0.09	0.014	0.07	0.05	0.2
Ac2/2	7.54	0.4298	0.3938	33.01	10.14	21.35	23.64	64.59
δ	0.12	0.0002	0.0002	0.27	0.06	0.17	0.18	0.08
Ac2/3	12.50	0.3889	0.36583	42.003	9.71	14.500	17.45	56.20
δ	0.01	0.0002	0.00006	0.013	0.04	0.007	0.03	0.11
Ac2/4	36.79	0.3757	0.3781	67.12	5.63	21.98	22.69	75.62
δ	0.26	0.0003	0.0002	0.20	0.01	0.04	0.05	0.02
Ac2/5	17.47	0.4453	0.3961	48.85	16.32	31.32	35.32	62.48
δ	0.24	0.0015	0.0004	0.30	0.16	0.19	0.24	0.09
Ac2/6	6.57	0.4838	0.3665	30.80	23.53	22.21	32.35	43.3
δ	0.07	0.0016	0.0006	0.16	0.07	0.23	0.20	0.2
Ac3/1	17.92	0.4775	0.4059	49.401	21.009	40.07	45.25	62.33
δ	0.00	0.0002	0.0002	0.004	0.014	0.07	0.06	0.04
Ac3/2	22.29	0.4593	0.4378	54.34	10.40	48.17	49.28	77.82
δ	0.06	0.0002	0.0004	0.07	0.02	0.18	0.17	0.06
Ac3/3	52.38	0.3779	0.3824	77.51	5.634	26.46	27.05	77.98
δ	0.23	0.0004	0.0003	0.14	0.013	0.13	0.13	0.03
Ac3/4	43.49	0.3749	0.3851	71.89	3.35	25.09	25.31	82.4
δ	0.20	0.0002	0.0004	0.13	0.10	0.16	0.15	0.3
Ac4/1	9.95	0.4227	0.3962	37.76	9.30	22.96	24.77	67.95
δ	0.06	0.0003	0.0002	0.11	0.05	0.03	0.05	0.10
Ac4/2	23.66	0.31877	0.3485	55.75	-3.69	4.73	6.00	128.0
δ	0.16	0.00012	0.0003	0.16	0.09	0.05	0.09	0.5
Ac4/3	53.66	0.35773	0.3723	78.26	1.81	19.91	19.99	84.80
δ	0.41	0.00006	0.0002	0.24	0.06	0.10	0.09	0.19
Ac4/4	4.88	0.4130	0.3681	26.37	10.54	13.03	16.76	51.04
δ	0.30	0.0047	0.0013	0.87	0.29	0.36	0.46	0.03

FIGURE 8.5 (Continued).

Colorimetric Characterization

Nombre	Coordenadas Fisicas			Coordenadas Psicofisicas			
	Y	x	y	L*	a*	b*	C*	h
Ac5/1	29.36	0.4708	0.4477	61.10	11.67	59.36	60.49	78.88
δ	0.13	0.0032	0.0020	0.11	0.28	1.79	1.81	0.06
Ac5/2	4.82	0.5181	0.4021	26.21	19.590	31.32	36.94	57.97
δ	0.01	0.0003	0.0003	0.03	0.014	0.09	0.07	0.08
Ac5/3	13.80	0.3751	0.3931	43.95	0.55	18.68	18.68	88.3
δ	0.05	0.0002	0.0002	0.07	0.08	0.04	0.04	0.3
Ac5/4	26.22	0.3594	0.36007	58.25	5.54	12.96	14.10	66.9
δ	0.05	0.0003	0.00006	0.05	0.09	0.03	0.06	0.3
Ac6/1	8.75	0.3719	0.4063	35.50	-2.58	17.90	18.09	98.20
δ	0.04	0.0002	0.0002	0.07	0.02	0.06	0.05	0.09
Ac6/2	21.79	0.38770	0.4018	53.80	1.75	25.58	25.65	86.08
δ	0.04	0.00010	0.0002	0.04	0.03	0.05	0.05	0.08
Ac6/3	2.61	0.3147	0.3573	18.40	-3.59	3.01	4.68	140.1
δ	0.02	0.0002	0.0005	0.10	0.05	0.06	0.07	0.3
Ac6/4	7.87	0.2738	0.3159	33.72	-6.32	-5.64	8.47	221.8
δ	0.07	0.0006	0.0005	0.15	0.09	0.13	0.14	0.5
Ac7/1	3.09	0.4882	0.3853	20.39	15.92	20.47	25.93	52.12
δ	0.02	0.0006	0.0004	0.07	0.03	0.10	0.08	0.12
Ac7/2	34.21	0.3225	0.35110	65.13	-3.69	6.53	7.50	119.46
δ	0.04	0.0001	0.00010	0.03	0.01	0.04	0.04	0.08
Ac7/3	18.85	0.33917	0.4169	50.51	-14.26	20.99	25.38	124.19
δ	0.05	0.00006	0.0002	0.06	0.04	0.03	0.04	0.06
Ac7/4	52.10	0.40290	0.3890	77.343	12.04	33.33	35.44	70.13
δ	0.02	0.00010	0.0002	0.014	0.02	0.06	0.05	0.06
Ac8/4	20.36	0.3940	0.3497	52.24	17.41	14.03	22.36	38.86
δ	0.05	0.0004	0.0003	0.06	0.04	0.11	0.10	0.17
Ac8/5	23.27	0.4033	0.36577	55.35	15.89	19.94	25.50	51.45
δ	0.08	0.0002	0.00006	0.08	0.03	0.02	0.03	0.03
Ac8/6	11.22	0.5132	0.4069	39.93	24.04	41.70	48.14	60.0
δ	0.63	0.0063	0.0019	1.06	0.24	1.19	1.15	0.5
Ac8/7	29.83	0.4078	0.42773	61.51	0.636	38.72	38.72	89.060
δ	0.05	0.0001	0.00012	0.04	0.009	0.05	0.05	0.012
Ac9/1	44.02	0.4067	0.4091	72.24	6.07	38.24	38.72	80.99
δ	0.06	0.0005	0.0003	0.04	0.06	0.20	0.20	0.05
Ac9/2	3.18	0.4899	0.3809	20.75	16.94	20.20	26.37	50.0
δ	0.03	0.0013	0.0008	0.11	0.05	0.19	0.15	0.3
Ac9/3	10.50	0.34317	0.4307	38.729	-13.28	20.00	24.01	123.59
δ	0.01	0.00006	0.0001	0.013	0.02	0.02	0.02	0.03

FIGURE 8.5 (Continued).

Nombre	Coordenadas Fisicas			Coordenadas Psicofisicas			
	Y	x	y	L*	a*	b*	C*	h
Ac10/1	9.81	0.3109	0.3507	37.48	-5.11	3.21	6.04	147.9
δ	0.54	0.0004	0.0003	1.00	0.06	0.04	0.03	0.7
Ac10/2	63.57	0.33507	0.35040	83.74	1.23	9.94	10.02	82.93
δ	0.05	0.00006	0.00010	0.03	0.02	0.04	0.03	0.13
Ac10/3	6.92	0.39797	0.3720	31.63	8.43	13.79	16.16	58.57
δ	0.01	0.00012	0.0002	0.03	0.03	0.04	0.03	0.17
Ac10/4	28.44	0.3751	0.3761	60.3	5.58	19.60	20.38	74.11
δ	0.92	0.0004	0.0002	0.8	0.03	0.13	0.13	0.07

FIGURE 8.5 Chromatic coordinates (SCE). *Source:* Graphical record of the R&D Project PUCM, 2013.

Nombre	Coordenadas Fisicas			Coordenadas Psicofisicas			
	Y	x	y	L*	a*	b*	C*	h
Ac1/1	23.11	0.31860	0.3485	55.19	-3.69	4.67	5.95	128.3
δ	0.16	0.00010	0.0003	0.17	0.09	0.04	0.09	0.5
Ac1/2	53.1	0.35823	0.37267	77.9	1.87	20.04	20.13	84.67
δ	0.4	0.00006	0.00012	0.2	0.05	0.09	0.09	0.18
Ac1/3	4.47	0.4217	0.3710	25.2	11.1	13.9	17.7	51.43
δ	0.30	0.0058	0.0017	0.9	0.3	0.5	0.6	0.12
Ac1/4	28.88	0.473	0.450	60.68	11.8	60.6	61.7	79.00
δ	0.13	0.003	0.002	0.12	0.3	1.9	1.9	0.07
Ac2/1	4.451	0.5312	0.40280	25.11	20.603	32.70	38.65	57.79
δ	0.012	0.0003	0.00017	0.04	0.008	0.05	0.05	0.03
Ac2/2	13.33	0.3767	0.39460	43.26	0.59	18.96	18.97	88.2
δ	0.05	0.0003	0.00010	0.08	0.09	0.03	0.03	0.3
Ac2/3	25.69	0.36010	0.36027	57.74	5.65	13.01	14.18	66.5
δ	0.05	0.00026	0.00006	0.05	0.09	0.02	0.05	0.3
Ac2/4	8.30	0.37460	0.40983	34.59	-2.65	18.45	18.64	98.17
δ	0.04	0.00010	0.00006	0.07	0.02	0.03	0.03	0.07
Ac2/5	21.27	0.38913	0.40303	53.24	1.81	25.87	25.93	86.00
δ	0.03	0.00006	0.00006	0.04	0.03	0.03	0.03	0.06
Ac2/6	2.27	0.3135	0.3597	16.87	-3.91	3.06	4.96	142.0
δ	0.02	0.0002	0.0007	0.07	0.06	0.09	0.10	0.4
Ac3/1	7.42	0.2713	0.3146	32.74	-6.53	-5.92	8.82	222.2
δ	0.05	0.0006	0.0003	0.14	0.09	0.10	0.13	0.3
Ac3/2	2.72	0.5057	0.3854	18.88	17.19	21.40	27.45	51.22
δ	0.02	0.0005	0.0002	0.07	0.02	0.06	0.05	0.05
Ac3/3	33.65	0.32237	0.35110	64.68	-3.69	6.48	7.45	119.66
δ	0.03	0.00006	0.00010	0.03	0.02	0.04	0.04	0.06
Ac3/4	18.31	0.33953	0.4191	49.87	-14.48	21.26	25.72	124.27
δ	0.05	0.00006	0.0002	0.06	0.05	0.02	0.04	0.06

FIGURE 8.6 (Continued)

Colorimetric Characterization

	Coordenadas Físicas			Coordenadas Psicofísicas				
Nombre	Y	x	y	L*	a*	b*	C*	h
Ac4/1	51.62	0.40410	0.3896	77.051	12.19	33.65	35.79	70.08
δ	0.02	0.00010	0.0002	0.013	0.02	0.06	0.05	0.06
Ac4/2	19.85	0.3958	0.3498	51.67	17.71	14.17	22.68	38.67
δ	0.05	0.0004	0.0003	0.05	0.06	0.11	0.10	0.17
Ac4/3	22.75	0.4052	0.36613	54.82	16.14	20.153	25.82	51.31
δ	0.08	0.0002	0.00006	0.08	0.02	0.013	0.02	0.03
Ac4/4	10.8	0.520	0.4086	39.30	24.59	43.3	49.8	60.41
δ	0.5	0.006	0.0018	0.79	0.22	1.3	1.2	0.50
Ac5/1	29.24	0.4095	0.4293	60.99	0.68	39.19	39.19	89.01
δ	0.04	0.0002	0.0001	0.04	0.02	0.04	0.04	0.02
Ac5/2	43.50	0.4080	0.4100	71.89	6.16	38.6	39.1	80.93
δ	0.07	0.0005	0.0003	0.04	0.06	0.2	0.2	0.05
Ac5/3	2.81	0.5074	0.3810	19.28	18.23	21.28	28.02	49.42
δ	0.03	0.0014	0.0005	0.13	0.04	0.14	0.12	0.15
Ac5/4	10.062	0.34393	0.43483	37.954	-13.63	20.483	24.604	123.64
δ	0.003	0.00006	0.00006	0.006	0.02	0.005	0.013	0.03
Ac6/1	9.56	0.3104	0.3506	37.03	-5.15	3.12	6.02	148.8
δ	0.52	0.0003	0.0004	0.98	0.06	0.03	0.04	0.6
Ac6/2	63.13	0.33527	0.35053	83.51	1.251	9.98	10.06	82.85
δ	0.05	0.00006	0.00012	0.03	0.014	0.03	0.03	0.10
Ac6/3	6.505	0.40287	0.37407	30.65	8.72	14.308	16.757	58.64
δ	0.012	0.00006	0.00006	0.03	0.02	0.005	0.005	0.06
Ac6/4	27.9	0.3760	0.3765	59.81	5.69	19.70	20.51	73.90
δ	0.9	0.0004	0.0002	0.83	0.03	0.12	0.13	0.07
Ac7/1	22.63	0.4591	0.44300	54.69	9.17	49.90	50.74	79.59
δ	0.07	0.0003	0.00010	0.07	0.06	0.15	0.16	0.04
Ac7/2	30.01	0.3744	0.3618	61.66	9.91	16.17	18.96	58.48
δ	0.09	0.0004	0.0002	0.08	0.07	0.08	0.10	0.07
Ac7/3	7.49	0.3288	0.3587	32.89	-2.37	5.66	6.14	112.7
δ	0.03	0.0003	0.0004	0.07	0.02	0.07	0.06	0.4
Ac7/4	26.0	0.3404	0.3656	58.1	-1.91	11.70	11.85	99.3
δ	0.3	0.0006	0.0003	0.2	0.10	0.14	0.12	0.6
Ac8/4	28.54	0.3585	0.3493	60.38	8.80	10.49	13.69	50.0
δ	0.09	0.0002	0.0002	0.08	0.02	0.07	0.04	0.2
Ac8/5	7.09	0.43693	0.3973	32.0	10.49	22.4	24.7	64.86
δ	0.12	0.00012	0.0002	0.3	0.05	0.2	0.2	0.06
Ac8/6	11.995	0.3913	0.36657	41.209	9.94	14.735	17.77	55.99
δ	0.005	0.0001	0.00006	0.008	0.04	0.012	0.03	0.10
Ac8/7	36.2	0.3766	0.3786	66.67	5.747	22.14	22.88	75.45
δ	0.3	0.0003	0.0003	0.20	0.008	0.05	0.05	0.04

FIGURE 8.6 (Continued)

| | Coordenadas Fisicas ||| Coordenadas Psicofisicas ||||
Nombre	Y	x	y	L*	a*	b*	C*	h
Ac9/1	17.0	0.449	0.3976	48.2	16.61	31.98	36.0	62.56
δ	0.2	0.002	0.0004	0.3	0.18	0.19	0.3	0.11
Ac9/2	6.15	0.495	0.3684	29.80	24.34	23.6	33.9	44.08
δ	0.06	0.002	0.0005	0.14	0.08	0.2	0.2	0.19
Ac9/3	17.406	0.48220	0.40763	48.767	21.37	41.14	46.35	62.55
δ	0.007	0.00010	0.00012	0.008	0.02	0.06	0.05	0.05
Ac10/1	21.77	0.4626	0.4400	53.79	10.54	49.23	50.35	77.91
δ	0.07	0.0002	0.0003	0.07	0.02	0.16	0.15	0.06
Ac10/2	51.8	0.3788	0.3829	77.18	5.73	26.67	27.28	77.88
δ	0.3	0.0004	0.0003	0.15	0.02	0.13	0.13	0.03
Ac10/3	42.90	0.3757	0.3857	71.49	3.44	25.29	25.52	82.3
δ	0.19	0.0002	0.0005	0.13	0.11	0.18	0.17	0.3
Ac10/4	9.50	0.4276	0.3988	36.92	9.53	23.70	25.55	68.09
δ	0.06	0.0004	0.0002	0.11	0.04	0.06	0.07	0.04

FIGURE 8.6 Chromatic coordinates (SCI). *Source:* Graphical record of the R&D Project PUCM, 2013.

	Nombre	L*(SCE)	L*(SCI)	ΔL*	a*(SCE)	a*(SCI)	Δa*	b*(SCE)	b*(SCI)	Δb*	ΔE*
1	Ac1/1	55.75	55.19	-0.56	-3.69	-3.69	0.00	4.73	4.67	-0.06	0.6
2	Ac1/2	78.26	77.94	-0.32	1.81	1.87	0.06	19.91	20.04	0.14	0.4
3	Ac1/3	26.37	25.2	-1.21	10.54	11.1	0.52	13.03	13.9	0.83	1.6
4	Ac1/4	61.10	60.68	-0.42	11.67	11.8	0.10	59.36	60.6	1.20	1.3
5	Ac2/1	26.21	25.11	-1.10	19.590	20.603	1.01	31.32	32.70	1.38	2.0
6	Ac2/2	43.95	43.26	-0.69	0.55	0.59	0.04	18.68	18.96	0.29	0.7
7	Ac2/3	58.25	57.74	-0.51	5.54	5.65	0.11	12.96	13.01	0.04	0.5
8	Ac2/4	35.50	34.59	-0.91	-2.58	-2.65	-0.07	17.90	18.45	0.55	1.1
9	Ac2/5	53.80	53.24	-0.56	1.75	1.81	0.05	25.58	25.87	0.28	0.6
10	Ac2/6	18.40	16.87	-1.53	-3.59	-3.91	-0.32	3.01	3.06	0.05	1.6
11	Ac3/1	33.72	32.74	-0.98	-6.32	-6.53	-0.21	-5.64	-5.92	-0.28	1.0
12	Ac3/2	20.39	18.88	-1.52	15.92	17.19	1.27	20.47	21.40	0.93	2.2
13	Ac3/3	65.13	64.68	-0.45	-3.69	-3.69	0.00	6.53	6.48	-0.05	0.5
14	Ac3/4	50.51	49.87	-0.65	-14.26	-14.48	-0.22	20.99	21.26	0.27	0.7
15	Ac4/1	77.343	77.05	-0.29	12.04	12.19	0.15	33.33	33.65	0.32	0.5
16	Ac4/2	52.24	51.67	-0.57	17.41	17.71	0.30	14.03	14.17	0.14	0.7
17	Ac4/3	55.35	54.82	-0.53	15.89	16.14	0.25	19.94	20.153	0.21	0.6
18	Ac4/4	39.93	39.3	-0.63	24.04	24.6	0.55	41.70	43.3	1.63	1.8
19	Ac5/1	61.51	60.99	-0.52	0.636	0.68	0.04	38.72	39.19	0.47	0.7
20	Ac5/2	72.24	71.89	-0.35	6.07	6.16	0.09	38.24	38.6	0.37	0.5
21	Ac5/3	20.75	19.28	-1.47	16.94	18.23	1.28	20.20	21.28	1.08	2.2
22	Ac5/4	38.729	37.954	-0.78	-13.28	-13.63	-0.35	20.00	20.483	0.48	1.0

FIGURE 8.7 (Continued)

Colorimetric Characterization

	Nombre	L*(SCE)	L*(SCI)	ΔL*	a*(SCE)	a*(SCI)	Δa*	b*(SCE)	b*(SCI)	Δb*	ΔE*
23	Ac6/1	37.48	37.03	-0.45	-5.11	-5.15	-0.03	3.21	3.12	-0.09	0.5
24	Ac6/2	83.74	83.51	-0.23	1.23	1.251	0.02	9.94	9.98	0.04	0.2
25	Ac6/3	31.63	30.65	-0.98	8.43	8.72	0.30	13.79	14.308	0.52	1.1
26	Ac6/4	60.3	59.8	-0.46	5.58	5.69	0.11	19.60	19.70	0.10	0.5
27	Ac7/1	55.24	54.69	-0.55	9.08	9.17	0.09	48.90	49.90	1.00	1.1
28	Ac7/2	62.13	61.66	-0.47	9.76	9.91	0.16	16.09	16.17	0.08	0.5
29	Ac7/3	33.85	32.89	-0.96	-2.31	-2.37	-0.06	5.63	5.66	0.04	1.0
30	Ac7/4	58.60	58.1	-0.53	-1.93	-1.91	0.02	11.69	11.70	0.01	0.5
31	Ac8/4	60.91	60.38	-0.53	8.644	8.80	0.16	10.46	10.49	0.03	0.6
32	Ac8/5	33.01	32.0	-1.00	10.14	10.49	0.35	21.35	22.36	1.00	1.5
33	Ac8/6	42.003	41.209	-0.79	9.71	9.94	0.23	14.500	14.735	0.24	0.9
34	Ac8/7	67.12	66.7	-0.44	5.63	5.747	0.11	21.98	22.14	0.16	0.5
35	Ac9/1	48.85	48.21	-0.64	16.32	16.61	0.29	31.32	31.98	0.66	1.0
36	Ac9/2	30.80	29.80	-1.00	23.53	24.34	0.81	22.21	23.6	1.36	1.9
37	Ac9/3	49.401	48.77	-0.63	21.009	21.37	0.36	40.07	41.14	1.06	1.3
38	Ac10/1	54.34	53.79	-0.55	10.40	10.54	0.14	48.17	49.23	1.06	1.2
39	Ac10/2	77.51	77.18	-0.33	5.634	5.73	0.09	26.46	26.67	0.21	0.4
40	Ac10/3	71.89	71.49	-0.40	3.35	3.44	0.09	25.09	25.29	0.20	0.5
41	Ac10/4	37.76	36.92	-0.83	9.30	9.53	0.23	22.96	23.70	0.74	1.1

FIGURE 8.7 Assessment of brightness in Seade's painting. *Source:* Graphical record of the R&D Project PUCM, 2013.

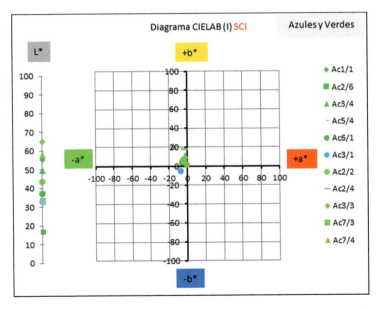

FIGURE 8.8 Graphic representation of the CIELAB coordinates. Blues and greens. *Source:* Graphical record of the R&D Project PUCM, 2013.

and they are distributed within a chroma range between 10 and 50 units.

With regard to the lightness axis, we can observe that, again there is a variety of lightness, ranging this time from 20 and 65 units.

The yellow and ochre colors (Figure 8.9), composed mostly of chrome orange and iron oxides, show a similar chromatism to that of the orange and red colors, although they are brighter colors, mostly situated between 55 and 85 CIELAB units, with some exceptions that reach lower values.

8.4.2 SPECTRAL DATA

The spectral graphs confirm the results obtained in the colorimetric analysis. They show again very varied colors in terms of hue, chroma key and lightness, with maximum reflectance around 70% (Figures 8.11 and 8.12).

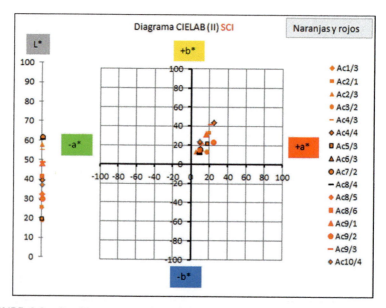

FIGURE 8.9 Graphic representation of the CIELAB coordinates. Oranges and reds.
Source: Graphical record of the R&D Project PUCM, 2013.

Colorimetric Characterization

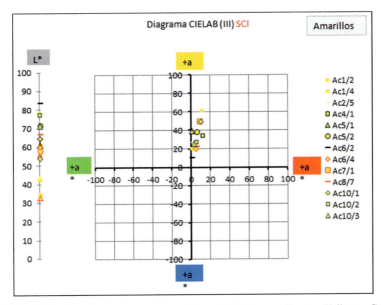

FIGURE 8.10 Graphic representation of the CIELAB coordinates. Yellows. *Source:* Graphical record of the R&D Project PUCM, 2013.

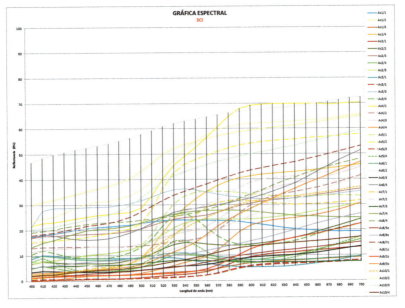

FIGURE 8.11 Graphic representation of the spectral data SCI. *Source:* Graphical record of the R&D Project PUCM, 2013.

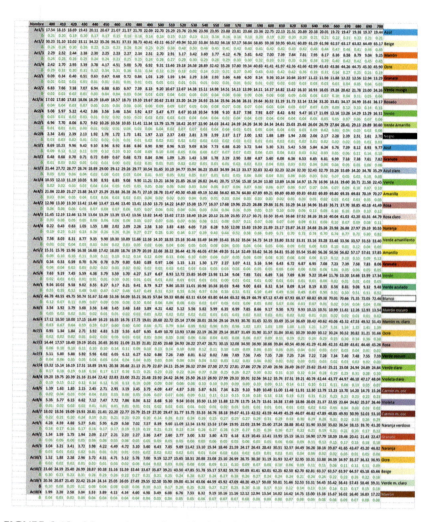

FIGURE 8.12 Mean values and standard deviation of the spectral data SCI. *Source:* Graphical record of the R&D Project PUCM, 2013.

KEYWORDS

- Allegory to work
- chromatic data

- colorimetric studies
- colors
- Cultural Centre Colonia Del Sacramento Felipe Seade
- chromatic variation

REFERENCES AND BIBLIOGRAPHY

Aguilar, M., & Blanca, V. (1995). *Iluminación y Color*. Servicio de Publicaciones (UPV) Valencia. ISBN 8477213542.

Bomford, D., & Staniforth, S., (1981). *Wax-Resin Lining and Color Change: An Evaluation*, In: National Gallery Technical Bulletin 5, pp. 58–65. ISSN: 0140-7430.

Bomford, D., & Staniforth, S., (1981). *Lining and Color Change: Further Results*, In: National Gallery Technical Bulletin 5, pp. 65–69. ISSN: 0140-7430.

Capillas, P; Artigas, J. M., & Pujol, J., (2002). *Fundamentos de Colorimetría*. Universitat de Valencia, ISBN 8437054206.

Gilabert, E. (1992). *Medida del color*. UPV. ISBN 847721185X.

Hita Villaverde, E., (2001). *El mundo del color. Desde lo perceptivo y artístico a lo científico*. Ed. Universidad de Granada, Granada. ISBN 8433827251.

Melgosa, et al., (2001). *Algunas reflexiones y recientes consideraciones internacionales sobre evaluación de diferencias de color*. In: **Óptica** Pura y Aplicada. Vol. 34, pp. 1–10.

Martínez- Bazán, M. L. (2001). *Determinación de los colores existentes en la decoración al fresco, ejecutada por A. Palomino, en un fragmento de la nave central de la Iglesia de los Santos Juanes de Valencia*. Depósito legal: V-1742-2001 ISBN: 84-699-3405-8.

CHAPTER 9

STUDY OF THE CHEMICAL COMPOSITION THROUGH CROSS SECTIONS: OPTICAL MICROSCOPY, SCANNING ELECTRON MICROSCOPY, AND X-RAY MICROANALYSIS

D. J. YUSÁ-MARCO,[1] X. MAS-I-BARBERÀ,[2] M. FERNÁNDEZ-ÓSCAR,[3] and M. J. GUIRADO-RUANO[4]

[1]*Associate Professor, Department of Conservation and Restoration of Cultural Heritage, UPV, 3N Building, Camino de Vera s/n, 46022 Valencia, Spain, Tel.: +34-3877000/Ext. 73129, E-mail: doyumar@crbc.upv.es*

[2]*Associate Professor, Department of Conservation and Restoration of Cultural Heritage, UPV, 3N Building, Camino de Vera s/n, 46022 Valencia, Spain, Tel.: +34-963877000/Ext. 73128, E-mail: jamasbar@upvnet.upv.es*

[3]*Phd Student, Department of Conservation and Restoration of Cultural Heritage, UPV, 3N Building, Camino de Vera s/n, 46022 Valencia, Spain. Telephone+34-661685561, E-mail: mirferoscr@gmail.com*

[4]*Phd Student, Department of Conservation and Restoration of Cultural Heritage, UPV, 3N Building, Camino de Vera s/n, 46022 Valencia, Spain, Tel.: +34-635814197, E-mail: mariajguirado@gmail.com*

CONTENTS

9.1 Introduction 182
9.2 Experimental 183
9.3 Results and Discussion 185
9.4 Conclusions 191
Acknowledgment 193
Keywords 193
References and Bibliography 193

9.1 INTRODUCTION

This chapter is focused on the chemical characterization of some mural painting works, published by different authors, in order to establish the more suitable conservation treatments. Elemental determination of pigments from layers of artworks is possible to be evaluated by SEM/EDX and XRF. Bersani et al. (2014) worked with the combination of analytical techniques of the type noninvasive and microdestructive in the case of the most famous work of art in Parma cathedral, the *Assumption of the Virgin Mary* by Correggio. Their study allowed the characterization of pigments, the identification of the binding media, the restoration materials and the degradation products (Bersani et al., 2014). Another case of study, developed by Amadori et al. (2015), were the Roman wall paintings of the Villa of the Papyri in Herculaneum. Moreover, Perez-Rodriguez et al. (2015) reported the results obtained by different analytical techniques (OM, colorimetry, FTIR, μ-Raman, XRD and SEM/EDX) of many samples of green wall paintings from Seville Alcázar (Pérez-Rodríguez et al., 2015). In addition, another case analyzed by this type of analytical techniques was the Madonna con Bambino (XIII–XV century) mural painting (Fontecchio – L'Aquila, Italy) (Sfarra et al., 2015). Finally, the same way, Proietti et al., published a paper about a multianalytical research of Nubian mural paintings of the church of Sonqi Tino, Sudan (Proietti et al., 2016).

A mix method, including optical microscopy (OM) in combination with scanning electron microscopy–X-ray microanalysis (SEM-EDX), is described for the chemical determination of micro samples from the "Allegory to work" mural painting (Felipe Seade). These microinvasive analytical techniques were to obtain optimum results using the minimum amount of sample. These techniques are selected based on microscopic observation of cross sections for sample under visible light that could provide the color and thickness information of each layer, while SEM-EDX analysis is proved to give elemental compositions of tested area at microscale coating the sample surface with conducting material.

9.2 EXPERIMENTAL

9.2.1 SAMPLES AND SAMPLE PREPARATION

Six samples were collected from the "Allegory to work" mural painting (Felipe Seade) (sampling points are reported in Figure 9.1 and in Table 9.1). Micro samples were prepared as cross sections by embedding them in polyester resin (Ferpol-1973 made by Comercial Feroca, S. A. (Madrid-Spain) and provided by Agar Agar, S. L. (Pontevedra-Spain),

FIGURE 9.1 Sampling points from the "Allegory to Work" mural painting (Felipe Seade). Graphical Record of the R&D Project PUCM, 2013.

TABLE 9.1 The Samples Collected and Their Description (numbers refer to the different layers by starting from the lowest layer: 1 = ground; 2 and 3 = paint layers)

Sample name	Color	Description
FS1C	Brown	1. White ground
		2. Brown paint layer
FS3C	White	1. [substrate missing]
		2. White-Orange paint layer
		3. White paint layer
FS4C	Red	1. White ground
		2. Brown-Red paint layer
FS6C	Blue	1. White ground
		2. Blue paint layer (seems a mixture of two pigments, dark blue and white)
FS7C	Stucco onto ochre layer	1. White ground
		2. Ochre paint layer
		3. White stucco layer
FS9C	Yellow ochre	1. [substrate missing]
		2. Thin ochre paint layer
		3. Yellow paint layer

Then, they were cut and polished. Thus, they can be observed and analyzed transversely.

9.2.2 INSTRUMENTATION

Cross sections of the samples were observed with a Leica DMR microscope (reflected visible light, X25 to X400 magnifications) and were chemically analyzed with a Jeol JSM 6300 SEM (scanning electron microscope), working in high vacuum conditions, an accelerating voltage of 20 kV, a beam current of 2×10^{-9} A and a working distance of 15 mm (back scattered electrons), and operating with a Link-Oxford-Isis X-ray microanalysis system to evaluate its elemental composition. Elemental semiquantitative analysis was obtained using the method of correction ZAF (Osete-Cortina et al., 2010). All samples were coated with carbon to minimize charging effects.

9.3 RESULTS AND DISCUSSION

From the analysis results of the cross sections, similar structure was detected in the pigmented polychromic samples collected from the "Allegory to work," generally including the white ground layer, the preparation layer made of gypsum and quartz, and finally, the paint layer (one or two layers).

The cross section of FS1C sample was observed with reflected visible light (Figure 9.2). One can recognize from the bottom upwards a layer of white ground and a brown layer. The SEM/EDX analysis (Figure 9.3) highlighted the presence of a gypsum ($CaSO_4 \cdot 2H_2O$) (33.65% CaO, 51.73% SO_3) and quartz (14.62% SiO_2) in the ground (layer 1). Above the ground, there is a layer 2 of lithopone (barium sulfate and zinc sulfide) (5.18% BaO, 1.92% ZnO, %.91% SO_3) mixed with chrome orange (lead chromate, $PbCrO_4$) (53.83% PbO, 2.10% Cr_2O_3) and umber (7.60% FeO, 0.46% MnO). Similar composition was observed in FS4C sample. A gypsum ($CaSO_4 \cdot 2H_2O$) (40.00% CaO, 58.27% SO_3) and quartz (1.73% SiO_2) in the ground and lithopone (barium sulfate and zinc sulfide) (4.90–1.90% BaO, 2.42–6.01% ZnO, 4.27–5.75% SO_3), chrome orange (lead chromate, $PbCrO_4$) (18.10–33.14% PbO, 0.50–2.09% Cr_2O_3) and umber (18.65% FeO, 1.17% MnO) and iron oxide (III) (18.26%FeO) in the paint layer (Figures 9.4 and 9.5).

FIGURE 9.2 Microphotograph of the sample FS1C, 63X. *Source:* Graphical record of the R&D Project PUCM, 2013.

186 Conservation, Tourism, and Identity of Contemporary Community Art

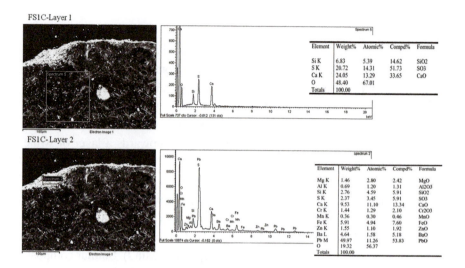

FIGURE 9.3 SEM-BSE image and X-ray spectrum of the cross section of sample FS1C. *Source:* Graphical record of the R&D Project PUCM, 2013.

A ground layer was not observed in the case of FS3C sample (Figure 9.6 and 9.7). However, a second white paint layer (calcite, $CaCO_3$ (59.19% CaO) and zinc white (23.26% ZnO)) can be seen over original paint layer (lithopone (barium sulfate and zinc sulfide) (25.27% BaO, 31.95% ZnO,

FIGURE 9.4 Microphotograph of the sample FS4C, 63X. *Source:* Graphical record of the R&D Project PUCM, 2013.

Study of the Chemical Composition Through Cross 187

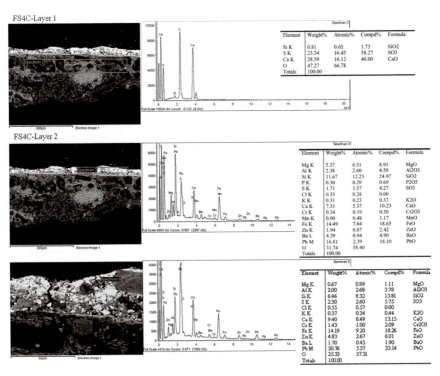

FIGURE 9.5 SEM-BSE image and X-ray spectrum of the cross section of sample FS4C. *Source:* Graphical record of the R&D Project PUCM, 2013.

FIGURE 9.6 Microphotograph of the sample FS3C, 63X. *Source:* Graphical record of the R&D Project PUCM, 2013.

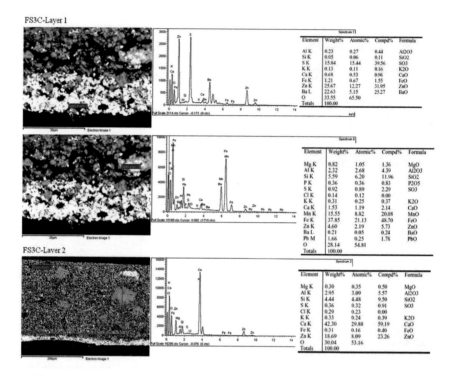

FIGURE 9.7 SEM-BSE image and x-ray spectrum of the cross section of sample FS3. *Source:* Graphical record of the R&D Project PUCM, 2013.

39.56% SO_3), chrome orange (lead chromate, $PbCrO_4$) (1.78% PbO, n.d.% Cr_2O_3) and umber (48.70% FeO, 20.08% MnO). This suggests a repaint.

The blue color was obtained by a mixture of Prussian blue ($Fe_4(Fe(CN)_6)_3$) (ranging from 0.89 to 10.20% FeO) and lithopone (barium sulfate and zinc sulfide) (4.90–11.78% BaO, 0.19% ZnO, 4.37% SO_3) and lead white ($2PbCO_3 \cdot Pb(OH)_2$) (78.68–76.56% PbO). Under a ground layer it was analyzed gypsum ($CaSO_4 \cdot 2H_2O$) (39.53% CaO, 58.88% SO_3) and quartz (1.59% SiO_2), (Figures 9.8 and 9.9).

Generally, in most samples it has been observed a single paint layer, while the FS7C and FS9C samples could be seen two or three layers."

As to the FS7C sample, on a basis layer containing gypsum ($CaSO_4 \cdot 2H_2O$) (36.33% CaO, 54.74% SO_3) and clay minerals (6.57% SiO_2, 0.36% Al_2O_3, 0.27% FeO), we applied (Figures 9.10 and 9.11) two colored layers (layers 2–3). They were composed of lithopone (barium sulfate and zinc sulfide)

Study of the Chemical Composition Through Cross   189

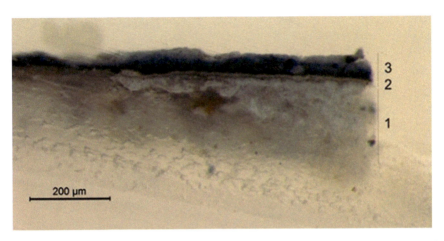

FIGURE 9.8 Microphotograph of the sample FS6C, 63X. *Source:* Graphical record of the R&D Project PUCM, 2013.

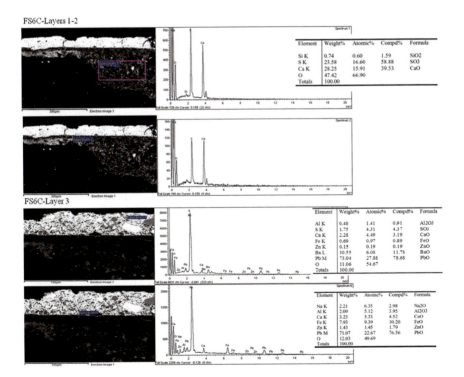

FIGURE 9.9 SEM-BSE image and *x*-ray spectrum of the cross section of sample FS6C. *Source:* Graphical record of the R&D Project PUCM, 2013.

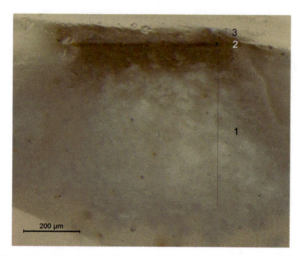

FIGURE 9.10 Microphotograph of the sample FS7C, 63X. *Source:* Graphical record of the R&D Project PUCM, 2013.

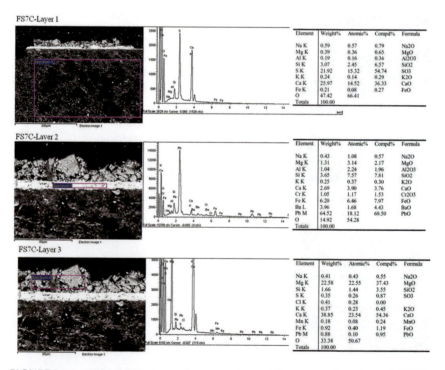

FIGURE 9.11 SEM-BSE image and *x*-ray spectrum of the cross section of sample FS7C. *Source:* Graphical record of the R&D Project PUCM, 2013.

(4.43% BaO, n.d.% ZnO, n.d.% SO$_3$), lead white (2PbCO$_3$·Pb(OH)$_2$) (69.50% PbO), chrome orange (lead chromate, PbCrO$_4$) (1.53% Cr$_2$O$_3$) and dolomite (CaMg(CO$_3$)$_2$, 54.36% CaO, 37.43% MgO$_2$), umber (1.19% FeO, 0.24% MnO).

A cross section of a FS9C sample is shown in Figures 9.12 and 9.13. Three colored layers were analyzed. First, lithopone (barium sulfate and zinc sulfide) (23.43% BaO, 10.39% ZnO, 23.15% SO$_3$), chrome orange (lead chromate, PbCrO$_4$) (4.17% PbO), 1.04% Cr$_2$O$_3$), and clay materials with iron oxide (2.72% FeO) (layer 1). Second, zinc white (30.91% ZnO), chrome orange (lead chromate, PbCrO$_4$) (34.47% PbO), 8.46% Cr$_2$O$_3$), and clay minerals (1.31% FeO) (layer 2). And, the last one, zinc white (68.42% ZnO), chrome orange (lead chromate, PbCrO$_4$) (17.95% PbO), 3.45% Cr$_2$O$_3$), and clay minerals (1.17% FeO).

9.4 CONCLUSIONS

This chapter was focused on the chemical characterization of mural painting samples from the "Allegory to work" (Felipe Seade). A mix method including optical microscopy (OM) in combination with scanning electron microscopy – X-ray microanalysis (SEM-EDX), is described for the chemical determination of micro samples.

FIGURE 9.12 Microphotograph of the sample FS9C, 63X. Graphical Record of the R&D Project PUCM, 2013.

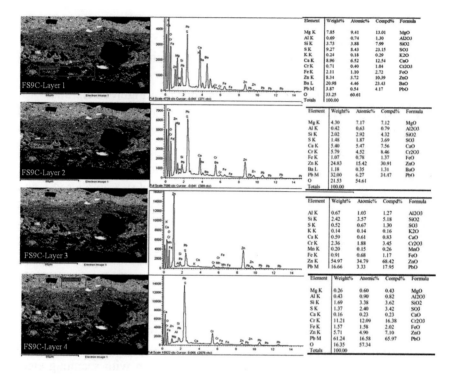

FIGURE 9.13 SEM-BSE image and *x*-ray spectrum of the cross section of sample FS9C.
Source: Graphical record of the R&D Project PUCM, 2013.

Similar structure was detected in the pigmented polychromic samples, generally including the white ground layer, the preparation layer made of gypsum and quartz, and finally, the paint layer (one or two layers). Several pigments could be identified by SEM-EDX, including clay minerals, chrome orange (lead chomate), lead white or lithopone. In the yellow and ochre colors, chrome orange, umber or iron oxides mixed with lithopone and zinc white were used. In the brown colors, clay minerals, umber and chrome orange were identified. In the case of red colors, Seade used clay minerals, lead chomate, minium and iron oxide. Two kinds of blue were identified, ultramarine and Prussian blue, mixed with lead white and lithopone, and clay minerals. Ultramarine was identified in the green samples extracted from the "Allegory to work" mural painting (F. Seade). Lithopone and lead white were main pigments used for white. However, Seade added zinc white to obtain a different kind of white.

ACKNOWLEDGMENT

The authors would like to thank M. Planes and J. L. Moya (Microscopy Service, UPV) for their technical assistance.

KEYWORDS

- "Allegory to work" mural painting
- chemical characterization
- cross section
- optical microscopy
- pigments
- scanning electron microscopy
- x-ray microanalysis

REFERENCES AND BIBLIOGRAPHY

Amadori, M. L., Barcelli, S., Poldi, G., Ferrucci, F., Andreotti, A., Baraldi, P., & Colombini, M. P. (2015). Invasive and noninvasive analyzes for knowledge and conservation of Roman wall paintings of the Villa of the Papyri in Herculaneum. *Microchem. J.*, *118*, 183–192.

Bersani, D., Berzioli, M., Caglio, S., Casoli, A., Lottici, P. P., Medeghini, L., Poldi, G., & Zannini, P. (2014). An integrated multianalytical approach to the study of the dome wall paintings by Correggio in Parma cathedral, *Microchem. J.*, *114*, 80–88.

Osete-Cortina, L., Doménech-Carbó, M. T., Doménech, A., Yusá-Marco, D. J., & Ahmadi, H. (2010). Multimethod analysis of Iranian Ilkhanate ceramics from the Takht-e Soleyman palace, *Anal Bioanal Chem*, *397*, 319–329

Pérez-Rodríguez, J. L., Jiménez de Haro, M. C., & Siguenza, B., (2015). Martínez-Blanes, J. M. Green pigments of Roman mural paintings from Seville Alcazar. *Appl Clay Sci.*, *116–117*, 211–219.

Proietti, N., Di Tullio, V., Presciutti, F., Gentile, G., Brunetti, B. G., & Capitani, D. (2016). A multianalytical study of ancient Nubian detached mural paintings. *Microchem. J.*, *124*, 719–725.

Sfarra, S., Ibarra-Castanedo, C., Tortora, M., Arrizza, L., Cerichelli, G., Nardi, I., & Maldague, X. (2015). Diagnostics of wall paintings: A smart and reliable approach, *J. Cult. Herit.* http://dx.doi.org/10.1016/j.culher.2015.07.011].

CHAPTER 10

TECHNICAL DOCUMENTATION SHEET OF PAINTING: SCIENTIFIC CATALOGUING

M. SÁNCHEZ-PONS[1], M. FERNÁNDEZ-OSCAR[2],
J. C. VALCÁRCEL-ANDRÉS[3] and M. L. MARTÍNEZ-BAZÁN[4]

[1]*Associate Professor, Department of Conservation and Restoration of Cultural Heritage, UPV, 3N Building, Camino de Vera s/n, 46022 Valencia, Spain, Tel.: +34-963877000/Ext. 73136, E-mail: mersanpo@crbc.upv.es*

[2]*Phd Student, Department of Conservation and Restoration of Cultural Heritage, UPV, 3N Building, Camino de Vera s/n, 46022 Valencia, Spain, Tel.: +34-661685561, E-mail: mirferoscr@gmail.com*

[3]*Associate Professor, Department of Conservation and Restoration of Cultural Heritage, UPV, 3N Building, Camino de Vera s/n, 46022 Valencia, Spain, Tel.: +34-963877000/Ext. 73136, E-mail: jvalcara@crbc.upv.es*

[4]*Associate Professor, Department of Conservation and Restoration of Cultural Heritage, UPV, 3N Building, Camino de Vera s/n, 46022 Valencia, Spain, Tel.: +34-963877000/79311, E-mail: martine@crbc.upv.es*

CONTENTS

10.1 Introduction 196
10.2 Objectives and Methodology 196
10.3 Design of a Cataloguing Model 197

10.4 Completed Sheets Related to the Painting "Allegory to Work" 200
10.5 Conclusions... 200
Keywords... 206
References and Bibliography... 206

10.1 INTRODUCTION

All technical documentation of an artistic work implies a respectful and progressive study, which if possible, is reproducible and adaptable to the circumstances of the other pieces that form the whole work.

With the mural "Allegory to work" by Felipe Seade it has been possible to develop all phases of study proposed in the model developed for the project documentation *"Social function of Uruguayan mural painting of the twentieth century as a mean and model of sustainable heritage activation. Decentralization, identity and memory"* and to complete, in this way, the different forms designed for this purpose (Valcárcel et al., 2015).

The different phases of preliminary studies have been done gradually, and the results interconnected. Conclusions drawn from each of the historic, artistic and social context of the work have been combined with the physicochemical study of the painting and its surroundings. First, work started with an organoleptic study, performing a detailed inspection with front light under different light radiation, with the corresponding photographic record of the whole surface. In addition, colorimetric measurements at different points of the work have been taken and finally micro samples have been extracted for analysis by light microscopy and SEM/EDX, in order to determine the constituting materials and additives of the work. From the correlation of all data, a complete diagnosis was possible, with which the proposed intervention on the mural has been developed.

10.2 OBJECTIVES AND METHODOLOGY

The cataloging of Uruguayan contemporary murals of the above-mentioned project has as fundamental goal the knowledge of the works for a proper conservation. This implies a deep knowledge at different levels: Socially seen, to which part they belong to in order to evaluate and identify these as part of its heritage and hence their collective identity; from the point of view of heritage managers who are responsible for establishing safeguard measures, as the specialists in defining protocols and maintenance handling. Therefore, this cataloging model intends to be a tool to coordinate these actions in an orderly and systematic way.

The working method is based on the coordination of an interdisciplinary team working on different aspects of the mural paintings, which covers both the analysis of the meaning of each work with the contextualization at the time it was realized and the value at present time. Additionally the technical study of the materials show how it was created and the conditions of exposure where it is located in order to allow a correct diagnosis of its state of conservation.

This team has been studying the works *in situ*, carrying out a complete fieldwork, analyzing both each mural and the community in which they are situated. To gather all the collected information from each of the works, different work sheets have been designed which helped to collect and present data in a synthesized and useful form for the different stakeholders involved in the management, conservation and enjoy of the murals.

10.3 DESIGN OF A CATALOGUING MODEL

The designed cataloging model consists of three sheets: inventory, technical documentation and diffusion. The first two maintain a common format, while the latter one is intended to be used in other ways to approach key data of each painting to the public.

10.3.1 INVENTORY SHEET

The inventory card is meant to have an identification record of each painting, of either a single work or a scene from a set. Questions related to the management of the cataloged contemporary mural collection are included.

The following fields are to be filled:
- Record data:
  Inventory No.
  Unique numerical identification code for each work of the collection, preceded by an acronym referring to the category of the work:
  – (U) Unique
  – (E) Scene of a set
  Incorporation date
  Date of last update
  Person(s) who made the registry
- General data:
  Author, title, date of realization, typology, size, location, owner, state of conservation, preliminary restorations.
- Realized registrations:
  Technical photographic record (R1), colorimetric (R2), physiochemical (R3) (indicate whether they have been made and specific studies):
  Artistic contextualization (E1), constituent materials (E2), state of conservation (E3), property study (E4) (indicate whether they have been realized, these include other types of records that may be appropriate).
- Annexed documents:
  Space to indicate documents located on the work, such as sketches, photographs of various moments through time, contracts, references in press, restoration reports, legal documents, etc.

10.3.2 TECHNICAL DOCUMENTATION SHEETS

These are documents that complement the inventory sheet, in which both realized technical records as well as specific studies arising from them are reflected, namely:
  a. *Records:*
     – Technical photographic record (R1)
       Both used equipment and number of photographs with related characteristics (oblique light, reflected UV, reflectography, macro) are recorded, leaving a space for a photo index reference.

- Colorimetric record (R2)
  Describes the equipment used for registration, the exact coordinates of the measuring points, and data from the same.
- Physicochemical record (R3)
  This sheet is divided into two parts, the first is relating to the taking of environmental data of the site where the work is and its surface (temperature, relative humidity, lumens and acoustic measurement), and the second registers and describes the exact points where micro samples have been taken for further analysis.
- Damage and causes record (R4)
  A frame of systematic implementation for recording all possible damage present in the work, both structural and esthetic and interpretative, as well as the cause either derived from the property, its geographic location, the technique itself, or actions of human or other living beings. The option of attaching a damage map and diagrams that illustrate graphically the observed damages is included.

b. *Studies:*
   Through these records, conclusions are collected in a systematic way, reviewing other data sources and the relationship established with these and the realized records.
   - Artistic contextualization (E1)
     A brief biography of the author is included, the theme of the work, an iconographic description and its repercussions in terms of knowledge by the public, and the main references where it has been cited
   - Technical analysis and materials (E2)
     In this study, the conclusions on the technique and used materials by the artist are discussed from reviewing documentary sources, the organoleptic and physicochemical analyzes.
   - State of conservation (E3)
     Finally, the working hypothesis is shown which allows corroborating the information obtained from the registry and studies in order to be able to perform a reliable diagnosis of the work.

10.4 COMPLETED SHEETS RELATED TO THE PAINTING "ALLEGORY TO WORK"

For illustrative purposes Figures 10.1–10.11 are presented for the completed sheets which summarize the main results of the preliminary studies on the painting.

10.5 CONCLUSIONS

Thanks to a coordinated work of an interdisciplinary team of professionals from different areas (curators, restorers, historians, chemists, experts in colorimetry, analytical photographer, heritage managers, economists, and sociologists), it has been possible to obtain the necessary information for understanding, knowing and conserving the mural "Allegory to work," painted by Felipe Seade in 1938, a key work in the artistic and cultural history of the twentieth century of Uruguay and, in particular, of Colonia del Sacramento.

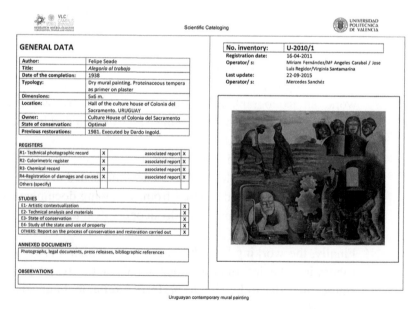

FIGURE 10.1 Inventory sheet. *Source:* Graphical record of the R&D Project PUCM.

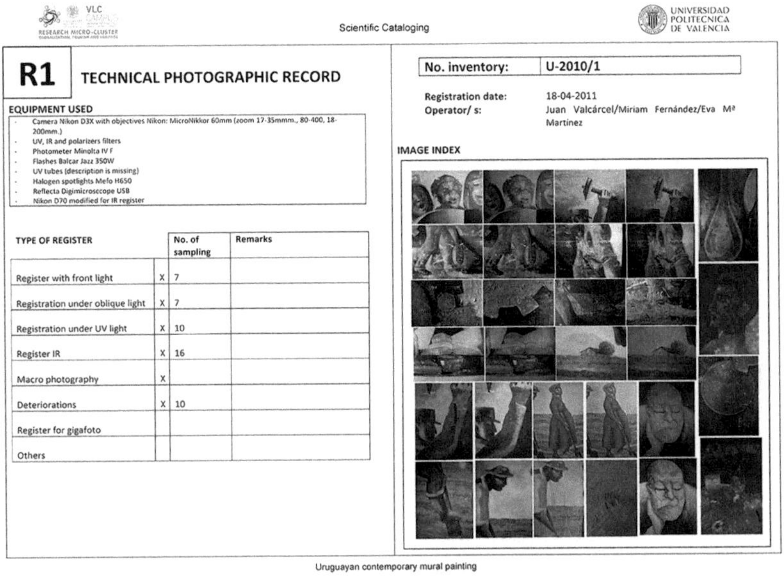

VLC CAMPUS RESEARCH MICRO-CLUSTER

Scientific Cataloging

UNIVERSIDAD POLITECNICA DE VALENCIA

R1 TECHNICAL PHOTOGRAPHIC RECORD

EQUIPMENT USED

- Camera Nikon D3X with objectives Nikon: MicroNikkor 60mm (zoom 17-35mmm., 80-400, 18-200mm.)
- UV, IR and polarizers filters
- Photometer Minolta IV F
- Flashes Balcar Jazz 350W
- UV tubes (description is missing)
- Halogen spotlights Mefo H650
- Reflecta Digimicrosccope USB
- Nikon D70 modified for IR register

TYPE OF REGISTER		No. of sampling	Remarks
Register with front light	X	7	
Registration under oblique light	X	7	
Registration under UV light	X	10	
Register IR	X	16	
Macro photography	X		
Deteriorations	X	10	
Register for gigafoto			
Others			

No. inventory:	U-2010/1
Registration date:	18-04-2011
Operator/ s:	Juan Valcárcel/Miriam Fernández/Eva Mª Martinez

IMAGE INDEX

Uruguayan contemporary mural painting

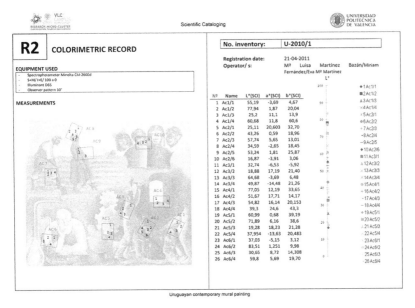

FIGURE 10.2 Technical documentation sheet: R1 Photographic record (2); R2 Colorimetric record a (3). *Source:* Graphical record of the R&D Project PUCM.

VLC CAMPUS RESEARCH MICRO-CLUSTER

Scientific Cataloging

UNIVERSIDAD POLITECNICA DE VALENCIA

R2 COLORIMETRIC RECORD

EQUIPMENT USED

- Spectrophotometer Minolta CM-2600d
- S+M/ I+E/ 100 a 0
- Illuminant D65
- Observer pattern 10°

MEASUREMENTS

No. inventory:	U-2010/1
Registration date:	21-04-2011
Operator/ s:	Mª Luisa Martínez Bazán/Miriam Fernández/Eva Mª Martínez

Nº	Name	L*(SCI)	a*(SCI)	b*(SCI)
1	Ac1/1	55,19	-3,69	4,67
2	Ac1/2	77,94	1,87	20,04
3	Ac1/3	25,2	11,1	13,9
4	Ac1/4	60,68	11,8	60,6
5	Ac2/1	25,11	20,603	32,70
6	Ac2/2	43,26	0,59	18,96
7	Ac2/3	57,74	5,65	13,01
8	Ac2/4	34,59	-2,65	18,45
9	Ac2/5	53,24	1,81	25,87
10	Ac2/6	16,87	-3,91	3,06
11	Ac3/1	32,74	-6,53	-5,92
12	Ac3/2	18,88	17,19	21,40
13	Ac3/3	64,68	-3,69	6,48
14	Ac3/4	49,87	-14,48	21,26
15	Ac4/1	77,05	12,19	33,65
16	Ac4/2	51,67	17,71	14,17
17	Ac4/3	54,82	16,14	20,153
18	Ac4/4	39,3	24,6	43,3
19	Ac5/1	60,99	0,68	39,19
20	Ac5/2	71,89	6,16	38,6
21	Ac5/3	19,28	18,23	21,28
22	Ac5/4	37,954	-13,63	20,483
23	Ac6/1	37,03	-5,15	3,12
24	Ac6/2	83,51	1,251	9,98
25	Ac6/3	30,65	8,72	14,308
26	Ac6/4	59,8	5,69	19,70

Uruguayan contemporary mural painting

FIGURE 10.3 Technical documentation sheet: R1 Photographic record (2); R2 Colorimetric record a (3). *Source:* Graphical record of the R&D Project PUCM.

202   Conservation, Tourism, and Identity of Contemporary Community Art

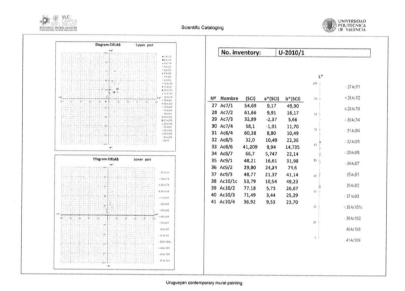

FIGURE 10.4 Technical documentation sheets: R2 Colorimetric record b (4); R3 Registration of physicochemical data (5). *Source:* Graphical record of the R&D Project PUCM.

FIGURE 10.5 Technical documentation sheets: R2 Colorimetric record b (4); R3 Registration of physicochemical data (5). *Source:* Graphical record of the R&D Project PUCM.

RESEARCH MICRO-CLUSTER VLC CAMPUS — Scientific Cataloging — UNIVERSIDAD POLITECNICA DE VALENCIA

R4 REGISTRATION OF DAMAGES AND CAUSES

DERIVED FROM PROPERTY

[ ] Structural movements	[X] Humidity leaks caused by defects: Covers [X], Drainage [X], Facings [ ], Windows or holes [ ]	Others (specify)

DERIVED FROM ITS LOCATION (GROUND AND ENVIRONMENT)

[ ] Especially wet ground settlement	[ ] Exposure conditions: Sunlight [ ], Wind and rain [ ], Heavy traffic [ ], Proximity to the sea [ ]	Others (specify)
[ ] Floods		
[ ] Seismic movements		
[ ] Fire		

DERIVED FROM PROPER TECHNIQUE

[X] Use of low quality materials	[ ] Ignorance of the technique used	Others (specify)
[ ] Incompatible materials	[X] Especially degradable technique	
[ ] Inappropriate choice of technique		

DERIVED FROM HUMAN ACTION

[X] Previous restoration: Inadequate repainting [X], Protective varnishes altered [ ], Excessive cleaning [ ], Tearing [ ]	[ ] Interventions in the building for remodeling	Others (specify)
	[X] Vandalism	
	[ ] Changes in the use of space	

DERIVED FROM ACTION OF OTHER LIVING BEINGS

[ ] Animal droppings: Insects [ ], Birds [ ]	[ ] Microorganisms: Mushrooms [ ], Lichens [ ]	Others (specify)
	[ ] Plants and roots	

No. inventory: U-2010/1

Registration date: 18-04-2011
Operator/ s: Miriam Fernández/Eva Mª Martínez

STRUCTURAL DAMAGES

- [ ] Fissures
- [X] Cracks
- [X] Separation between layers
- [ ] Hollows
- [ ] Salt efflorescence — At the surface [ ], Sub-surface efflorescence [ ] | Fine film [ ], Concretions [ ] | Soluble [ ], Insoluble [ ], undetermined [ ]
- [ ] Crackle
- [X] Disintegration and powdering of the surface — ~~Area of bulging~~
- [X] Missing material

Other effects – not described:

AESTHETIC AND INTERPRETIVE DAMAGES

- [ ] Chromatic alterations — Discoloration [ ], Yellowed [ ] | Tonal decompensation [x], Others [ ]
- [X] Stains — Paint [ ], Plaster [X], Cement [ ] | Organic [ ], Unidentified [ ]
- [X] Missing parts and lagoons — Partial pictorial surface abrasion [ ], General erosion [X], Punctual loss of pictorial film [ ] | Significant losses of paint layer [X], Loss of preparatory layers [X], Partial mutilation
- [ ] Decontextualisation

Other damage not described:

Repainting

OBSERVATIONS

Uruguayan contemporary mural painting

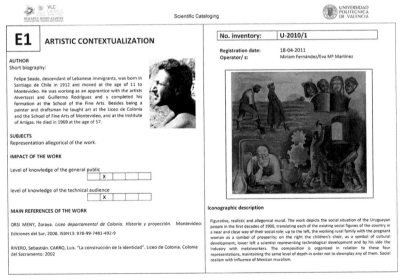

FIGURE 10.6 Technical documentation sheets: R4 Registration of damages and causes; E1 Artistic contextualization. *Source:* Graphical record of the R&D Project PUCM.

RESEARCH MICRO-CLUSTER VLC CAMPUS — Scientific Cataloging — UNIVERSIDAD POLITECNICA DE VALENCIA

E1 ARTISTIC CONTEXTUALIZATION

AUTHOR
Short biography:

Felipe Seade, descendant of Lebanese immigrants, was born in Santiago de Chile in 1912 and moved at the age of 11 to Montevideo. He was working as an apprentice with the artists Alvertazzi and Guillermo Rodríguez and y completed his formation at the School of the Fine Arts. Besides being a painter and draftsman he taught art at the Liceo de Colonia and the School of Fine Arts of Montevideo, and at the Institute of Artigas. He died in 1969 at the age of 57.

SUBJECTS
Representation allegorical of the work.

IMPACT OF THE WORK

Level of knowledge of the general public

	X			

level of knowledge of the technical audience

	X			

MAIN REFERENCES OF THE WORK

ORSI MENY, Zoraya. *Liceo departamental de Colonia. Historia y proyección.* Montevideo: Ediciones del Sur, 2008. ISBN13: 978-99-7481-492-9

RIVERO, Sebastián. CARRO, Luis. "La construcción de la identidad". Liceo de Colonia. Colonia del Sacramento: 2002

No. inventory: U-2010/1

Registration date: 18-04-2011
Operator/ s: Miriam Fernández/Eva Mª Martínez

Iconographic description

Figurative, realistic and allegorical mural. The work depicts the social situation of the Uruguayan people in the first decades of 1900, translating each of the existing social figures of the country in a near and close way of their social role: up to the left, the working rural family with the pregnant woman as a symbol of prosperity; on the right the children's choir, as a symbol of cultural development; lower left a scientist representing technological development and by his side the industry with metalworkers. The composition is organized in relation to these four representations, maintaining the same level of depth in order not to downplay any of them. Social realism with influence of Mexican muralism.

Uruguayan contemporary mural painting

FIGURE 10.7 Technical documentation sheets: R4 Registration of damages and causes; E1 Artistic contextualization. *Source:* Graphical record of the R&D Project PUCM.

VLC CAMPUS RESEARCH MICRO-CLUSTER

Scientific Cataloging

UNIVERSIDAD POLITECNICA DE VALENCIA

E2 TECHNICAL ANALYSIS AND MATERIAL

TECHNIQUE: Protein temple with egg yolk on polished plaster primer

Direct observation	X
Documentary consultation	X
Physicochemical studies	X

MURAL STRUCTURE AND SURFACE FEATURES

Wall anchor system:		Volumentric:		Surface:		Aspect:	
Painted	X	Two-dimensional	X	Simple (1 technique)	X	Mate	
Adherent		Three-dimensional		Mixed (2 or more)		Brillant	
Inserted		Combined				Combined	X
Hanging							

MATERIALS USED

		Probable	Identified
Support	x	Brick Wall	
Plasters	x		Plaster preparation
Adhesive material	x		Egg yolk
Primer			
Surface	x		Polished Plaster
Protective layer	x		Without protection layer
Repainting	x		Polyvinyl Acetate

OBSERVATIONS:

No. inventory:	U-2010/1

Registration date: 26-06-2011
Operator/ s: Mª Dolores Yusa-Marco/Miriam Fernández/Eva Mª Martínez

IDENTIFICATION OF PIGMENTOS	Extraction system	Notes / Description
Microsample FS1C Brown	Scalpel	Lead chromate, burnt umber
Microsample FS3C White	Scalpel	Calcite, zinc white, lead white
Microsample FS4C Reddish	Scalpel	Burnt umber, clay, iron oxides
Microsample FS6C Blue	Scalpel	Prussian blue, ultramarine
Microsample FS9C Yellow	Scalpel	Lead chromate, iron oxide, burnt umber

ANALYTICAL STUDY

YELLOWS

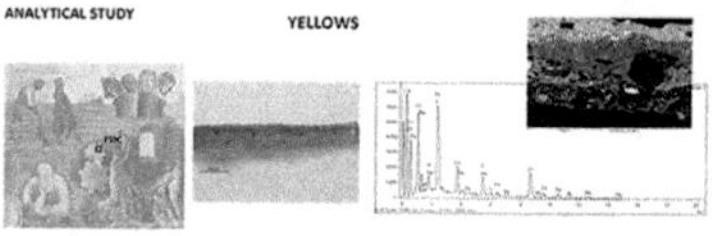

Lead chromate, iron oxide, burnt umber, zinc white

REDDISH

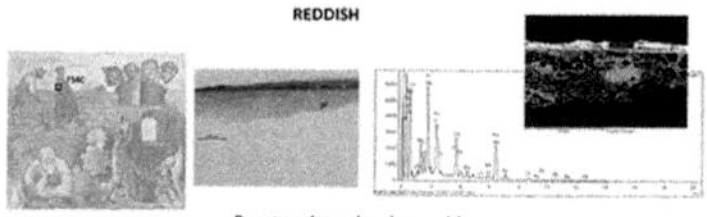

Burnt umber, clay, iron oxide

Uruguayan contemporary mural painting

FIGURES 10.8 Technical documentation sheets: E2 technical analysis and materials; E3 State of conservation (a). *Source:* Graphical record of the R&D Project PUCM.

VLC CAMPUS RESEARCH MICRO-CLUSTER

Scientific Cataloging

UNIVERSIDAD POLITECNICA DE VALENCIA

E3 STATE OF CONSERVATION

STRUCTURAL STATE

		Probable causes	Defined causes
Separation of the substrate			
Separation between layers	x		Moisture leaks
Decohesion	x		Technical defect
Disintegration	x		Technical defect
Fractures			
Cracks	x		mortars instability
Others			

STATE OF THE SURFACE

		Probable causes	defined causes
Darkening			
Discoloration			
Tonal decompensation			
Whitish veils			
Missing parts	x		Destruction of parts, Vandalism

PRESENCE OF MATERIAL NOT BELONGING TO THE ORIGINAL WORK

		Probable causes	Defined causes
Repainting or replacement	x		Restoration in 1981
Oxidized protections			
Stains	x		Plaster replacements, intentional depositions
Surface dirt	x	Natural particle deposition	Lack of maintenance

Observations
The work presents numerous incisions affecting the paint layer and the preparatory mortar.

No. inventory:	U-2010/1

Registration date: 18-04-2011
Operator/ s: Miriam Fernández/Eva Mª Martínez

Good condition	
Acceptable	
Poor condition	X
Requires urgent action	
Decontextualized	

Registration date: 22-07-2014
Operator/ s: Virginia Santamarina

Good condition	X
Acceptable	
Poor condition	
Requires urgent action	
Decontextualized	

Uruguayan contemporary mural painting

FIGURES 10.9 Technical documentation sheets: E2 technical analysis and materials; E3 State of conservation (a). *Source:* Graphical record of the R&D Project PUCM.

Technical Documentation Sheet of Painting 205

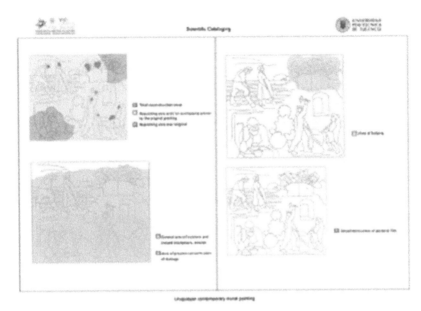

FIGURE 10.10 Technical documentation sheets: E3 State of conservation (b). *Source:* Graphical record of the R&D Project PUCM.

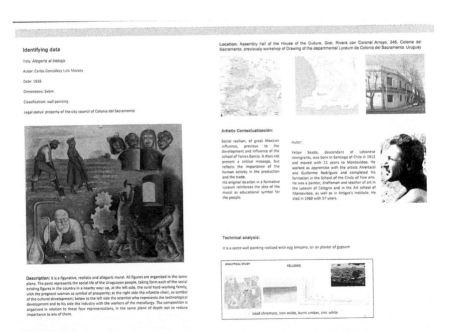

FIGURE 10.11 Diffusion sheet. *Source:* Graphical record of the R&D Project PUCM.

The presentation of the collected data through an inventory, technical documentation and dissemination sheets, is highly effective for managing this kind of heritage, constituting an essential tool for the conservation of this mural, as well as for other modern and contemporary wall paintings, which are a significant Uruguayan cultural heritage of the twentieth century.

With this model of technical documentation the value of the works is highlighted, having a deep knowledge of them, allowing consideration in their artistic context, knowing their conservation state, conveying those values and establishing the most adequate strategies for their preservation, either through preventive conservation plans or specific restoration proposals.

KEYWORDS

- **cataloguing**
- **contemporary wall paintings**
- **diffusion sheets**
- **inventory sheet**
- **mural painting**
- **technical documentation sheets**

REFERENCES AND BIBLIOGRAPHY

Baca, M. (2006). *Cataloguing Cultural Objects. A Guide to Describing Cultural Works and their Images.* Visual Resources Association, Chicago, ISBN-10: 0-8389-3564-8.

DeCarli, G., & Tsagaraki, C. (2006). *Un Inventario de Bienes Culturales: ¿por qué y para quién?* Web del SENIP [Online]. Published online www.ilam.org Ediciones ILAM San José, Costa Rica. Retrieved from: http://senip.gob.ar/wp-content/uploads/2011/09/Uninventariodebienesculturales.porqueyparaquien.pdf (accessed Nov 22, 2012).

Harpring, P., & Baca, M. (2014). *Categories for the Description of Works of Art.* Web of J. Paul Getty Trust, [Online]. Published online: 2014. Retrieved from: http://www.getty.edu/research/conducting_research/standards/ cdwa (accessed May 20, 2012).

Nagel, L., & Núñez, G. (2005). *La normalización de vocabulario: preservación de la información* En: *Revista Conserva* No. 9, Ed. Centro Nacional de Conservación, Web del Centro Nacional de Conservación y Restauración de Chile, [Online]. Published online: 2005. Retrieved from: http://www.dibam.cl/dinamicas/DocAdjunto_700.pdf (accessed Jan 22, 2011).

Sánchez-Pons, M; Fuster-López, L., & Mata, A. (2013). *Contemporary Murals: Growing Awareness on Their Values and Potential as Community Heritage*, in *Procedings of the Workshop Tourism & Creative Industry*, Editorial UPV, Valencia. ISBN 978-84-9048-153-0.

Sánchez-Pons, M. (2011). *Murals valencians dels segles XX i XXI. La web com a plataforma de difusió del seu coneixement*, en Urtx: revista cultural de l'Urgell, ed Arxiu Comarcal de l'Urgell, Lleida, pp. 109–125. ISSN 1130-0574.

Sánchez-Pons, M., Clavel, I., Vicente, T., Nebot, E. (2006). *El conocimiento del mural contemporáneo: un paso previo a su restauración: proyecto de catalogación de murales contemporáneos en la ciudad de Valencia*, in *Arché*, Editorial UPV, Valencia, pp. 53–59, ISSN 1887–3960.

Valcarcel-Andrés, J., Más-Barberà, X., Sánchez Pons, M., & Yusa-Marco, D. (2015). *Función social del muralismo uiriguayo del siglo XX como vehículo de activación patrimonial sustentable: Catalogación Técnica*, in *Conservation Issues in Modern and Contemporary Murals*, Cambridge Scholar Publishing, New Castle upon Tyne, pp. 513–525. ISBN 978-1-4438-7233-1.

PART IV

INTERVENTION PROCESS OF THE PAINTING "ALLEGORY TO WORK"

CHAPTER 11

STATE OF CONSERVATION

J. L. REGIDOR-ROS,[1] M. A. ZALBIDEA MUÑOZ,[2] and M. FERNÁNDEZ-OSCAR[3]

[1]*Associate Professor, Department of Conservation and Restoration of Cultural Heritage, UPV, 3N Building, Camino de Vera s/n, 46022 Valencia, Spain, Tel.: +34-963877000/73132, E-mail: jregidor@crbc.upv.es*

[2]*Associate Professor, Department of Conservation and Restoration of Cultural Heritage, UPV, 3N Building, Camino de Vera s/n, 46022 Valencia, Spain, Tel.: +34-963877000/73132, E-mail: manzalmu@crbc.upv.es*

[3]*Phd Student, Department of Conservation and Restoration of Cultural Heritage, UPV, 3N Building, Camino de Vera s/n, 46022 Valuncia, Spain, Tel.: +34-661685561, E-mail: mirferoscr@gmail.com*

CONTENTS

11.1 Introduction 212
11.2 Objectives 213
11.3 Methodology 213
11.4 Results of the Study and Evaluation of the State of Conservation 213
11.5 Conclusions 223
Keywords 224
References and Bibliography 224

11.1 INTRODUCTION

Situated within the movement of Uruguayan social realism, the work "Allegory to work" by the artist Felipe Seade, placed at the emblematic house of culture (former departmental Liceo) in Colonia de Sacramento witnesses the different historical events and transformations of the Uruguayan society in the early twentieth century.

Ever since its creation in 1936, the mural has reflected the outcome of the sociopolitical events, eventually fading into oblivion and lack of social recognition, which led to an attempt of complete destruction of the artwork in 1985 (Figure 11.1, general view of the mural before the intervention). Such was the damage endured by the mural that Dardo Ingold, former pupil of the artist, played an active role in 1981 with an intervention aimed to improve its state of conservation. He reinterpreted his master by recreating new color schemes, volumes, shapes and tonalities. Nevertheless, the aggressions against the painting have continued to occur to the present day.

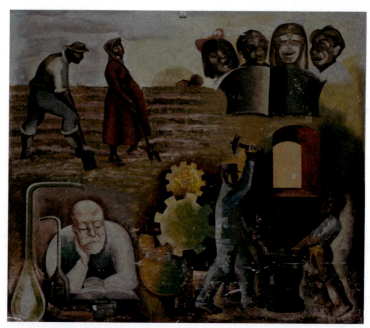

FIGURE 11.1 General view of the mural before the intervention. *Source:* Graphical record of the R&D Project PUCM, 2010.

11.2 OBJECTIVES

This chapter is aimed to draw a diagnosis of the state of conservation of the different layers and parts of the mural, in order to present a proposal of optimal intervention, adapted to the needs of the painting towards its future preservation, and contributing to guarantee the dissemination and promotion of this cultural asset as a symbol of collective identity.

11.3 METHODOLOGY

The conservation issues affecting the mural were determined through the analysis and evaluation of the different *in situ* studies that took place in April, 2011. These studies were carried out within the framework of the project "The social purpose of Uruguayan mural painting in the twentieth century as a carrier and activation model of sustainable heritage. Decentralization, identity and memory." A wide range of tests were performed, such as Organoleptic study, photographic study (general photography, grazing, macro, UV, IR), colorimetric study, environmental study (RH, temperature, Lux, dB), sample extraction for subsequent chemical analysis (of pigments and binders) and, lastly, cleaning tests (tests of solubility and suitability of the cleaning processes) to determine the material from which the inpainting is made and thus proceed to its proper disposal.

11.4 RESULTS OF THE STUDY AND EVALUATION OF THE STATE OF CONSERVATION

The first visual approach to the work conveyed a confusing perception of both the material structure and the esthetic values. The countless aggressions such as incisions, *sgraffitto* signatures and all kinds of erosions, together with the clumsy attempts to conceal them contributed to extremely irregular reading.

The assessment of the state of conservation of the work "Allegory to work" revealed that, due to the great amount and extent of the damage on the painting, it showed signs of structural instability and a poor state of conservation in all of its layers, both the preliminary and the pictorial surfaces.

As a result of the previous studies, the different issues affecting the mural painting are evaluated and quantified on Table 11.1.

TABLE 11.1 Conservation Issues Affecting the Mural Painting

Damage Factor	Causes	Consequences
Human	Deactivation	Gaps on several areas of the mural
	Lack of protection	Superficial damage, erosions, incisions, etc.
	Inappropriate interventions	Disguising the original.
Structural	Moisture leaks	Baggy effect and detachment of the pictorial layers
Caused by the technique	Loss of binding capacity	Pulverization and leakage of the pictorial layer

The first cause of the damage affecting the painting by Felipe Seade is the technical execution of the work itself, performed with a dry-painting technique. The artist made a protein-based tempera mixture, consisting of egg white on a polished preparation of plaster (Orsi, 2008). This painting technique used by Felipe Seade in the creation of the mural, pointing out that Seade used a pre-renaissance technique, is allegedly obsolete due to the laborious complexity it implied: "He used colored earth for potters and an organic binder (egg white) that used to be applied on plaster and was known as encaustic egg tempera..." (Orsi, 2008).

The original pictorial layer applied through egg white exposes notorious damage, resulting in negative responses to the values of physical and chemical resistance, due to the loss of cohesiveness of the binder (Figure 11.2, detail of the damaged area on the pictorial layer).

It is well known that the use of this material as a paint binder does not respond properly in humid environments and, over time, it generates detachment and powdery effects on the pictorial layer. Doerner remarks on those effects: "Egg white is water-soluble, but easily breakable and detachable like glue. It should neither be used in successive layers, nor as bottom painting in the transparency technique" (Doerner, 2005).

Nevertheless, the most significant issue affecting the work relate to human factors after its creation. On the one hand, the mural suffered serious damage essentially since its very execution, due to its location on a highly frequented area aimed at teaching children. On the other hand, the failed attempts of total destruction and the intervention in 1981 by Ingold, who inpainted a great extension of the original pictorial layer. Regarding this intervention, Ingold himself explained:

State of Conservation

FIGURE 11.2 Detail of the damaged area on the pictorial layer. *Source:* Graphical record of the R&D Project PUCM, 2011.

"One day I noticed the workers were breaking the mural at the Viejo Liceo. Then I went to the Council and talked to the Mayor […], about the importance of the work they were destroying […] he entitled me to stop the (destruction) works and restore it. Then the workers stopped, having removed already all the plaster up to the bricks, in order to build a new plaster. What did we do then? … It took us more than two months to fix. First, we refilled all the gaps with a trowel (some of them had been scratched with a compass); we used plaster trying to respect all the intact parts, in order to preserve Seade's work. Luckily, I was familiar with the colors he had used, since he had been my teacher in art school: cosolico red, brown, black… and a bit of ochre. Then we covered fissures, let it aerate, dry and then prepare the colors, which I did not mix with egg white as in the original, which belonged to a previous time. I used proper glue as a binder, made with a bit of Cascola© glue, and the colors. Then we proceeded to "touch," only in the damaged parts, trying to be as respectable as possible; although we needed to nearly re-create some figures, such as the scientist in the lab, which was no longer visible. To do so, Miguel Ángel Odriozola granted me a black and white picture, since color photography didn't exist at that time" (Informant 61).

From the interview, we assume that Dardo Ingold took care of the stucco of the most significant gaps and the reconstruction of the damaged areas by means of thin plaster or mastic. Mastic is traditionally known in the territory as a binder to refill the damaged murals, a mortar used to cover thin layers with plaster and vinyl synthetic resin. Once the mastic was applied, Ingold performed a general pictorial inpainting with a vinyl binder. These types of general inpainting, aimed to save and protect the original paints, are often found in mural painting interventions in South America.

During the visual test, the broadness and morphology of the inpainting were established in three different typologies (Figure 11.3, inpainting application typologies). Firstly, the areas where the inpainting overlaps with the original layer. Secondly, the areas presenting full reconstruction of both the preparatory and the pictorial layer, due to damage of a specific area or overall erosion and damage. Finally, areas that display the overlapping of a thin layer of primer and inpainting on the original pictorial layer.

Ultraviolet photography and cleaning tests helped to verify and understand the reach of Ingold's intervention in 1981, as shown in the pictures below (Figures 11.4 and 11.5, sighting of the morphology and the extent of the inpainting through ultraviolet photography).

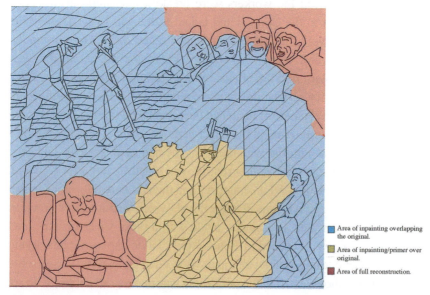

FIGURE 11.3 Inpainting application typologies. *Source:* Graphical record of the R&D Project PUCM, 2013.

State of Conservation 217

FIGURES 11.4 Sighting of the morphology and extent of the inpainting through ultraviolet photography. *Source:* Graphical record of the R&D Project PUCM, 2013.

FIGURES 11.5 Sighting of the morphology and extent of the inpainting through ultraviolet photography. *Source:* Graphical record of the R&D Project PUCM, 2013.

Despite the great extent of the inpainting and the fact that a wide part of the perimeter zones of the restored areas reveals slopes, caused by the overlapping of the stucco on the original layer, other areas show traces of the layer by Felipe Seade.

The organoleptic analysis detected structural instability due to the detachment of the layers on the top right area of the mural (Figure 11.6, sketch specifying the baggy effect area), caused by leaking out of the facade and the external roof towards the pictorial structure, risking a future loss of the affected layers.

As previously noted, during the period between 1936 and 2013, the mural painting suffered several damages, caused by vandalism and misconduct. Such factors resulted in the presence of scratches, inscriptions both carved and made with graphite, beatings and erosions caused intentionally and widespread all over the mural, with a higher concentration of damage on the bottom of the work (Figure 11.7, sketch showing the location of the scratched area).

FIGURE 11.6 Sketch specifying the baggy effect area. *Source:* Graphical record of the R&D Project PUCM, 2013.

State of Conservation

FIGURE 11.7 Sketch showing the location of the scratched area. *Source:* Graphical record of the R&D Project PUCM, 2013.

The different scratches carved on the mural surface present different depth on the pictorial layer (Figures 11.8–11.10, scratches and carving damage on the mural surface).

On the picture below of Figure 11.11 (scratching damage and inscriptions), the grazing light photography unveiled the extent and depth of the inscriptions and scratches executed when the mural location was used as a drawing class and recreation area of the nursery school.

To a lesser extent, remains of the graphite used to commit specific inscriptions and graphics were also found on the bottom area of the mural, as well as carved inscriptions, which usually refer to the proper name of the person and the date of performance.

Less abundant are small holes (Figures 11.11 and 11.12, holes on the mural) distributed across different areas of the mural, originated by using the mural as a target against which sharp objects were projected.

Professor Lyda Martín, a student of Dardo Ingold's and assistant during the intervention performed in 1981, explains on this fact:

"There was less, it was really damaged. He, who knew well the professor's work, was able to restore a lot, because it was seriously eroded by the

FIGURES 11.8 Scratches and carving damage on the mural surface. *Source:* Graphical record of the R&D Project PUCM, 2013.

FIGURES 11.9 Scratches and carving damage on the mural surface. *Source:* Graphical record of the R&D Project PUCM, 2013.

State of Conservation

FIGURE 11.10 Scratches and carving damage on the mural surface. *Source:* Graphical record of the R&D Project PUCM, 2013.

FIGURE 11.11 Scratching damage and inscriptions. *Source:* Graphical record of the R&D Project PUCM, 2013.

FIGURE 11.12 Holes on the mural. *Source:* Graphical record of the R&D Project PUCM, 2013.

compasses that had been projected against it [...] 30 years ago there were big dry point compasses made out of wood which they projected as spears. I don't know how the students were allowed to commit such damage, I don't know who was in charge… the mural wasn't given its appropriate value until Ingold saw it and claimed "this needs to stop." Then the room was closed and the entrance forbidden until later on, when the restoring project started, together with the reconstruction, but it was really damaged, not sure if that much, I couldn't remember exactly, but I thought there was less…" (Informants 73).

Other issues inherent to the mural itself were the passing of time or the imperfections of the pictorial technique, such as the powdery effects of the original pigment in different areas and after the inpainting. The damage appears on the complete pictorial layer, which hinders any kind of intervention on the mural.

The considerable weakening of the mural layer favored detachments, located mostly towards the top right-hand of the mural.

Superficial dirt widely stuck to the pictorial layer is noticeable, even more visible on the brighter tonalities (Figure 11.13, detachment and loss of pictorial layer).

State of Conservation 223

FIGURE 11.13 Detachment and loss of pictorial layer. *Source:* Graphical record of the R&D Project PUCM, 2013.

11.5 CONCLUSIONS

The artistic movement of Social Realism in Uruguay during the twentieth century, more specifically the work by the artist Felipe Seade, represents invaluable evidence of the Uruguayan history. The study developed through the piece "Allegory to work" proves the strong connection and presence of history in this painting, which conveys strong cultural values.

The mural belongs to a period of national recession and a loss of identity, stimulated by the great amount of conflicts taking place in and out of the country. In this context, Felipe Seade describes and depicts the Uruguayan lifestyle as the living testimony of history. The different phases of recording and analysis on the mural have proved that, in spite of the proper environmental conditions of the location and the building, its state of conservation is worrying due to the frequent and serious damage and aggressions.

After the completion of the study, we conclude that the mural painting located at the former Liceo in Colonia del Sacramento holds major symbolic and social value, representative of the Uruguayan people, and therefore, any further intervention techniques should guarantee the proper conservation of the mural, rescuing its essence and identity.

As a final point, it is appropriate to point out that the intervention on the mural by Dardo Ingold in 1981, must be understood within its own context, and justified since had it not been for it, the mural would most likely have disappeared completely.

KEYWORDS

- **Allegory to work**
- **Colonia**
- **Felipe Seade**
- **intervention process**
- **mural**
- **restoration**

REFERENCES AND BIBLIOGRAPHY

Doerner, M. (2005). *Los materiales de pintura y su empleo en el arte.* 6ª Edición. Ed. Reverte S. A.: Barcelona.

Fernández Oscar, M. (2011). "Allegory to work" de Felipe Seade: Activación Patrimonial, Estudios Previos y Propuesta de Intervención. Master Thesis. Departamento de Conservación y Restauración de Bienes Culturales. UPV.

Orsi Meny, Z. (2008). *Liceo departamental de Colonia. Historia y proyección.* Ediciones del Sur: Montevideo. ISBN13: 978-99-7481-492-9.

INTERVIEWS

- Informants 61: Dardo Ingold Bernardi. Profile: Artists. Date of Interview: June 11, 2013.
- Informants 73: Lyda Martín Cutinela. Profile: Artists. Date of Interview: June 11, 2013.

CHAPTER 12

RESTORATION PROCESS

M. A. ZALBIDEA MUÑOZ,[1] J. L. REGIDOR-ROS,[2] V. MUHVICH-MEIRELLES,[3] and A. R. BENÍTEZ-ALCIERI[4]

[1]Associate Professor, Department of Conservation and Restoration of Cultural Heritage, UPV, 3N Building, Camino de Vera s/n, 46022 Valencia, Spain, Tel.: +34-963877000/73136, E-mail: jregidor@crbc.upv.es

[2]Associate Professor, Department of Conservation and Restoration of Cultural Heritage, UPV, 3N Building, Camino de Vera s/n, 46022 Valencia, Spain, Tel.: +34-963877000/73134, E-mail: manzalmu@crbc.upv.es

[3] Curator at the Department of Restoration of Cultural Heritage, Commission of the Nation, ECM of Uruguay. Canelones 968–111000, Montevideo, Uruguay, Tel.: +598-2900-7415, E-mail: vladimirmuhvich@gmail.com

[4] Curator at the Department of Restoration of Cultural Heritage, Commission of the Nation, ECM of Uruguay. Canelones 968–111000, Montevideo, Uruguay, Tel.: +598-2708-7606/27080764, E-mail: alejandraberrielbenvenuto@hotmail.com

CONTENTS

12.1	Introduction	226
12.2	Objectives	226
12.3	Methodology of Work	228
12.4	Conclusions	249
Keywords		252
References and Bibliography		252

12.1 INTRODUCTION

This chapter describes the technical processes and the decision making of the data collection and intervention campaigns carried out in the mural "Allegory to work."

Conducting a proposed intervention so that it results logical and suits the specific needs of a work, is a key factor in developing direct intervention projects on heritage assets. Therefore, tracing the development of a structured protocol and preprocess of restoring the mural "Allegory to work," executed by Felipe Seade, allows selecting the appropriate method to carry out the painting's rescue, within the framework of collaboration, which involved the intervention.

Initially, the research covered several stages that defined the historical, technical and material reality of the mural "Allegory to work." Along with the analytical and historical studies shown in previous chapters, the work was subject to a series of suitability tests that confirmed the viability of the different restorative techniques.

The complex intervention program tried to mitigate the continuous assaults on the work by Felipe Seade, probably caused by not being considered as cultural heritage. The aggressions, to which we refer, are mainly incisions and cuts on the painting made by schoolchildren. Those attacks reflect the aim of destruction and mutilation this mural painting was exposed to along its existence.

The work was submitted to different restoration processes that prevented its complete destruction, but contributed to hiding the existing original painting in large surfaces. The assembly evidenced a bleak, inhomogeneous and difficult reading panorama (see Figures 12.1–12.3 that reveal the amount of over painting veiled on the surface).

12.2 OBJECTIVES

The main objective proposed was to recover, as far as possible and depending on its historical development, the original painting by Felipe Seade entitled "Allegory to work," located in the iconic House of Culture in Colonia de Sacramento.

Restoration Process

FIGURE 12.1 Over painting veiled on the surface 1. Source: Graphical record of the R&D Project PUCM, 2013.

FIGURE 12.2 Over painting veiled on the surface 2. Source: Graphical record of the R&D Project PUCM, 2013.

FIGURE 12.3 Over painting veiled on the surface 3. Source: Graphical record of the R&D Project PUCM, 2013.

This objective was carried out through a selective process, based on criteria as well as treatments tailored to the characteristics and needs of each area, without losing thus the vision of a pictorial set.

The restoration process carried out in the work "Allegory to work" during the months of June and July, 2013, by the analysis and intervention team of the Mural Heritage Restoration Institute of the Polytechnic University of Valencia, together with a team of local artists and restorers. Vladimir Muhvich and Alberto Benítez from the Restoration studio of the Uruguay's Nation Cultural Heritage Committee collaborated as restorers, as well as Adriana Ramos, from the Municipality of Colonia, who collaborated as teacher.

Moreover, as secondary objectives, it was established:
1. To revalue the work for its proposed activation as a National heritage.
2. To expand the cultural offerings in Colonia del Sacramento.

12.3 METHODOLOGY OF WORK

After the process of analyzing the results and the evaluation of the state of the mural painting, the phases of the proposed intervention were established, aimed to restore the original work by Felipe Seade, and then contribute to its optimal preservation and diffusion.

The methodology used in this study step was divided into the following points:
1. Design of a general test protocol.
2. Dry and physicochemical cleaning tests.
3. Evaluation and assessment of the effectiveness of the performed tests.

Once the initial tests on the work characteristics and conditions were made, the cleaning tests were carried out in order to know the compatibility limits and interaction of the diverse paint layers (both the original and the overlapping) with intervention processes. This test campaign, performed in April, 2011, was an essential element to complete an intervention proposal adapted to the mural painting needs, and it located and delimited the area of the diverse pictorial registries.

Based on the action proposal designed, the effective recovery of the mural painting was structured in phases, adapted to the present timing for the intervention (Table 12.1), and executed simultaneously and in an open and reversible process.

The cleaning tests conducted during the campaign of April 2011 (Table 12.2 – Cleaning tests) were performed on the mural, and gathered as follows (Figure 12.4):

12.3.1 TEST EVALUATION

As it had been anticipated, based on the historical and analytical data obtained, at least two well-defined paint layers coexist in the work. One corresponding to the original execution by Felipe Seade and the other one carried out by Dardo Ingold during his intervention in 1981. The Felipe

TABLE 12.1 Phases of the Intervention Process

Previous actions	Specific protections in areas from the original exposed to be damaged
Phase 1	Consolidation process of the paint layers
Phase 2	Process of cleaning and elimination of over paintings
Phase 3	Process of plastering and filling the gaps
Phase 4	Retouching and pictorial finishing process

TABLE 12.2 Cleaning Test Processes Proposed to Clear the Over Painting

Sample group/Process type	Application typology
Dry Cleaning	Adhesion traction system
	Mechanical work with scalpel and rubber
Aqueous cleaning	Soft contact with a sponge
	Soft contact with a sponge filtered by Japanese paper
	Application of Agar-Agar
	Mechanical work with swab
Non-aqueous solvent cleaning	Application of solubility test
Aqueous/mechanical combined system	Adhesion-traction + Soft contact with a sponge and demineralized water through Japanese paper

Seade original painting shows a subtle brush stroke, painted in watercolor and with a lot of transparency above a smooth prime typical from tempera paintings.

On the other hand, the intervention by Dardo Ingold present a stronger brush touch which, in spite of the original intention to respect the

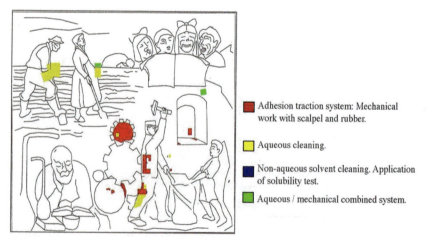

FIGURE 12.4 Location and distribution of cleaning tests by groups. *Source:* Graphical record of the R&D Project PUCM.

chromatics and the technique by his teacher (Orsi, 2008), it was revealed more bold, subjective and invasive in the end.

The set of technical solutions experienced to release the Felipe Seade's pictorial film from the repainting by Dardo Ingold proved partially effective. The heterogeneity of the cohesion level from both layers and the number of incisions, cuts and scratches on the entire surfaces made extremely challenging any cleaning methodologies, including the controlled pull up.

12.3.2 INTERVENTION PROPOSAL

The intervention proposal got over some progressive work phases, with the intention of generating a controlled process at any time. Therefore, the first work phase was based on the development of a selective cleaning process or painting removal in zones with presence of the original paint layer.

1. Elimination of incision leveling stucco and graffiti, with scalpel in areas with the original paint layer hidden.
2. Soft contact with a sponge of the intervention zone, employing a natural sponge and water or an aqueous-alcoholic mixture applied with Japanese paper.
3. Accurate elimination and cleaning of the remaining overlapping without preparation by scalpel and Whishab® [7] of different strength.

Afterwards, the second phase of the project was performed, where the processes of the pictorial consolidation and film layers were activated. The pictorial consolidation intended to reinforce the mechanical stability of the pictorial layer that Felipe Seade executed, and consolidate the susceptible areas likely to suffer future detachment.

For the fixation and consolidation of the different layers, the use of acrylic resins at low concentration applied by injection, impregnation and spraying was expected, depending on the structural needs of the work. The use of these resins is justified by the impossibility of introducing any inorganic material due to the thickness and body that those mixtures create that in this case would only produce a regrowth of the volume between the painting layer and the support, generating detachment of the same film.

As for the third phase of the work: the process of coating lapses and chromatic reintegration, there was a first work with leveling gaps, incisions and graffiti by using a commercial filling product with mechanical characteristics similar to the original gypsum plaster and the one used by Dardo Ingold to ensure both stability and durability.

Low tone glazes were used for the implementation of the chromatic reintegration, applied with watercolor and finished with a graphical texture by the *tratteggio* technique.

In large monochrome areas where the color was swiped or burnt, it was estimated to perform a chromatic reintegration by applying glazes with spraying systems or airbrush color application.

12.3.3 RECOVERY PROCESS OF "ALLEGORY TO WORK" BY FELIPE SEADE

As mention before, the restoration process of the mural painting was structured in phases, solved by a team of eight technicians, in an established timing, generating and contributing to close collaboration between Uruguay and Spain.

The first phase of the work was focused on the implementation of the different consolidation processes of the pictorial layers that are set out on Table 12.3, and on the map (see Figure 12.5) of consolidation of strati and paint layers.

The consolidation of the mural painting areas affected by the separation between the pictorial layer and the physical support was determined by injecting and adhesive mixture of an acrylic emulsion and a load (Acril

TABLE 12.3 Consolidation of Strati and Paint Layers

Features of the intervention zone	Process carried out	Materials
Separation of internal and preparatory layers	Consolidation and filling Injection	Acril AC 33® 20% diluted in water thickened with Creta
Dustiness of pigment and detachment of pictorial film	Consolidation: Impregnation by brush	Micro-emulsion. Acril ME®

Restoration Process

FIGURE 12.5 Consolidation of strati and paint layers. *Source:* Graphical record of the R&D Project PUCM, 2011.

AC 33® diluted into 20% water, mixed with Creta -gypsum-depending on the filler to replenish). The treatment area was previously protected provisionally with moisturized Japanese paper filters and the existing large amount of holes was used for its pouring. A slight back strain secured the adhesion of the paint layers (see Figures 12.6–12.8).

The layer areas presenting dustiness and high disunion were fixed by brush impregnation (see Figures 12.9 and 12.10 the application of the binder with a brush and Japanese paper, buffered with natural sponge afterwards) and filtered through an acrylic micro-emulsion Japanese paper (Acril ME®) at concentrations below 5%. This task was repeated in areas where the original paintings were weakened after the over painting had been removed. Fixing the original layer represents also a layer that facilitates the reversibility of the successive pictorial retouching processes.

The most complex process of the intervention was the pictorial surface cleaning process, more specifically, the removal of the overlapping that hid the original painting. The precarious conservation state of the painting's layer and the intolerance to the many cleaning

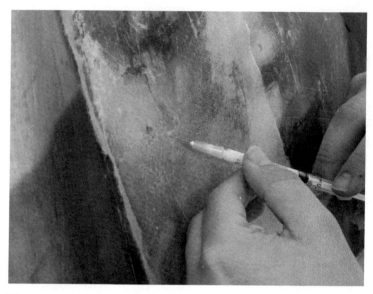

FIGURES 12.6 Application of the consolidating with a brush and Japanese paper.
Source: Graphical record of the R&D Project PUCM, 2012.

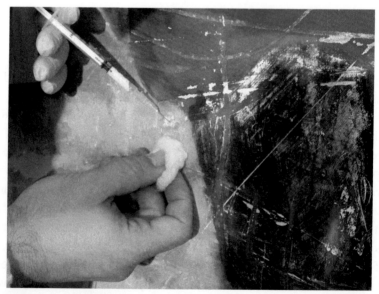

FIGURES 12.7 Application of the consolidating with a brush and Japanese paper.
Source: Graphical record of the R&D Project PUCM, 2012.

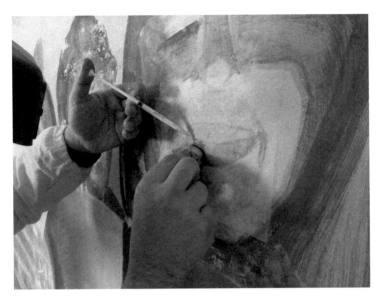

FIGURES 12.8 Application of the consolidating with a brush and Japanese paper. *Source:* Graphical record of the R&D Project PUCM, 2012.

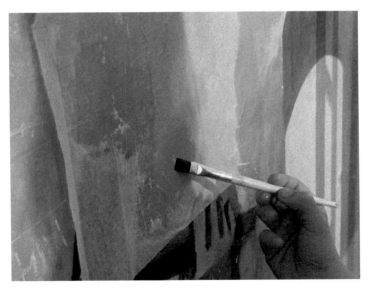

FIGURES 12.9 Application of the consolidating with a brush and Japanese paper, buffered with natural sponge afterwards. *Source:* Graphical record of the R&D Project PUCM, 2012.

FIGURES 12.10 Application of the consolidating with a brush and Japanese paper, buffered with natural sponge afterwards. *Source:* Graphical record of the R&D Project PUCM, 2012.

FIGURES 12.11 Application of the consolidating with a brush and Japanese paper, buffered with natural sponge afterwards. *Source:* Graphical record of the R&D Project PUCM, 2012.

processes, aspects that have been exposed in previous chapters, challenged the different cleaning operations that were specifically adapted to each treated area.

With deep respect, and with the aim to strengthen the coexistence of the original painting with its historical events (overlapping, assaults, etc.), the cleaning and elimination of the over painting was performed selectively, focused on areas where the original paint layer was hidden continuously and with relevant esthetic charge (FigureS 12.12–12.18).

The different types of set-off were treated with the following methodologies described in the Table 12.4.

Approximately 50% of incisions and missing pictorial surface was plastered, depending on the figurative element damaged, the magnitude and size of the incision, the need to interrupt visually the identification of the text and due to the limited space and time to execute the intervention.

The adopted criteria for the treatment of the graffito incised cuts and signatures was: to provide compatibility between the original materials and the "fillings" used in the performance by Dart Ingold, the products used in the coating process of the mural were Polyfilla® [6] and Modostuc® [4]. The deepest holes were treated firstly with a mixture of two volumes of Polyfilla® per one of water to form a paste that was applied by spatula, previously moistening with water the area of application of the stucco. The Modostuc® was used for filling shallow incisions or after the Polyfilla® clogging, once the depth of the holes was reduced (see Table 12.5; Figures 12.20 and 12.21). Subsequently, the stucco areas were treated using scalpel and sandpaper low abrasiveness to obtain a lower level.

The color retouching was carried out (see Table 12.6) with Artist Water Color Winsor & Newton® watercolors in pill and tube [1], with ranges of cadmium, red, blue, green earth, sienna yellow, etc. The colors for the retouching task were selected based on their index of light stability or *lightfatnes*, using in this case, the more stable ones.

Reintegration was carried out in two different ways (see Figures 12.22–12.24). On the one hand, and as the main procedure for reintegration, was the tratteggio (Figures 12.25–12.28) applied in a modulated stroke and according to the color needs of each area.

On the other hand, in areas of large extension of color wearing, a mimetic retouching reintegration was chosen, trying to generate a broad

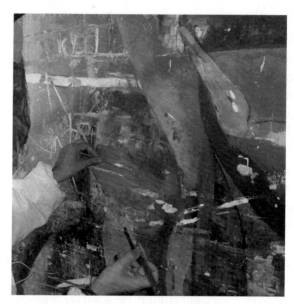

FIGURE 12.12 Aqueous repaint and mechanical removal of the overlapping by using swab and scalpel. *Source:* Graphical record of the R&D Project PUCM, 2013.

FIGURE 12.13 mechanical removal of the overlapping on an incision without stucco. *Source:* Graphical record of the R&D Project PUCM, 2012.

Restoration Process

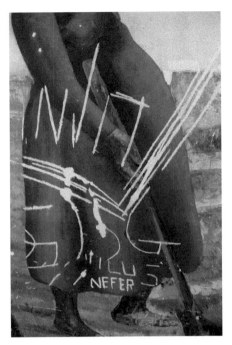

FIGURES 12.14 Incision areas without stucco after the removal of the overlapping.
Source: Graphical record of the R&D Project PUCM, 2013.

FIGURES 12.15 Incision areas without stucco after the removal of the overlapping.
Source: Graphical record of the R&D Project PUCM, 2013.

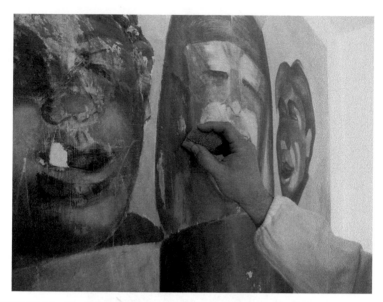

FIGURE 12.16 Removal of the overlapping by surface abrasion with Wishab® rubber. *Source:* Graphical record of the R&D Project PUCM, 2012.

FIGURE 12.17 Removal of the superimpose repaint directly on the original. *Source:* Graphical record of the R&D Project PUCM, 2012.

Restoration Process

FIGURE 12.18 Mechanical removal of stucco on the original. *Source:* Graphical record of the R&D Project PUCM, 2012.

FIGURE 12.19 Removal of the superimpose repaint in incision sites. *Source:* Graphical record of the R&D Project PUCM, 2013.

TABLE 12.4 Removal of Over Painting

Characteristics of the area to intervene	Process executed	Materials
Stucco and polychrome in areas that hid the original	Mechanical removal	Scalpel
Concretions and incisions repainted and uncoated	Mechanical removal	Scalpel
Repaint performed directly on original layer	Soft contact with a sponge	Hydro-alcoholic mixture at 70%
Incohesive repaints	Mechanical removal	Wishab® Gums

TABLE 12.5 Processes of the Applied Stucco

Features of the intervention area	Process executed	**Materials**
Deeper erosions	Internal filling	Polyfilla®
	Surface filling	Modostuc®
Superficial erosions	Surface filling and leveled	Modostuc®

TABLE 12.6 Application of Chromatic Reintegration

Characteristics of the area to intervene	Process	Materials
Complete lacks of the original paint layer shaped bounded	Tratteggio	Watercolor Artist Water Color Winsor & Newton®
Large areas of pigment weariness	Airbrush	Watercolor Artist Water Color Winsor & Newton®

reading of the whole mural with greater coherence and consistency. This was applied by airbrush watercolor (Figure 12.29) to adjust the gaps by integrating the Figure and offer an easier reading.

12.3.4 RESULTS

The restoration tasks work carried out in the "Allegory to work" imply the starting point to the approach of new projects and interventions in the

Restoration Process

FIGURES 12.20 Plastering of incisions and holes. *Source:* Graphical record of the R&D Project PUCM, 2012.

Uruguayan mural national heritage, thus promoting the interpretation and valuation of the country's cultural identity.

The retrieval of the painting (Figures 12.30–12.35), respecting its identity as a historical testimony, resulted in social interest and important diffusion movements by the local and national media (website of the Ministry of Culture, newspaper El País, Museos.uy, Uypress, Coloniatotal, etc.), which enhanced the appreciation and acceptance of the painting as part of the

FIGURES 12.21 Plastering of incisions and holes. *Source:* Graphical record of the R&D Project PUCM, 2012.

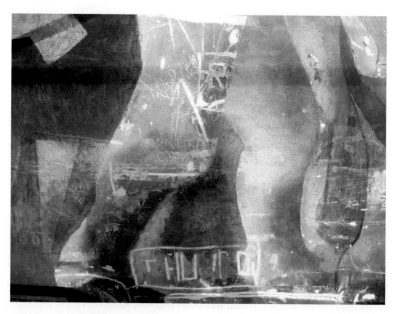

FIGURE 12.22 Process and detail of the chromatic reintegration. *Source:* Graphical record of the R&D Project PUCM, 2012.

Restoration Process

FIGURE 12.23 Process and detail of the chromatic reintegration. *Source:* Graphical record of the R&D Project PUCM, 2013.

FIGURE 12.24 Process and detail of the chromatic reintegration. *Source:* Graphical record of the R&D Project PUCM, 2012.

FIGURE 12.25 Chromatic reintegration with paintbrush using tratteggio. *Source:* Graphical record of the R&D Project PUCM, 2013.

FIGURE 12.26 Chromatic reintegration with paintbrush using tratteggio. *Source:* Graphical record of the R&D Project PUCM, 2013.

Restoration Process

FIGURE 12.27 Chromatic reintegration with paintbrush using tratteggio. *Source:* Graphical record of the R&D Project PUCM, 2013.

FIGURE 12.28 Chromatic reintegration with paintbrush using tratteggio. *Source:* Graphical record of the R&D Project PUCM, 2013.

FIGURE 12.29 Chromatic reintegration with airbrush. *Source:* Graphical record of the R&D Project PUCM, 2013.

FIGURE 12.30 Painting details after restoration. *Source:* Graphical record of the R&D Project PUCM, 2013.

FIGURES 12.31 Painting details after restoration. *Source:* Graphical record of the R&D Project PUCM, 2013.

Uruguayan artistic heritage and contributed to the expansion of the cultural and artistic offer in Colonia del Sacramento as world heritage value.

The work developed cooperatively by the team formed by the UPV (Spain) teachers and technicians and the members of the National Cultural Heritage Commission (Uruguay) restoration workshop, together with local professionals, implied a fruitful exchange of ideas and ways of work. This coexistence was crucial for the intervention on the national Uruguayan pictorial heritage and the professional education in projects involving conservation and restoration of mural paintings.

12.4 CONCLUSIONS

The design of the intervention process, together with the technical conditions described, presents a specific action framework. Since it

FIGURES 12.32 Painting details after restoration. *Source:* Graphical record of the R&D Project PUCM, 2013.

FIGURES 12.33 Painting details after restoration. *Source:* Graphical record of the R&D Project PUCM, 2013.

Restoration Process

FIGURES 12.34 Painting details after restoration. *Source:* Graphical record of the R&D Project PUCM, 2013.

FIGURE 12.35 Painting details after restoration. *Source:* Graphical record of the R&D Project PUCM, 2013.

belongs in a cooperation project, the intervention must be subjected to specific temporary and economic parameters, which is why a truly enforceable and effective proposal should be considered without compromising the quality of the performance.

The different phases of the restoration project on Felipe Seade's "Allegory to work" are to be completed within a maximum of one month.

Establishing a coherent conservation proposal is principal for accomplishing a favorable intervention development, offering optimal answers in the results of the work.

After the evaluation of the results obtained and through a complete assessment of them all, it was determined that Felipe Seade's "Allegory to work," due to its historical and cultural value, contributes to enhance the identity signs of world heritage Colonia del Sacramento.

The restoration of this mural painting must be the starting point of new activities aimed to promote new models of heritage management, based on sustainable development through the management of mural assets.

The cornerstone of this new proposal should be an engine of progress towards the protection of mural pictorial heritage, transforming this concept into a product of the Uruguayan collective identity, thus to encouraging the accessibility to a new concept of cultural tourism.

KEYWORDS

- **Colonia**
- **mural painting**
- **restoration**
- **retrieval**
- **Seade**

REFERENCES AND BIBLIOGRAPHY

Artist Water Color Winsor & Newton®. Watercolors Winsor & Newton®. Retrieved from: http://www.winsornewton.com/assets/catawcspanishccFeb2013.pdf (accessed: December 14, 2013).

Doerner, M. (2005). *Los materiales de pintura y su empleo en el arte.* 6ª Edición. Ed. Reverte S. A.: Barcelona.

Fernández Óscar, M. (2011). "Allegory to work" de Felipe Seade: Activación Patrimonial, Estudios Previos y Propuesta de Intervención. Master Thesis. Departamento de Conservación y Restauración de Bienes Culturales. UPV.

Modostuc®. Commercial paste made with wáter, cellulosic additives, resin emulsion, plasticizers, calcium carbonates and natural calcium sulfate, according to data sheet: 6.6. *Prodotti per stuccature, sigillature e finiturevarie* by C. T.S S.r.l p.134. Retrieved from: http://www.ctseurope.com/catalogo.asp?lingua=ITA&gruppo=5&capitolo=6&paragrafo=6 (accessed: Desember 14, 2013).

Orsi Meny, Z. (2008). *Liceo departamental de Colonia. Historia y proyección.* Ediciones del Sur: Montevideo. ISBN13: 978-99-7481-492-9. p. 281.

Polyfilla®. White plaster reinforced cellulose, according to data sheet: 6.6. *Prodotti per stuccature, sigillature e finiture varie* by C. T.S S.r.l. p. 136. Retrieved from: http://www.ctseurope.com/catalogo.asp?lingua=ITA&gruppo=5&capitolo=6&paragrafo=6 (accessed: December 14, 2013).

Whishab®. Product marketed as rubber, based on a mass of vulcanized rubber. Retrieved from: http://www.ctseurope.com/catalogo.asp?capitolo=8&lingua=ESP (accessed December 13, 2013).

PART V

MUSEOGRAPHIC AREA AND SUSTAINABLE TOURISM OF THE PAINTING "ALLEGORY TO WORK"

CHAPTER 13

THE USE AND SOCIAL ENJOYMENT OF MURALS: 'THE PEOPLE'S ART,' ITS PUBLICS AND CULTURAL HERITAGE

S. CARDEN

Research Assistant, School of Planning, Architecture and Civil Engineering, Queen's University Belfast. David Keir Building, Stranmillis Road, Belfast, Northern Ireland, BT7–5AG, E-mail: s.carden@qub.ac.uk

CONTENTS

13.1	Introduction	257
13.2	The People's Blackboard': Mural Art and Its 'Publics'	258
13.3	Murals, Tourism, and City Branding	262
13.4	Conclusion	266
Keywords		267
References and Bibliography		267

13.1 INTRODUCTION

The relationship of murals to public space and the built environment makes them relevant to a more diverse range of audiences than gallery-based art-forms, but presents particular challenges around the use, management and maintenance of artworks whose ownership and accessibility can be complex, whose content or location may be politically sensitive, and whose inscription in the very fabric of cities leaves them vulnerable to all the flux and contestation of everyday civic life. Whether originally created as private commissions, public art or ephemeral political statements, and whether interior or exterior, murals' survival is contingent on wider processes in the built environment as well as changing perceptions of their style and content. The audience for murals today includes the cultural tourists so desired by urban and regional policy-makers around the world. Competition for tourist attention has led to the reassessment of previously overlooked or controversial murals as heritage artifacts. Tourism and communications technology mean that the publics addressed by murals are now international. However, due to the site-specific nature of murals, whether they are located in a public building or a city street, they inevitably say something about the people of that place, addressing an 'imagined community' (Andersen, 1991) of citizens or residents. When located in public buildings or outdoor space, murals form a visual platform for the circulation of ideas through the 'public sphere' (Habermas, 1991; see also Greeley, 2012: 3). They can therefore function as tools for nation- or solidarity-building and become a focus of debate about the nature of the public they address, engaging audiences in reflection on intra and inter-communal relationships. This is the case of Seade's mural that has a strong community focus.

13.2 THE PEOPLE'S BLACKBOARD': MURAL ART AND ITS 'PUBLICS'

Mural art is often distinguished by its orientation towards the 'democratic,' the communal, the 'popular,' in opposition to 'the elitist, exclusive, and academic character of the "fine art" tradition' (Marschall, 1999: 58) aligned with official state and artistic institutions. Pablo Neruda is reported to have said that 'murals are the people's blackboard' (Braun-Reinitz and Weissman, 2009: 1) and advocates of 'community' murals often refer to them as a 'people's art' (Cockcroft et al., 1977; Barnett, 1984; Drescher, 1998; Bogside Artists, 2001: 2). The association of murals with 'the people,' the collaborative methods sometimes used to create them, their locations and content all imply a communal audience, a 'public' (Indych-López, Anna. 2008: 208; Iveson, 2007:21, Zebracki, 2013: 303) rather than an individual viewer. Different types of mural address themselves to different publics, enabling varying kinds of audience engagement.

In the case of the 'community mural movement' (Braun-Reinitz and Weissman, 2009: 3) in the USA, murals are often made by or with and addressed to the residents of a particular neighborhood, constructing a vision of cohesiveness based around shared goals and/or a common heritage. The process of this type of mural-making is as important as the end result, aspiring to engage artists and local people as 'equal participants' and to build and express a 'community consensus' (Braun-Reinitz and Weissman, 2009: 7) through the negotiation and creation of the mural. The decorative function of these murals is often presented as a response to unattractive cityscapes and their social aims include both increased communal pride or political awareness and a changed relationship between residents and the fabric of the city: their advocates suggest that these mural projects present an 'alternative to graffiti' or dissuasion from antisocial behavior among young people (Mueller, 1979: 74; Braun-Reintz and Weiss, 2009: 65).

Murals located inside public or municipal buildings as public art often address an imagined ideal citizenry, constructing particular visions of nationhood. These murals offer a platform for 'envisioning the national polity' (Greeley, 2012: 3) through their imagery and location: from the grandeur of London's Palace of Westminster (Willsdon, 2000: 94) to the everyday bureaucracy of the US Postal Service (Marling, 1983), murals in public buildings assert a vision of the nation as its citizens and officials go about their business. This nation-building function is particularly prominent in the mural art of nation-states which are recently established or in the process of redefining themselves. In the first decades of Canadian independence from the British Empire, a mural tradition developed which 'glorified the salient features of Canada as a modern nation-state' (McKay, 2002: 4). During the Great Depression in the USA, artists were put to work creating murals in post offices as part of President Roosevelt's New Deal (Marling, 1983). Most famously, the development of Mexican mural art was intimately connected to the Mexican Revolution, the authoritarianism of the post-revolutionary government, and disparate reactions to that (Coffey, 2012: 179; Greeley, 2012: 13; Campbell, 2012: 282). The evolving relationship between mural art and the Mexican state demonstrates the contested nature of 'cultural patrimony – the forms of symbolic and cultural capital associated with national identity' (Campbell, 2012: 277).

The role of state patronage in the creation and management of murals is often controversial. A mural may be used as outright state propaganda but is more often the result of a complex set of negotiations around access to public space, legitimacy and authorship. For example, while the imagery and ideology of the USA 'community mural movement' discussed above focuses on the neighborhood or 'community' rather than the state, and the model of mural-making developed by this movement emphasizes grassroots solidarity and collaboration (Drescher, 2002: 7), direct or indirect state support for such projects through funding, official commissioning programs or the use of government-owned space leads Merriam (2011: 2) to question why these artworks have not been subject to the sort of legal challenges frequently faced by other officially mandated ideological expression (such as religious symbols in public schools), arguing that 'inner-city murals represent "government speech"...funded and selected through government programs.'

While styles of mural painting vary widely, mural artists have primarily worked in modes that prioritize legibility and populism, from Mexican social realism to the 'realist styles, story-telling, history painting, and symbolism' which dominated British mural painting between 1840–1940 (Willsdon, 2000: 384) to the rough-and-ready draftsmanship of most paramilitary murals in 1980s Northern Ireland (Rolston, 1992: v). (During the so-called 'Troubles,' painting styles developed based on speed, with the painters' priority being to complete the work to a legible standard without being seen, stopped or even attacked.) Marling (1983: 312) argues that federally funded Depression-era murals in post offices across the USA turned away from both the 'academic' artistic tradition with its obscure references and the 'modernistic' trend towards abstraction, privileging the more universally accessible 'center of the esthetic spectrum.' Golden (2002: 22) suggests that allegorical subject matter like that found in nineteenth century 'history paintings' continues to be a frequent feature of contemporary murals long after falling out of favor in easel art because 'Allegories speak to our moral and spiritual aspirations.' Representing communal moral consensus to audiences whose individual aspirations inevitably vary invites challenge, as the diversity of experiences within any public 'set up a "way of seeing" that makes them inherently an openly agonistic, critical audience" (Zebracki et al., 2010: 305). By attempting to speak for 'the people,' murals prompt discussion of who 'the people' really are.

Conflict around the boundaries or status of the community a mural addresses, whether this be national or otherwise, can make the mural's existence provocative. In Northern Ireland during the period of violent political conflict known as the 'Troubles,' for example, murals projected ethno-national claims about the legitimacy of paramilitary groups, both through their content and through their location, asserting community consensus in residentially segregated neighborhoods. Loyalist murals coopted British military imagery to express an uncompromising commitment to the Northern Irish state within working class Protestant neighborhoods (Rolston, 2012: 450), while Republican murals in working class Catholic neighborhoods presented Republican paramilitarism as a legitimate response to state oppression (Sluka, 1992: 214). A local government scheme to replace paramilitary murals with less violent imagery (after the peace process culminated in the 1998 Good Friday Agreement and 2006 St. Andrews Agreement) was called 'Reimaging Communities' (Hill and White, 2012: 79; Hocking, 2015: 98). It is perceptions of 'the community,' from within and outside it that are at stake in decisions about murals. The relationship of Northern Irish murals to the communities in which they are situated (like the nature of 'community' itself REF Cohen) is a matter of ongoing debate (Jarman, 2005:175; Bryan and Gillespie, 2005: 5).

The use of walls in place of canvas enables mural art (along with other forms of street art and graffiti) to circumvent some of the gatekeeping functions of 'institutional frames' like galleries and exhibitions (Coffey, 2012: 22). In escaping the restrictions of the gallery-based fine art establishment, murals also fail to benefit from its protective qualities. As the spaces they occupy are not primarily devoted to their preservation, the existence of murals is often dependent on rapidly changing pressures on city space: 'the people's blackboard' is easily erased (see McCormick and Jarman, 2005). Site-specific in a way that gallery art is not, murals are not easily tradable physical commodities, nor are they collectable in the same way as other painting or sculpture (Willsdon, 2000: vii; Indych-López, 2009). The relationship of murals to the market is therefore different from that of easel painting and individual responsibility for and benefit from their preservation is not necessarily easy to identify.

13.3 MURALS, TOURISM, AND CITY BRANDING

While murals do not have the same relationship to the market as more easily tradable art forms, their site-specific nature means they can be commoditized as visitor attractions through the tourism industry. The local distinctiveness of murals and the spectacle they produce within otherwise mundane landscapes makes them a useful resource for place marketing more broadly, as images of cities are used to attract investors, developers and affluent new residents as well as tourists.

Murals were undertaken as 'small-town promotion projects' in the USA, Canada and New Zealand in the late twentieth century (Bell, 1997: 145; see also Widdis, 2000: 246; Koster and Randall, 2005: 42; Drescher, 1997: 17). Drescher (2009: xiv) reports that in the USA, 'more than two dozen "mural towns" previously dependent on single industries have muralized their walls as a means of encouraging tourism to combat economic devastation caused by the shutdown of those industries.' Such schemes share a celebratory ethos, emphasizing positive features of the locality, omitting intracommunal tensions and orienting themselves towards a romanticized past (Widdis, 2000: 248). In this nostalgic portrayal of societal harmony, Dresher (1997: 17) argues that these murals have more in common with murals funded by the USA federal government as part of the 1930s New Deal than with their urban contemporaries.

While contemporary murals in cities include more overtly political and contentious works than those in small rural towns, contemporary cities compete fiercely for cultural capital (Kearns and Philo, 2003; Miles and Paddison, 2005), so urban murals of all descriptions are being reframed as the kind of cultural heritage and creativity prized by local authorities and private developers. Murals have an especially pervasive effects on place identity because rather than being the object of a visit to a gallery or museum, murals can be experienced in passing, as a spectacular backdrop to city life. As Zebricki (2013:305) points out, 'public art's publics' are distinguished by the fact that 'the bulk of them are undirected observers in the open urban field.' It is not even necessary to leave one's car in cities like Los Angeles, for example, as 'the windshield becomes the entrée to a many-faceted, free art show' (Levick and Young, 1988: 32). Murals are therefore not only valuable as visitor attractions in their own right, but as contributions to the vibrant ambience that planners and developers aspire to project. Murals enrich the built environment, intensifying 'the viewers' experience as they "read" a particular architectural site' (McKay, 2002: 15), reinforcing the impact of imposing state buildings, lending cultural cachet to utilitarian official architecture or relieving the gray monotony of nondescript urban landscapes.

The scramble to identify and commoditize cultural heritage in cities has led to the reevaluation of types of mural art that were originally conceived of as ephemeral, that had been all but forgotten, or that were until recently regarded as symptomatic of societal problems rather than cultural richness. Some murals created as temporary interventions in the cityscape rather than long-term installations are now targeted for restoration or conservation (Merrill, 2015: 369). Murals in public buildings which were long overlooked by art historians are increasingly recognized and analyzed as part of the artistic heritage of the nation (i.e., Marling, 1983; Willsdon, 2000). Revolutionary murals are commoditized and institutionalized (Coffey, 2012: 192). Even murals which play a role in violent conflict by laying claim to disputed territory can come to be seen as heritage artifacts and tourist attractions during post-conflict periods or processes of conflict transformation. In both Belfast and Derry/Londonderry, murals related to the 'Troubles' have become a significant part of the city's brand identity and are regarded by many visitors as 'a *matèriel* remnant of the conflict… that should not be forgotten or concealed' (Simone-Charteris and Boyd, 2010: 187).

The enjoyment of murals by tourists does not neutralize their political complexity for local residents and authorities. Indeed, the introduction of a lucrative global audience to the contested cultural realm of a divided society has the potential to reinforce division; in Northern Ireland, some fear that so-called 'terror tourism' encourages the 'legitimization of sectarian politics and sectarian landscapes' (McDowell, 2008, 406). Public bodies such as the Northern Ireland Tourist Board and government structures such as Belfast City Council have not been active or enthusiastic in selling

'Troubles Belfast' (O'Dowd and Komarova, 2009: 10). Given the sensitivity of this traumatic history and the state's complex role in it, official authorities look on rather awkwardly as private businesses and neighborhood-level organizations promote the sites and relics of the 'Troubles' that chime with their own perspectives and priorities (Simone-Charteris and Boyd, 2010: 184, 189).

In places where a mural tradition has become a strong part of the national or urban brand, its styles and techniques can inspire local artists and be utilized by private business people in unexpected ways. In Belfast, while delicate negotiation about which 'Troubles' murals to preserve as heritage artifacts and which to remove or transform continues, an artist called Ciaran Gallagher has gradually lined the walls of a city center courtyard with paintings which combine his own style with what he calls the 'legible, realist, almost generic' styles of local political murals (author's interview with the artist, 2016). Rejecting the blandness of 'this reimaging thing with the flowers' (Gallagher, 2016) he combines recognizable elements of Belfast history, culture and current affairs in a riotous collage-like series of murals. Some elements (like the industrial heritage of ship factories or the TV series Game of Thrones) are features of official 'Titanic Belfast' (Ramsey, 2012: 173) marketing, but are here interwoven with local in-jokes, recognizable Belfast characters and references to darker aspects of the city. This work engages with the context of mural painting in a self-conscious way, even including a play on the advocacy of community murals as an alternative to youth crime in a graffiti-style scrawl instructing the viewer to 'stay in drugs, eat your school and don't do vegetables.' Some of the subjects touched on are very sensitive indeed; one scene is labeled 'Romper Room,' in a reference to some of the most notorious violence of the 'Troubles' in Belfast (see Dillon, 1990: 22–23).

At a time when symbols of the conflict are bitterly contested and Northern Ireland's whole political system frequently appears frozen in the face of 'dealing with the past' (Amnesty International, 2013) it is striking that these murals exist as a largely unremarked backdrop to Belfast's nightlife and feature of its visitor tours. The 'Romper Room' reference has attracted a small amount of negative feedback (from a fellow artist objecting on the behalf of people who were tortured in rooms like that), to which Gallagher responds by acknowledging the harrowing nature of the subject but asserting the importance of artistic freedom and satire, given that everyone sees 'worse things on the news' (interview, 2016). Such an approach is only possible in this case because of the geography of the murals' location: in a privately owned, almost enclosed courtyard at the heart of an area redeveloped in the 2000s as an 'up and coming cultural hotspot' called the Cathedral Quarter, far from the city's segregated working-class neighborhoods (Discover Northern Ireland 2015). These murals are commissioned by a long-established bar owner whose private resources and embeddedness in local networks are both essential to enable such unconstrained mural art; in this case, private business allows the muralist to abandon the usual concern with communal consensus.

Some of those who prize the radical potential of mural painting regard the contemporary emphasis on tourist audiences with suspicion. For example, the Bogside Artists, a small collective whose most famous work is within an Irish nationalist neighborhood of the city of Derry/Londonderry, write in their 'Manifesto' (2001: 34–36) that 'you could be forgiven for thinking it is the Tourist Board that controls modern Irish culture,' suggesting that this touristic perspective entails a rejection of the 'truly contemporary.' Nonetheless, as Coffey (2012: 192) writes of Mexican mural art, 'the popularity of this artform is achieved through participation in the rituals of heritage.' The Bogside Artists' representations of local experiences of the 'Troubles' and communal resistance to British state forces have become a regular stop on the city's tourist trail and were highlighted in the city's bid to become UK City of Culture, 2013 (Derry City Council, 2010: 96).

Murals are popular with the media in places like Northern Ireland, as an efficient way to communicate 'a sense of distinctiveness, place and authenticity' (Simone-Charteris and Boyd, 2010: 187) in news bulletins, documentary, drama and film. While images of murals may be repurposed or exploited for ends other than those envisaged by the painters, causing resentment and anxiety around ownership (White, 1995; see also Greaney, 2002: 44), the reproduction of murals 'in books, posters and postcards' (McCormick and Jarman, 2005: 67) means that even their physical destruction does not necessarily mean oblivion. Tourist audiences also extend murals' reach, as 'once they go home, tourists become propagators of messages and their own experiences to their friends and relatives' (Simone-Charteris and Boyd, 2010: 183). The role of tourists in promoting mural sites has grown closer to the role of the media as tourist photography and social media have come together in travel blogs, Facebook albums and online reviews. Ubiquitous mobile internet offers new ways for tourists and others to experience murals, such as the *Belfast Mural Guide* (Kerr, 2014) which allows individuals to guide themselves around the city's murals via GPS coordinates.

13.4 CONCLUSION

While mural art varies greatly, one characteristic that carries across its different manifestations is an orientation towards a communal audience, a 'people' or 'public.' Another is a site-specific quality; while the blank walls of an art gallery are designed to be all but interchangeable so as not to distract from the (portable) work, the walls on which murals are painted are part of the structure of the built environment and the identity of particular places. As Willson (2000: 383) argues, this means that sociological perspectives are more central to the analysis of murals than of other forms of art: being created 'for a certain audience and place, murals cannot be viewed solely as mere esthetic objects' (Willsdon, 2000: 383, emphasis in original). As Campbell (2012: 277) argues, when a mural is viewed in its social context, we can see it as not just an image but 'a locus of social struggle, a point of articulation for collective opinion and public space, and a moment of esthetic adaptation to changing cultural circumstances.' Murals resist or escape some of the restrictions and exclusions of the gallery-based art establishment, but in doing so they enter into broader political processes. The public nature of murals makes their content open to debate, conflict, even sabotage (McCormick and Jarman, 2005: 42; Indych-López, 2008: 210). While murals often become a focal point for the conflicting demands of local residents, tourists, the media, and elite cultural consumers, they create space for a wide range of public engagement and interaction between these interest groups and the broader society around them.

KEYWORDS

- cultural heritage
- murals
- public art
- tourism

REFERENCES AND BIBLIOGRAPHY

Amnesty International. (2013). *Northern Ireland: Time to Deal with the Past*. Amnesty International: London.

Anderson, B. (1991). *Imagined Communities: Reflections on the Origin and Spread of Nationalism*. Verso: London.

Barnett, A. (1984). *Community Murals: The People's Art*. Art Alliance Press: California.

Bell, C. (1997). "The "real" New Zealand: Rural Mythologies Perpetuated and Commodified." *The Social Science Journal, 34*(2), 145–158.

Braun-Reinitz, J., & Jane Weissman (2009). *On the Wall: Four Decades of Community Murals in New York City*. Univ. Press of Mississippi: Mississippi.

Bryan, D., & Gordon, G. (2005). *Transforming Conflict: Flags and Emblems*. Institute of Irish Studies, Queen's University Belfast: Belfast.

Campbell, B., (2012). "An Unauthorized History of Post-Mexican School Muralism." In *Mexican Muralism: A Critical History*, edited by Alejandro Anreus, Robin Adele Greeley, and Leonard Folgarait, University of California Press: Berkeley. pp. 263–282.

Cockcroft, E., Weber, J., & Cockcroft, J., eds. (2012). *Towards a People's Art: The Contemporary Mural Movement*. New York: E. P. Dutton and Co.

Coffey, M., (2012). *How a Revolutionary Art Became Official Culture: Murals, Museums, and the Mexican State*. Durham: Duke University Press.

Conrad, D., (1995). "Community Murals as Democratic Art and Education." *Journal of Aesthetic Education. 29*(1), 98–102.

Derry City Council. *Cracking the Cultural Code: Our Bid*. Derry/Londonderry: Derry City Council, 2010.

Dillon, Martin (1990). *The Shankill Butchers: A Case Study of Mass Murder*. Random House: London.

Discover Northern Ireland. *The Cathedral Quarter* [Online]. Published online: 2016. Retrieved from: http://www.discovernorthernireland.com/The-Cathedral-Quarter A504?Layout=Explore (accessed Jan 31, 2015).

Drescher, T., (1997). "Introduction." In *Painting the Town: Murals of California*, edited by Robin Dunitz and James Prigoff. RJD Enterprises: Los Angeles, pp. 7–20.

Drescher, T., (2009). "Introduction." In: Braun-Reinitz, J., & Weissman, J. *On the Wall: Four Decades of Community Murals in New York City.* ix–xvi. University Press of Mississippi: Mississippi.

Golden, J., (2002). "Cool Jane." In: *Philadelphia Murals and the Stories they Tell*, edited by Jane Golden, J., Robin Rice, R., & Monica Yant Kinney, Temple University Press: Philadelphia, pp. 18–32.

Greaney, M., (2002). "The Power of the Urban Canvas: Paint, Politics, and Mural Art Policy." *New England Journal of Public Policy, 18*(1), 7–48.

Greeley, R. A., (2012). 'Muralism and the State in Post-Revolution Mexico.' In *Mexican Muralism: A Critical History*, edited by Alejandro Anreus, Robin Adele Greeley, and Leonard Folgarait. University of California Press: Berkeley, pp. 13–36.

Habermas, J., (1991). *The Structural Transformation of the Public Sphere: An Inquiry into a Category of Bourgeois Society*. Translated by Thomas Burger. Cambridge: The MIT Press.

Hill, A., & White, A. (2012). "Painting Peace? Murals and the Northern Ireland Peace Process." *Irish Political Studies, 27*(1), 71–88.

Hocking, Bree. (2015). *The Great Reimagining: Public Art, Urban Space, and the Symbolic Landscapes of a "New" Northern Ireland*. Berghahn Books: London.

Indych-López, A. (2008). "Mexican Muralism in the United States: Controversies, Paradoxes, and Publics." In *Mexican Muralism: A Critical History*, edited by Alejandro Anreus, Robin Adele Greeley, and Leonard Folgarait University of California Press: Berkeley, pp. 208–229.

Indych-López, A., (2009). *Muralism Without Walls: Rivera, Orozco, and Siqueiros in the United States, 1927–1940*. University of Pittsburgh Press: Pittsburgh.

Iveson, K., (2007). *Publics and the City*. Blackwell: Oxford.

Jarman, N., (2005). "Painting Landscapes: The Place of Murals in the Symbolic Construction of Urban Space." In *National Symbols, Fractured Identities: Contesting the National Narrative*, edited by Michel Geisler. University Press of New England: New Hampshire, pp. 172–192.

Kearns, G., & Philo, C., (1993). *Selling Places: The City as Cultural Capital, Past and Present*. Pergamon Press: Oxford.

Kerr, R., (2014). *The Belfast Mural Guide: Locate Series*. MSF Pres: Belfast.

Koster, R., & James Randall (2005). "Indicators of Community Economic Development through Mural-Based Tourism." *Canadian Geographer/Le Géographe Canadien. 49*(1), 42–60.

Levick, M., & Young, S., (1988). *The Big Picture: Murals of Los Angeles*. Thames and Hudson Ltd.: London.

Marling, K., (1983). *Wall-to-Wall America: A Cultural History of Post-Office Murals in the Great Depression*. University of Minnesota Press: Minneapolis.

McClellan, A., (2008). *Art and Its Publics: Museum Studies at the Millennium*. Blackwell: Oxford.

McCormick, J., & Jarman, N., (2005). "Death of a Mural." *Journal of Material Culture. 10*(1), 49–71.

McDowell, S., (2008). "Selling conflict heritage through tourism in peacetime Northern Ireland: transforming conflict or exacerbating difference." *International Journal of Heritage Studies. 14*(5), 405–421.

McKay, M., (2002). *National Soul: Canadian Mural Painting, 1860s–1930s*. McGill-Queen's Press: London.
Merriam, J., (2011). "Painting Black Spaces Red, Black, and Green: The Constitutionality of the Mural Movement." *Berkeley Journal of African-American Law & Policy*, *13*(1), 1–44.
Merrill, S., (2015). "Keeping It Real? Subcultural Graffiti, Street Art, Heritage and Authenticity." *International Journal of Heritage Studies*, *21*(4), 369–389.
Miles, S., & Paddison, R., (2005). "Introduction: The Rise and Rise of Culture-Led Urban Regeneration." *Urban Studies*, 42(5–6), 833–839.
Mueller, M., (1979). *Murals: Creating an Environment*. Davis Publications: Worcester, Massachusetts.
Ramsey, P., (2013). "A Pleasingly Blank Canvas: Urban Regeneration in Northern Ireland and the Case of Titanic Quarter." *Space and Polity*, *17*(2), 164–179.
Rolston, B., (1992). *Drawing Support: Murals in the North of Ireland*. Beyond the Pale Publications: Belfast.
Rolston, B., (2012). "Re-Imaging, Mural Painting and the State in Northern Ireland." *International Journal of Cultural Studies*, *15*(5), 447–66.
Simone-Charteris, M., & Boyd, S., (2010). "Northern Ireland Re-emerges from the Ashes: the Contribution of Political Tourism towards a more Visited and Peaceful Environment." In: *Tourism, Progress, and Peace*, edited by Omar Moufakkir & Ian Kelly. CABI: Oxfordshire, pp. 179–198.
Sluka, J., (1992). "The Politics of Painting, Political Murals in Northern Ireland." In *The Paths to Domination, Resistance, and Terror*, edited by Carolyn Nordstrom and JoAnn Martin. University of California Press: Oxford: pp. 190–216.
The Bogside Artists. *Murals*. Guildhall Press: Derry, 2001.
Widdis, R., (2000). "The murals of Moose Jaw: Commodification or articulation of the past?" *Historical Geography*, 28, 234–252.
Willsdon, C., (2000). *Mural Painting in Britain 1840–1940: Figure and Meaning*. Oxford University Press: Oxford.
Woods, O., (1995). *Seeing is Believing? – Murals in Derry*. Guildhall Press: Derry.
Zebracki, M., (2013). "Beyond public artopia: public art as perceived by its publics." *Geo Journal*, 78, 303–317.

CHAPTER 14

PREVENTIVE CONSERVATION POLICIES

X. MAS-I-BARBERÀ,[1] M. SÁNCHEZ PONS,[2] and J. OSCA PONS[3]

[1]*Associate Professor, Department of Conservation and Restoration of Cultural Heritage, UPV, 3N Building, Camino de Vera s/n, 46022 Valencia, Spain, Tel.: +34-963877000/Ext. 73128, E-mail: jamasbar@upvnet.upv.es*

[2]*Associate Professor, Department of Conservation and Restoration of Cultural Heritage, UPV, 3N Building, Camino de Vera s/n, 46022 Valencia, Spain, Tel.: +34-963877000/Ext. 73136, E-mail: mersanpo@crbc.upv.es*

[3]*Associate Professor, Department of Conservation and Restoration of Cultural Heritage, UPV, 3N Building, Camino de Vera s/n, 46022 Valencia, Spain, Tel.: +34-963877000/Ext. 73110, E-mail: juosca@crbc.upv.es*

CONTENTS

14.1	Introduction	272
14.2	Analysis and Evaluation of Risk of Deterioration of the Mural	277
14.3	Proposal for the Preventive Conservation Plan	280
14.4	Conclusions	281
	Keywords	282
	References and Bibliography	282

14.1 INTRODUCTION

Preventive conservation is a series of measures that are executed to monitor the environmental conditions in which the artworks or collectibles, someone wants to preserve, are situated, without making any direct intervention on the materials that make up the object. That means that it is a working method that seeks to prevent or minimize damage to the artworks or collections before it occurs by control of the parameters that surround the object to be protected.

Any process of restoring a heritage property should end with the implementation of a series of measures to ensure the future conservation of the work in a sustainable way. The elaboration of a maintenance plan is not only useful for preserving the cultural asset but is, also from the economic point of view, very profitable as it minimizes the risk of possible required interventions in the future.

One of the fundamental principles in the preventive conservation of a mural painting is to determine the condition of the building in which the object is located. Mural painting is a technique which depends on the building on which it was painted—it can indeed be classified as property as it belongs to the wall, and therefore to the architectural structure. This is what raises the greatest problems in controlling and identifying the risks of damage it could experience, since it is impossible to isolate it from the building, and therefore shares the deterioration factors. Consequently, the properly assess of possible damage risks is the key, which defines the priorities and monitoring procedures to raise the necessary preventive conservation actions on the property itself.

The relative humidity (RH) and ambient temperature are the two critical parameters responsible for most of the deterioration processes, be they physical, chemical or biological that may affect any material as they favor any thermodynamic transformations.

Thus, when assessing these factors, both parameters have to be taken into account. To measure the amount of water in the surroundings, the relative humidity (the measure in percentage) is used, which is defined as the relation between the amount of water vapor of a given air mass and the mass of the same volume of air which could be reached if it were completely saturated with water vapor at the same ambient temperature.

RH is used because it facilitates understanding and expresses better the interaction of ambient water vapor with the materials. The RH depends on the absolute humidity and temperature, such that the RH and temperature relationship is established as follows: if the moisture content (water vapor) of the environment is constant, and the temperature varies, the RH also varies, as the amount of water vapor that may contain this environment is different. That is to say, with the same conditions of water vapor in the atmosphere the RH decreases if the temperature increases; whereas RH increases if the temperature drops. If temperature decreases and thus air continues to cool down, the capacity to contain water vapor may decrease so far that the saturation point could be reached and water starts to condense, also called the dew point.

Lighting conditions also will be crucial, since they could influence both the ambient temperature and photochemical degradation processes, which should be studied and adapted to the needs of the studied property.

In order to propose a specific preventive conservation plan for the mural Seade it is necessary to identify the risks that may affect this artwork, and for that three related fundamental intrinsic aspects are addressed, namely:
- the nature of the mural painting;
- the building in which it is located and the given use; and
- the environmental conditions of the surroundings

The mural "Allegory to work," as already explained, is a painting executed with a dry painting technique on a gypsum plaster on a brick wall. The pigments are bound by protein means, especially sensitive to thermohygrometric changes and moisture, which can get to the paint by leaks either from the outside or by surface condensation. When moisture reaches directly the damage can be immediate, but in this case, particularly the progressive contribution of moisture condensation from inside is also dangerous. The constituent materials are highly hygroscopic and constant supply of water may gradually deteriorate the paint layer since this causes a loss of strength of the binder, which in turn can lead to the disintegration of the paint layer, which would weaken under ECMhanical stress. This determines the need to control the state of the roof and the wall where the mural is located, as well as thermohygrometric room factors.

The mural has no varnish protection which, given its nature, makes it even more vulnerable. In addition, the identified repaintings on the surface are executed with a different material and therefore with different hygroscopic and transpiring characteristics, cause the moisture to affect especially the original zones of the work.

The building that houses the painting, in origin was the Liceo de Colonia and the room that is the Aula de Dibujo (Hall of Drawing). Today this space is the Salón de Actos de la Casa de la Cultura de la ciudad (Conference room of the Culture House of the city).

This is an exempt building located in an urbanized and gardened terrain the floor in "u" shape, with no road traffic and close to the Río de la Plata (River Plate, literally: River of Silver).

The room is located on the first floor, occupying one of the side wings and the wall, specifically in the west wall of the same, thus it is one of the exterior walls of the building.

In the past, the building had serious problems were leaks led to the loss of an important part of the work in its upper right part, now rebuilt in a previous restoration.

The space has a not centralized air conditioning system through individual machines installed in different areas of the building.

The hall where the mural is located has a rectangular format of 5.8 x 30 m^2 and a height of 6.8 m and thus an internal volume of about 1,183.2 m^3 (Figure 14.1). It has four large windows in the wall to the left of the wall, leading to a balcony and three large doors, communicating with a covered side corridor, open towards the inner courtyard (Figure 14.2).

The windows and doors are woodwork and are somewhat deteriorated, so that the seal is not airtight. The window frame is divided into squares with a simple frosted glass pane and it has exterior wooden shutters (Figure 14.3).

The windows are covered internally with large curtains and the floor is carpeted. The area where the wall is located is slightly elevated through an existing step in the floor. Nowadays this space is illuminated through the large windows and small incandescent lamps with adjustable spotlights. In measurements made on the surface of the work recorded lighting conditions oscillating between 20 and 60 lux.

Preventive Conservation Policies

FIGURE 14.1 General view of the hall where the studied mural is located. *Source:* Graphical record of the R&D Project PUCM, 2016.

FIGURE 14.2 View of the open side passage which gives access to the room. *Source:* Graphical record of the R&D Project PUCM, 2016.

FIGURE 14.3 Detail view of one of the windows in the room. *Source:* Graphical record of the R&D Project PUCM, 2012.

The climate of the interior of this room is controlled via three separate air conditioning units, located next to the windows.

The site of Colonia del Sacramento in the north shore of the Río de la Plata is responsible for humid subtropical climate of the city, with distinct seasons and abundant rainfall throughout the year which are less frequent in the colder months. The temperature ranges between 8°C and 15°C from June to August and 17–29°C in January with a major relative environmental humidity. Measurements at one of the monitoring visits in April 2011, reflected an ambient temperature inside the room of about 19.5°C and a relative humidity of 52%, very adequate conditions for the maintenance of the work. But these measurements should be repeated at other times of the year, as well as during the celebration of certain activities in which many people could participate.

As already mentioned, this room is used as an event hall of the Culture House of the city, so different events are held in it (Figure 14.4). This use conditions could lead to some changes in temperature and humidity in different times, depending on the activity or its absence.

FIGURE 14.4 Children performing an educational workshop in the room. *Source:* Graphical record of the R&D Project PUCM, 2012.

This use, linked to ignorance of the importance of the mural for the collective identity of the Uruguayan people, has generated some of the most significant damages observed in the mural before restoration, such as the presence of numerous graffiti made by incision on the surface of the paint (Figure 14.5).

Finally, since the city is located in an area of low seismicity, it seems not necessary to develop a response plan adapted for the work in the case of seismic risk.

14.2 ANALYSIS AND EVALUATION OF RISK OF DETERIORATION OF THE MURAL

The following sections presents the risks that, in a direct way, interact in a greater extent with the artwork and the space in which it is located, and the central role that plays the building in safeguarding it.

FIGURE 14.5 Presence of numerous graffiti made by incision on the surface of the paint.
Source: Graphical record of the R&D Project PUCM, 2012.

14.2.1 MURAL PAINTING

Risk analysis study of the work of Seade, shows different aspects of both intrinsic nature like moisture by capillarity (material properties of the artwork) and extrinsic nature (environmental and derived data by the functionality of the building) to be considered in order apply the correct preservation approach:

a. The hygroscopicity of the constituent materials of the mural. It is discussed in previous sections, that there is a wall made from a plaster with protein binders. These material properties, due to the technique developed by the artist, makes the mural a truly sensitive and delicate work.
b. Moisture flow by capillary contained within the wall.
c. The ignorance of the importance of the property resulting in antisocial acts (graffiti and unfortunate actions).
d. Possible differences in behavior of the original materials and the materials used for restoration, caused by misjudgments of the environmental conditions.

14.2.2 SPACE: HALL

Knowledge of the characteristics of the space where the work is located is essential for a proper control of the resulting risks. In this regard, it is worth mentioning:
  a. The environmental conditions regarding temperature and relative humidity of the room are unstable. Visual observation demonstrates the lack of sealed doors and windows and improper use of air conditioning mechanisms. These devices are obsolete and do not receive the minimum maintenance (clogged filters, uneven airflow, etc.).
  b. Lighting is insufficient and inadequate. Incandescent lights are installed which modify environmental conditions and lead to a wrong observation. Besides, the distribution of points of light is inappropriate, costly and unsustainable.
  c. The cleaning service of the room lacks of information regarding materials and methods for cleaning to be applied for cleaning the room. In this regard, the staff is uninformed of any measure that alters the surface properties of the work.
  d. The room lacks a program for use where access and activities carried out are controlled and regulated. In addition, administration has no specialized training in basic preventive measures.
  e. The room does not warn of the existence of the mural painting and therefore, there is some ignorance by the public.
  f. The existence of unhygienic elements or their tendency to attract dust are observed. Carpet is on the pavement and inappropriate curtains.

14.2.3 BUILDING

Building architecture (covered terrace where water can accumulate) and the location of the mural (inside of the exterior façade) indicates that, in case of deterioration of these elements, exists a great risk of water leaks and pollutants from the outside directly to the inside (roofs and walls, etc.).

14.3 PROPOSAL FOR THE PREVENTIVE CONSERVATION PLAN

The most important recommendation to be included in the plan for preventive conservation, considering and estimating the risks that directly affect the preservation of the artwork are given in the following subsections.

14.3.1 MURAL PAINTING

Top priority will be to monitor the work every six months during the first two years after the restoration in order to register documentary any information on temperature and relative humidity of the surface. If the data are logical it may be repeated annually on a control model that meets the standard measures on prevention of wall works.

14.3.2 SPACE: HALL

a. It will be mandatory to maintain stable environmental conditions, avoiding abrupt changes between the inside and outside of the room. It is recommended not to open or close windows in an uncontrolled manner, except in order to regulate the humidity of the room and thereby prevent surface condensation, although it should not come in air from the entrance of the room. It is recommended to install an inverter air conditioning system inside with a constant renewal of air upon detection of a temperature below 12°C (±2) and RH above 65% (± 2) to be monitored via a digital hygrometer.

b. It is recommended to distribute the lighting system according to the room and, if necessary, replace it with another, more sustainable. Side installation of two spotlights with LED lighting system such that it allows observation of the work without interferences. Likewise, the rest of the room vertical illumination according to the functionality need will be employed.

c. It is advisable to keep the room clean, and inappropriate elements that favor the accumulation of dust and pollutants should be eliminated. Also, the cleaning staff will be formed in order to understand the basic principles of preventive conservation. In this regard, it is important to establish a control over the cleaning mode of this space (always aspiration), evaluating the products used (never sprays and vaporizers), giving precise instructions to the persons in charge of the cleaning service to not touch and manipulate the mural under any circumstances.

d. It will be necessary to train and educate members of the administration of the room in preventive measures through an organizational model and sustainable management. Activities and influx in the room will also be controlled without exceeding the permitted limits. The temperature and humidity measurements demonstrate appropriate conditions; however, these can abruptly change when an event with a large influx of people is celebrated.

e. It is recommended as a fundamental measure to inform the public and visitors of the value of the work through courses, training and dissemination activities. This will result in awareness-raising to make them part of the cultural property.

f. It will be necessary to install a physical security barrier to the work as an essential preventive measure and/ or volumetric sensors. Also, it is recommended to develop a monitoring and maintenance measure of the security systems through a log book prepared for such a purpose.

g. Finally, it is advisable to review annually all measures taken in order to observe strengths, identify shortcomings and propose improvements. All this will be recorded in the control and maintenance logbook. This text can only be completed by the responsible personnel administration and/or the conservation professional in the section reserved for this purpose.

14.3.3 BUILDING

a. It will be mandatory to check roofs and other construction elements that may accumulate water, especially during winter season and after heavy rain hail and strong winds.

b. It is recommended to monitor the walls and ceiling in order to detect stains of moisture and leaks.

14.4 CONCLUSIONS

The mural painting "Allegory to work," located in the old Liceo de Colonia del Sacramento is holder of a symbolic and social value, representative of all the Uruguayan people. Preventive conservation should ensure proper conservation of the mural, maintaining its essence and identity. Likewise, this mural stands out for its historical, artistic and social interest and which claims preservation through sustainable activities and art acting as a tourist attraction. This requires following a series of prevention and maintenance measures, not only to protect the work but also to make its environment accessible and visible for visitors. The design of a program of guided tours with conservative purposes will be an important aspect to be evaluated.

KEYWORDS

- preventive conservation
- deterioration factors
- mural painting
- risk assessment

REFERENCES AND BIBLIOGRAPHY

Ballart-Hernandez, J., & Juan-Tresserras, J. (2001). *Gestión del patrimonio cultural*. Colección Ariel Patrimonio. Barcelona: Ariel.

Cayetano-Valcarcel J. A., Martínez-Bazán, M. L., Mas-Barberà, X., & Sánchez-Pons, M. (2013). *Cataloguin the Twentieth Century Murals of Uruguay. Value Enhancement for Tourist Advertizing*. In: Tourism & Creative Industry. Workshop Proceedings; UPV, Servicio de Publicaciones. pp. 161–162.

Martínez-Carazo, E. M., Santamarina-Campos, V., De-Miguel-Molina, M., & Fernández-Óscar, M. (2013). *Sustainable Cultural Tourism: Museum Program of the Uruguayan Muralist Production of the Centuries XX and XXI*. In: Tourism & Creative Industry. Workshop Proceedings; UPV, Servicio de Publicaciones. pp. 79–81.

Mas-Barberà, X, Sánchez-Pons, M., & Osca-Pons, J. (2015). *Función social del muralismo uruguayo del siglo XX como vehículo y modelo de activación patrimonial sustentable: catalogación técnica*. Conservation Issues in Modern and Contemporary Murals. Cambridge Scholars Publishing, pp. 513–524.

Rainer, L., & Bass-Rivera A., (2006). *The Conservation of Decorated Surfaces on Earthen Architecture*. Getty Conservation Institute Series: Symposium Proceedings, USA.

Santamarina-Campos, V., Carabal-Montagud, M. A., & De-Miguel-Molina, M. (2013). *Design and Implementation of Inclusive Cultural Policies: Contemporary Uruguayan Muralism as Sustainable Assets Activation*. In: Tourism & Creative Industry. Workshop Proceedings; UPV, Servicio de Publicaciones. pp. 49–67.

CHAPTER 15

GUIDELINES TO STIMULATE USE AND SOCIAL ENJOYMENT

M. DE-MIGUEL-MOLINA,[1] B. DE-MIGUEL-MOLINA,[2] and M. SEGARRA-OÑA[3]

[1]*Associate Professor, Research Micro-Cluster Globalization, Tourism and Heritage, Department of Management, UPV, Camino de Vera, s/n, 46022, Valencia, Spain, Tel.: +0034963877680/76821, Ext. 76844, E-mail: mademi@omp.upv.es*

[2]*Associate Professor, Research Micro-Cluster Globalization, Tourism and Heritage, Department of Management, UPV, 7D building, Camino de Vera s/n, 46022 Valencia, Spain, Tel.: +34-963877680/ Ext. 76843, E-mail: bdemigu@omp.upv.es*

[3]*Associate Professor, Research Micro-Cluster Globalization, Tourism and Heritage, Department of Management, UPV, Camino de Vera, s/n, 46022, Valencia, Spain, Tel.: +0034963877000, Ext. 76844, E-mail: maseo@omp.upv.es*

CONTENTS

15.1	Introduction	284
15.2	Objectives	284
15.3	Methodology	289
15.4	Results and Proposals	290
15.5	Conclusions	298
	Keywords	299
	References and Bibliography	299

15.1 INTRODUCTION

The mural "Allegory to work" by Uruguayan artist Seade, restored by our research team, is one of the 600 murals that we have registered in the country. These murals were painted to be shown to the public because that is the social essence of murals and this, in particular, is classified in the social realism of contemporary Uruguayan muralism. Its location, inside the Cultural Centre of Colonia de Sacramento (Rivera Street, 346), led us to analyze how the intervention of the municipality (Santamarina et al., 2015) could help the municipality to attract tourism and to involve the community (Koster, 2008).

With a good strategy, we could also achieve not only a sense of social identity, but also a way of improving the local development using murals as a tourist attraction (De Miguel Molina et al., 2014). Figini and Vici (2012) and Herrero et al. (2011) studied the potential of cultural art and other related activities as a tool for leveling seasonality. Moreover, Plaza (2008) studied how heritage investment can result in being an effective employment creator if it becomes an effective tourist attraction. We have taken into account that the use of this mural can be influenced by the fact that Colonia de Sacramento next to the Silver River, has become a touristic location since UNESCO named it a World Heritage site (Figure 15.1). Moreover, we base our study on the practices that other locations have used to stimulate visits to the most famous murals around the world.

Therefore, following Ambrose and Paine (2012), it is worth considering the range of social, cultural, economic and regeneration benefits that a museological proposal could provide to the community.

15.2 OBJECTIVES

We have developed this study with two interconnected main goals:
Design a public policy strategy to use this mural to involve the community, increasing the type of citizens that normally go to the Culture Centre to attend different activities.

Design a marketing strategy to use this mural to attract tourism, bearing in mind that it is an indoor mural and this can have both advantages and disadvantages.

Firstly, we have analyzed which kind of objectives we have to promote, as this mural has the particularity of being indoors. In this case, we have followed Ambrose and Paine's definition and classification of museums (2012: 10–11). They propose a wide concept and classification of museums as a public service for collecting, preserving, and interpreting the things of this world (heritage, as we call it, taking the point of view of the American Association of Museums. If we were to classify this space, with its sole emblematic mural, we could describe it as an artistic and historic, and 'intangible heritage,' collection of municipal management, in a city area, with an educational purpose and located in a historic house.

FIGURE 15.1 Historical Quarter in Colonia del Sacramento. *Source:* Graphical record of the R&D Project PUCM, 2011.

On the one hand, the mural is located in a cultural space that has its own activities or others offered by some institutions and associations that the residents attend. These activities are diverse and are offered normally to adults (Table 15.1). Therefore, as we can observe, these could be the current targets of this space.

TABLE 15.1 Activities June–November, 2013 Offered at the Conference Room of the Culture House of Colonia

Date	Activity	Organization
28–30 June	Chess Open Competition Colonia	Centre Unión Cosmopolita
7 August	Preliminary Workshop of the Young Tourism Promoters Program	Tourism Board, Tourism Association
8 August	Medical Workshop	Orameco, Femi
9 August	Book presentation	Central Library
10 August	Seminar of Psychology	A. P. U. (Uruguayan Association of Psychology)
10 August	Cinema	Mec (Culture and Education Ministry)
16 August	Scientific Workshop	Medical Association, Uruguay
20 August	Monthly meeting	Architects Society
21–22 August	Expo Educa	Mides (Social Development Ministry)
27 August	Education talk	CTC ORT
5 September	Conference	Technological Institute of Plata
7 September	Workshop on Resources and Strategies for a Different Education	Silvia Lasplaces
13 September	Meditation	Onenees, Uruguay
18 September	Workshop	Municipal Comedy
23 September	Workshop of the Elderly in Movement Program	Social Action Board
24 September	Monthly meeting	Architects' Society
26 September	Meeting	Dance Group "Riachuelo"
27 September	Book presentation	Central Library
3 October	Meeting	Educational Departmental Committee

TABLE 15.1 (Continued)

Date	Activity	Organization
5 October	Workshop	Cooperation Board
7–11 October "Oceans separate, youth unite"	International Seminar Cooperation Board	
15 October	Museums competition	Culture Board
16 October	Young Tourism Promoters Program	Tourism Association
17 October	Meeting	Dance Group "Riachuelo"
19 October	Workshop	Cooperation Board
22 October	Teachers meeting	Culture Board
23 October	Meeting	Educational Departmental Committee
24 October	Meeting	Intendancy
25 October	Book presentation	Central Library
26 October	Workshop	Cooperation Board
4 November	Uruguay Concursa	Mec Centres
5 November	Home School Elections	Culture Board
8 November	Recognition of the Citizens of Colonia	Rotary Club Colonia
12 November	Workshop	Promotion and Development Board
15 November	Literature Competition Prizes	Casa de las Letras
16 November	Annual Meeting	Social Assistants Association Uruguay
18 November	Meeting	Educational Departmental Committee
23 November	Documental Fiction	Culture Board
27 November	Home School Elections	Culture Board
28 November	Meeting Idóneos Acción Social	Social Action Board
29 November	Corporal Expression Exhibition	Beatriz Zilavi
29 November	Workshop Museums Universal Accessibility	Pronadi
30 November	Workshop Football Training	Trainers Association Colonia

Source: Culture Center of Colonia.

However, since the mural intervention (Figure 15.2), we wondered whether other kinds of activities could be offered, focused on these associations listed on table 1 and other associations, in order to enhance the mural's heritage value. Moreover, it could be promoted as a touristic cultural attractor, as in the itinerary proposed by our team, to combine cultural muralism heritage with Silver River's natural assets (Figure 15.3). With this in mind, we looked at whether there were hospitality facilities and picturesque places offered near to the Culture House that could give support to a touristic promotion and, if not, what others could be proposed.

According to Koster (2008: 180–182), murals can be used for different purposes, although the best strategy is to combine some of them. This depends on our target and objectives:

- Covering a public service: promoting art and creative industries.
- Including the participation of young groups: creating jobs, enhancing identity, increasing history knowledge, combating illegal graffiti.
- Beautification of the city: murals show community identity and history and, at the same time, attract more tourists.

FIGURE 15.2 Conference Room of the Culture House (old High School of Colonia del Sacramento). Location of the mural "Allegory to work." *Source:* Graphical record of the R&D Project PUCM, 2016.

FIGURE 15.3 View of the Silver River from the Culture House. *Source:* Graphical record of the R&D Project PUCM, 2012.

- With a clear tourism purpose: murals as attractors. It will be necessary to differentiate the location for this cultural attraction. Murals are developed to depict history but also they focus on a specific historical or social symbolism that could attract more visitors, becoming a unique experience.

15.3 METHODOLOGY

As a theoretical model, we have applied the proposal of Koster et al. (2008) regarding the strategic marketing process for museums. This model follows the different steps of a basic strategic process. Moreover, we have borne in mind that this mural is not an isolated artwork but a mural that can be part of a cultural and touristic itinerary.

At the analysis stage, we have used the benchmarking method, which is the systematic and continuous process of evaluating the products, services and working processes of those organizations that are recognized as representing best practice, with the objective of performing organizational improvements (Spendolini, 1992). According to Camp (1992), we should be able to identify our objective by comparison, and the key steps to completing this task are to know what or who is going to be evaluated and with which information do we want to make comparisons. The way we complete these steps will influence the next ones.

Furthermore, when applying the benchmarking method in the tourism field, Wöber (2002) highlights that it is essential to classify the type of organization we want to assess, depending on our goals:

Business related to hospitality, such as accommodation suppliers (hotels, motels, B&B, hostels, camps, and so on), restaurants, tourism operators and travel agencies.

Other organizations without economic purposes, such as national or regional tourism agencies, leisure attractions managed by governments and Non-Governmental Organizations (NGOs).

Destination: national, regional or local (rural or urban).

As our object of study, we looked for murals, located in an urban context, our two goals being: to find murals that were public or social (not lucrative) and murals that enhanced local economic development.

As the first goal is difficult to compare, we have focused on the second one. We searched in the social network TripAdvisor, which ranks attractions depending on visitors' votes, for which murals receive the best votes by tourists. Although we have not got all the information, it is useful to observe what are the characteristics of the best ranked and most visited murals in the world, as valued by their visitors. With that information, we can compare the characteristics of those murals.

In addition, at an operational level, we have taken into account the cultural, social and economic benefits of museums identified by Ambrose and Paine (2012: 12–16).

15.4 RESULTS AND PROPOSALS

Being an indoor mural could influence us to explore it as a traditional museum, but mural art by its very essence provides us with the opportunity of taking a broader perspective of museums and the associated possibilities that a museological itinerary – combining murals located in different parts of the city – can contribute to e local community development. However, this advantage also becomes a disadvantage, as visitors have to make an additional effort to visit them. The challenge, then, is how to add value to the visit through the different services that are close to the itinerary proposed (Figure 15.4), or to suggest new activities that could attract other groups of the community to that space (Figure 15.5).

We have benchmarked the most visited murals of the world and those that are best valued. Without doubt, the murals of Belfast in Northern Ireland are first in the ranking (Table 15.2).

The first three tours are very similar and TripAdvisor ranks the companies that offer them as excellent. They are Belfast Private Mural Tours (http://www.belfastmuraltours.com), Official Black Taxi Mural Private Tours (http://www.taxitrax.net) and West Belfast Mural-Private Tours (http://www.westbelfastmuraltours.com). Their services are alike, they offer guided tours with a local guide using private transport (more or less exclusive) and providing information about the political history of Northern Ireland through the murals.

FIGURE 15.4 Terraces at the historical quarter of Colonia del Sacramento. *Source:* Graphical record of the R&D Project PUCM, 2012.

FIGURE 15.5 Courtyard of the Cultural Center (old High School of Colonia del Sacramento). *Source:* Graphical record of the R&D Project PUCM, 2016.

TABLE 15.2 Best Valued Mural Tours in TripAdvisor (2013)

Country	Attraction	Comments/ranked excellent	Tour	Additional services
Northern Ireland	Belfast Private Mural Tours	376/359	Guided	Transport
Northern Ireland	Official Black Cab Mural Private Tours	56/52	Guided	Transport
Northern Ireland	West Belfast Mural – Private Tours	42/41	Guided	Transport
USA	Portsmouth Floodwall Mural	55/51	Free	Audio guides

Also, the city of Portsmouth in Ohio (USA) receives "excellent' rating" punctuation (http://www.portsmouthohiomurals.com), but in this case the visitors are free to complete the tour by their own using, if they want, audio guides.

Therefore, in our object of study we could offer these two types of visits: free or guided. However, we will add additional services to the basic visit, as suggested by Kotler et al. (2008: 288). In the case of Chemainus in Canada, they argue that murals can only become competitive if they are combined with other additional services.

In addition, to create value for the targets (community and visitors), we have to quantify the benefits they could receive and maintain them as higher as possible (economic, time, energy and physical). Therefore, it depends on the target we want to reach. In our object of study, we could have two different groups:
- Visitors: people who want to follow the murals' itinerary or people who want to visit the city and, indirectly, see the murals. We could provide information through some digital resources (webpage, blog, and app) and offer audio/video guides. In this case, the objective is to generate economic benefits.
- Community: we could enhance local culture and identity, providing the opportunity for citizens to guide the visits voluntarily and, as users, organizing workshops, seminars and so on related to the topic and symbolism of the mural. In addition, other cultural activities could be added to the Cultural House Program, taking into account the students' target (children and teenagers). In this case, the objective is to generate social benefits.

In both the cases, we could also create cultural benefits.

Regarding the economic benefits, Ambrose and Paine (2012: 12–16) suggest that museums can play a role in economic regeneration. In urban areas, service and creative industries enhance the museum environment, which acts as an 'attractor' for a tourist destination. Moreover, such facilities make the area more attractive for workers and their families and can support job creation and continued employment. They can also attract part-time or temporary staff, as part of government training projects. Visitors will also spend money within the local economy (shops, cafes, restaurants, hotels, garages, markets). Museums may also attract financial investment from external agencies, such as government programs or international agencies' research projects. With a stronger destination economy, the museum can then benefit from continuing investment and the cycle is further reinforced.

In the case of Colonia, it has recently celebrated 20 years of the Word Heritage Declaration and this fact is an advantage in attracting visitors.

Since then, the tourism of the country has been increasing year by year and, at present, Colonia receives 9.9% of the visitors of the country (Uruguayan Tourism Ministry, 2015: 4). The majority of tourists come from Argentina and Brazil, but the number of visitors from Europe and other parts of the world are increasing. In the whole country, the contribution of tourism to the Uruguayan economy is going to be the highest in the last ten years with a rate of 7.7% (Uruguayan Tourism Ministry, 2015: 26). And at Colonia, 6.54% of the workforces are employed in the tourism sector (Uruguayan Tourism Ministry, 2015: 25).

Regarding social benefits, Ambrose and Paine (2012: 12–16) present museums as developers of a sense of identity and community cohesion, especially with those who are socially disadvantaged. They can serve as a place of shared 'memory' for the community, contributing to the preservation and conservation of the community's cultural heritage (including the history and culture of minority groups) and providing opportunities for community involvement through volunteer programs, friends' groups or training programs.

Finally, in terms of cultural benefits, Ambrose and Paine (2012: 12–16) show museums as important centers for learning because they provide access to local heritage resources along with the information and knowledge that help to enhance their significance. They can offer students of all ages many opportunities to learn through contact with original material. Furthermore, as a center of objective professional expertise, they can work in partnership with other cultural bodies, such as libraries, archives and arts centers, to develop joint programs and projects. They can also provide cultural facilities, such as exhibition spaces, meeting rooms and websites, as well as organize cultural events and activities on-site, off-site and online.

After analyzing the possible benefits of our object of study, we have examined the four Ps to know how to reach and improve our two goals: to involve the community and to gain visitors.

- Product: in this case, the mural "Allegory to work" by Felipe Seade. Its conservation has been improved thanks to our intervention team but the Culture House should take the necessary measures to maintain it and prevent deterioration (Fernández Óscar, 2011). Additionally, the design of a museological itinerary would be part of the product. Therefore, for this itinerary we should select interesting, from the artistic or the ethnography point of view, and well-conserved murals to visit. In the city of Colonia, there is still a lack of consciousness of the heritage value of this mural and, in general, of many murals located in high schools or old high schools, not only by citizens but also by the authorities. Some indoor murals are perceived as ephemeral and so they are not protected against the negligence of staff or vandalism of the students, who do not appreciate their value and social function. If something is not understood and valued and we do not perceive it as part of our identity, and therefore are unlikely to take care of it or conserve it.

- Price: if a charge is to be made, it could be associated to a fee to enter the Culture House or to receive a guided tour. In other cases, we think that the visit should be free and some local volunteers could explain the history expressed by the mural and recount the life of the artist.
- Place: the mural is located in the Meeting Room of the Cultural Centre and so it is necessary to visit it there. This is not a problem, as the Culture House is located near the historical quarter, a touristic and shopping area, so the effort required by the visitor to view the mural is limited. In addition, some online technologies could help us to provide information in advance. Through a specific or a shared website or social network – for example, www.facebook.com/muralismouruguayo.contemporaneo, www.twitter.com/MuralismoUY, www.muralism0contemporane0uruguay0.blogs.upv.es, www.gttp.blogs.upv.es (accessed November, 2015)—we could give more information about the mural. At present, the Culture House does not have a website. On the other hand, the physical space should be well maintained and prepared to appreciate the mural. It will be necessary to provide an open space with furniture that could be easily moved (Figure 15.6). Another important variable to consider is the timetable for visits, because we have to find out when our potential visitors could come.
- Promotion: depending on the target, the promotion could be local or touristic. Firstly, the Culture House should promote the mural's intervention through the press and to all the heritage agencies of the local,

regional and national governments. From the touristic point of view, they should contact the city's tourism office. Creating a website in order carry out these tasks could be useful. At present, the cultural center only has a Facebook account page with little activity—https://www.facebook.com/pages/Casa-De-La-Cultura-Colonia-Del-Sacramento/301645559981210 (accessed November, 2015). To renovate the Culture House's image, they could change the present logo, creating a new one linked to the mural. This new anagram logo should be included in all the events and activities' documents (certificates, brochures, reports…). The Meeting Room could also be named 'Allegory of Seade' to identify the mural and its location. A picture of the mural could be shown at the Culture House entrance (Figure 15.7). The same image could be inserted in special triptychs to promote the mural, adding information about the artwork and its artistic and identity values.

"Can the outside of the museum be made to seem more friendly, perhaps by flags and banners, by 'welcome' signs, or by pictures showing what is to be found inside?" (Ambrose and Paine, 2012: 29).

Furthermore, additional services can complement the main product (Kotler et al., 2008: 288), such as:

FIGURE 15.6 Present inside of the room. *Source:* Graphical record of the R&D Project PUCM, 2016.

FIGURE 15.7 Entrance to the culture house. *Source:* Graphical record of the R&D Project PUCM, 2016.

- Temporal exhibitions
- Talks related to the mural's symbolism
- Cultural activities
- Creation of a volunteers' group to plan the guided visits
- Concerts
- Partnerships with local restaurants and cafes
- Audio guides
- Webpage
- Virtual tour using apps.

Other complementary services could be a cafe with local food, toilets, and chairs to have a rest, and so on (Ambrose and Paine, 2012: 29).

Museums are in competition, not simply with one another, but with all other forms of leisure and learning time. They have to provide products and services that the public want to pay for, either directly or through their taxes. Successful museums are oriented towards the market (Ambrose and Paine, 2012: 27).

At the Culture House, all the events and activities should be planned directed to the four principal social groups: children, teenagers, adults and the elderly, and cover the value of the service in all of them. It could be more efficient to arrange special visits for existing groups and to arrange special talks or other activities suited to their interests (Ambrose and Paine, 2012: 29). Above all, they should give priority to activities related to cultural heritage. The main objective will be to identify the Culture House with quality and important events. It could be convenient, for example, to form a committee to select the most appropriate activities regarding some selected criteria, publicizing the entire process.

As Ambrose and Paine (2012: 25, 28–29) stress, users expect to have more participation, particularly if they are minority groups such as children or women. This involvement may take many forms: for example, serving as a volunteer or taking part in those management committees, even helping in some activities. The challenge is to combine the participation of local people at all levels, not only the 'elite,' with the presence of foreign tourists, without losing identity.

Along with all these activities, it would be possible to establish a preventive conservation of the mural, which will lead to impeccable management and maintenance of the space. To reach this goal, all the staff should be trained and, in addition, we could involve more local people, creating a special committee to safeguard the mural and to monitor the maintenance of the Culture Centre.

But sometimes the budget is not enough; therefore a charity could be formed with the different social groups that normally use the Culture House for their activities: the Architects' Society, the Rotary Club, the Culture and Tourism Boards, and so on, who could give funds as well as organize philanthropic activities to preserve the building and the mural.

15.5 CONCLUSIONS

We have developed this study with two main goals that, as far as we have seen, can be achieved through sharing some activities. On the one hand, the first goal has been to design a public policy strategy to use this mural to involve the community, increasing the type of citizens that normally go to the Culture House to attend different activities. At this level, we have observed that children and teenagers are targets that tend to be overlooked by the Culture Centre, so they should try to involve them in some way. Not only for learning or cultural purposes, but also to create a local identity using the mural and its history. Furthermore, there is currently a lack of planning in other activities, which needs to be addressed in order to enhance the mural's role in the local heritage.

On the other hand, our second goal has been to design a marketing strategy to use this mural to attract tourism, bearing in mind that it is an indoor mural and this feature can have advantages and disadvantages. Benchmarking our mural with the most visited murals of the world, we can observe many existing deficiencies in using this mural as a tourist attractor. First, the mural should be integrated in the mural itineraries of Colonia de Sacramento and be promoted through different channels. Moreover, some additional services around the mural could add value to the tourists' visit. To become known, the Culture House should use the necessary ways to work with the various government departments and the travel agencies.

It is possible to combine the two strategies in order to involve the community, to improve a common identity and to enhance tourism in order to achieve sustainable local economic development.

KEYWORDS

- community development
- cultural tourism
- local identity
- marketing places
- mural art

REFERENCES AND BIBLIOGRAPHY

Ambrose, T., & Paine, C. (2012). *Museum Basics, 3rd edition*; Routledge: New York.

Camp, R. C. (1992). Learning from the best leads to superior performance. *Journal of Business Strategy, 13*(3), 3–6.

De Miguel Molina, M., Santamarina Campos, V., Segarra Oña, M. V., & De Miguel Molina, B. (2014). *Marketing Places: Highlighting the Key Elements for Attracting Mural-Based Tourism*. In: *Sustainable Performance and Tourism: A Collection of Tools and Best Practices*; Mondéjar Jiménez, J., Ferrari, G., Segarra Oña, M. V., & Peiró Signes, A., Eds., Chartridge Books Oxford: Oxford, *3*, 37–46.

Fernández Óscar, M. (2011). "Allegory to work" de Felipe Seade: Activación Patrimonial, Estudios Previos y Propuesta De Intervención. Master Dissertation, UPV.

Figini, P., & Vici, L. (2012). Off-season tourists and the cultural offer of a mass-tourism destination: The case of Rimini. *Tourism Management, 33*, 825–839.

Herrero, L. C., Sanz, J. A., & Devesa, M. (2011). Measuring the economic value and social viability of a cultural festival as a tourism prototype. *Tourism Economics, 17*, 639–653.

Kotler, N. G., Kotler, J. R., Wheeler, Ph., & Kotler, W. I. (2008). *Museum Marketing & Strategy*, Jossey Bass: San Francisco.

Koster, R. L. P. (2008). *Mural-Based Tourism as a Strategy for Rural Community Economic Development*. In: *Advances in Culture, Tourism and Hospitality Research*. Woodside, A. G., Ed., Emerald: Bingley, *2*, 153–292.

Plaza, B. (2008). On some challenges and conditions for the Guggenheim Museum Bilbao to be an effective economic reactivator. *International Journal of Urban and Regional Research, 32*, 506–517.

Santamarina Campos, V., Carabal Montagud, M. A., De Miguel Molina, M., & Martínez Carazo, E. V. (2015). *Agentes sociales y muralismo contemporáneo uruguayo. Nuevas perspectivas de investigación y manejo patrimonial*. In: *Conservation Issues in Modern and Contemporary Murals;* Sánchez Pons, M., Shank, W., Fuster López, L., Eds., Cambridge Scholars Publishing: Newcastle upon Tyne, *26*, 406–430.

Spendolini, M. J., & Spendolini, M. J. (1992). *The Benchmarking Book*. Amacom: New York.

Uruguayan Ministry of Tourism. Annual Report, 2015. http://www.mintur.gub.uy/index.php/es/feed-ministerio/item/235256-anuario (accessed Nov 23, 2015).

Wöber, K. W. (2002). *Benchmarking in Tourism and Hospitality Industries: The Selection of Benchmarking Partners*. CABI Publishing: Wallingford.

CONCLUSIONS: MANAGEMENT, TOURISTIC PROMOTION, AND SOCIAL ENJOYMENT OF CONTEMPORARY MURAL PAINTING

V. SANTAMARINA-CAMPOS, M. Á. CARABAL-MONTAGUD, M. DE-MIGUEL-MOLINA, and B. DE-MIGUEL-MOLINA

[1]*Associate Professor, Research Micro-Cluster Globalization, Tourism and Heritage, Department of Conservation and Restoration of Cultural Heritage, UPV, 3N Building, Camino de Vera s/n, 46022 Valencia, Spain, Tel.: +34-963879314/Ext. 79414, E-mail: virsanca@upv.es*

[2]*Associate Professor, Research Micro-Cluster Globalization, Tourism and Heritage, Department of Conservation and Restoration of Cultural Heritage, UPV, 3N Building, Camino de Vera s/n, 46022 Valencia, Spain, Tel.: +34-963877000/73132, E-mail: macamon@crbc.upv.es*

[3]*Associate Professor, Research Micro-Cluster Globalization, Tourism and Heritage, Department of Management, UPV, Camino de Vera, s/n, 46022, Valencia, Spain, Tel.: +0034963877680/76821/Ext. 76844, E-mail: mademi@omp.upv.es*

[4]*Associate Professor, Research Micro-Cluster Globalization, Tourism and Heritage, Department of Management, UPV, 7D Building, Camino de Vera s/n, 46022 Valencia, Spain, Tel.: +34-963877680/Ext. 76843, E-mail: bdemigu@omp.upv.es*

CONTENTS

Introduction 302
Keywords 313
References and Bibliography 313

INTRODUCTION

Felipe Seade is one of the principal artists of the Social Realism artistic movement (Informants 1, 4, 14, 24, 30 and 74) that had a high tendency in the Uruguayan artistic environment of the 30's, when it started to be defined the perception of the social function of the artist and its plastic application (Informants 3 and 30). This was, in part, thanks to the influence of the Mexican muralist David Alfaro Siqueiros, who visited Uruguay those years and requested the public use of the mural against the paintings (Informant 1).

As the recognized plastic artist Miguel Ángel Battegazzore (informant 24) highlights, Seade's work "is Mexican muralism" and it influenced a lot his learning and experience. "I worked with two opposite mentors; maybe for this reason I have, you know, matured so slowly; because I had a social mentor, Seade (muralist, interested in the frescos, influenced by the Mexican muralists and the social message), and later I had Pareja who was, I don't mean hedonist, but with a French training and interested in the color. Therefore, although being between these opposite poles, I didn't want to refuse any of them (…), Seade lectured artistic techniques but Pareja was interested in the color."

This movement was not a cultural isolated phenomenon, but a mixture of artists with different ideological individualities and several esthetic and plastic learnings, being the most representative: Felipe Seade (1912–1969), Norberto Berdía (1900–1983), Luis Mazzey (1895–1983), Carlos González (1905–1993), Armando González (1912), Demetrio Urruchúa (1902–1978) or Esteban Garino (1919–2001). All of them defended a humanist realism, enhancing the ethical aspects of the artwork and the artist like social drivers. The most painted topics in the artworks of the social realism were, among others, the representation of the rural family, the ethnic-social figure, the war, and so on.

In the particular case of the muralist production of Felipe Seade, it was concluded that his predominant idea was to elaborate a social archetype to show a pictorial creation of the rural Uruguayan character. Thus, he developed a social language to reflect the human drama, enhancing the affirmation and exaltation of the essence of the anonymous person and defining the features of the rural population. He favored the reconstruction, conservation and popular dissemination of the community heritage, "he had a political idea similar to the one that the Cuba Republic could have settled and a worldwide vision, the different kinds of Marxism, and so on (…) obviously influenced by the Mexican muralism and, in general, by the revolutionary Mexican arts" (Informant 60).

All these data allowed us to justify and reinforce the iconographic description of the mural painting, where it is represented, by means of the social figures of the country related to the role that they represented in the society, the social situation of the Uruguayans in the first decades of 1900. According to Miguel Ángel Battegazzore (Informant 24) "Seade didn't understand the art as a hedonistic thing (…), like the Mexican muralists, that is, it was a driver of the political and social action. The content was important. (…) Seade had more than one political thinking and, besides, in a time when Uruguay only thought in European terms, he was interested in the American things; that is, if he saw a girl with American features, a mulatta, then he chose her as a model. A little Chinese of the countryside, with small braids… This in those days wasn't Uruguay for the Uruguayans, because Uruguay lived backwards to America (…) The origin of Seade was Chilean, he got the Uruguayan nationality but he was Chilean. Then he gave another local view (…) The epoch of Seade is maybe a little bit before the arrival of Torres García, he belongs to a group of artists that, in some way, were reluctant to the constructive universalism."

These representations are presented in the mural "Allegory to work" (Figures 1 and 2), in four clear different sectors: work, arts, science and industry. According to Carlos Deganello (Informant 51), Director of the Department of Culture of the Colonia Intendancy in 2011, "it is related to the work, to the family, (…) and an image of progress (…)." Therefore the mural "Allegory to work" represents the principal transformations that the

FIGURE 1 Detail of the artwork "Allegory to work" by Felipe Seade, located in the Conference Room of the Culture House (old High School of Colonia del Sacramento), after the intervention process. *Source:* Graphical record of the R&D Project PUCM, 2016.

FIGURE 2 Detail of the artwork "Allegory to work" by Felipe Seade, located in the Conference Room of the Culture House (old High School of Colonia del Sacramento), after the intervention process. *Source:* Graphical record of the R&D Project PUCM, 2016.

country has experiment in the twentieth century, and reflects the conceptualization of the arts that Seade shows in his work that, according to Carlos Deganello, "has a huge heritage value" (Informant 51), in this sense "he painted an important mural, about a national historical topic in the Liceo of Colonia" (Informant 74).

In relation to the authorship, the ethnographic research and the biographic documents reviewed let us to contextualize the beginnings of the artistic trajectory of Seade in 1920 and his arrival to Colonia de Sacramento in 1934, after accepting a position as a painting teacher of the Old departmental Liceo. As explained by Carlos Deganello (Informant 37), "Felipe Seade is not Uruguayan, he is Chilean and he came to live in that moment to Montevideo. Later he came to Colonia, he liked it and he started to study painting in the Fine Arts School. He became Painting lecturer working at the Liceo, because this house, before, was the Municipal Liceo. He was all his life a very well-recognized artist (…) in 1938 this mural was painted with specific characteristics as it isn't a common drawing." He passed away young, in 1969, probably in his most splendid moment "ready to paint murals in his conception (…) but he hasn't the opportunity of painting more murals" (Informant 60).

But the most important was dating reliably the mural painting *Alegoría al trabajo* at, 1938, and one year after his work *La marcha del pueblo a la piedra alta,* which is located in the main hall of the Liceo No. 2 of Florida (Uruguay, Figures 3 and 4). In contrast *Alegoría al trabajo* is located in the old drawing room oft the Departmental Liceo de Colonia, which later was adapted to the "Casa de Cultura" (Culture House, Figure 5), which allowed that "all generations that came here to the Liceo have seen it because it is located in a classroom, and as consequence everybody knows it. They had it as a backdrop" (Informant 37).

In the same way, we elaborated the framework of the principal data related to the technique and history of the artwork, as by the sources reviewed we knew that in previous interventions it was completely repainted. The most important restoration had been the professor's Dardo Ingold in 1981 as the state of conservation of the mural was very deficient. These documents and the graphical material that we found in previous researches were of fundamental historical evidence.

FIGURE 3 Liceo number 2 of Florida, Uruguay. *Source:* Graphical record of the R&D Project PUCM, 2011.

FIGURE 4 Detail of the artwork "The walk of the village to the high stone" in the Principal Room of the Liceo number 2 of Florida, Uruguay. Figure of 2011, after the remove of the paneling that covered it. *Source:* Graphical record of the R&D Project PUCM, 2011.

In conclusion, the compilation all of the data (documents, pictures and ethnographic material) around the past of the artwork, as well as its scientific register, let us obtain the necessary information to conduct a correct intervention and design the social use and enjoyment of the place. From the ethnographic analysis, even if the majority of the informants talked about Seade as one of the principal contemporary muralists (Informants 1, 4, 14, 24, 29 and 51), we highlight the interview to his sons Juan Felipe and Carolina Seade, on the 14th April 2011. That was a singular and relevant testimony to collect information

Conclusions

FIGURE 5 View of the front of the Culture House of Colonia del Sacramento. *Source:* Graphical record of the R&D Project PUCM, 2016.

regarding the life and work of this important twentieth century artist (Informant 32). Finally, we stress the comments of Carlos Deganello (Informant 51) who, in reference to the artwork "Allegory to work," pointed out: "It is my real pleasure that it could be rebuilt, because its significance and for this artist who represented us in such a good way, and that, without being Uruguayan, but he lived here and became a Uruguayan and gave the best from himself because his life was dedicated to paint and teach (…). From here, from the Culture, we always are going to explain to the people to know him; today we say who Seade is (…). It's good that we give him here the impulse that is required."

In the case of the heritage activation process, as identity symbol of the Uruguayans, we accelerate the process with some sensibility action meetings and a module of the Postgraduate Course "Sustainable Management of Latin American Cultural Heritage," celebrated in Colonia. With these activities, we approached the artwork to the public as the principal sessions took place in the Painting Room while the researchers were working on the mural, and it was used as a practical case in the Postgraduate Course. Promoting that this space became a Colonia meeting point after its restoration process, hosting recently numerous cultural events, such as the "200 Years after the Foundation of the Colonia Department" conference, the departmental literary contest "Carlos Martínez Moreno" or the workshop "Gender and violence" (Figure 6), hold in 2016.

Moreover, the ethnographic research had also an activation effect as we asked for information related to muralism and the topics of this mural. All of it generated the openness of a dialog in several levels, not only in the Colonia community, but also in the rest of the country that started to reflect on the Seade's work and other forgotten murals. Therefore, we obtained more information in relation to some of his murals such as "The walk of the village to the high stone," located at the Liceo number 2 of Florida (Figures 3 and 4). As described by Ángel Kalenberg (informant 4): "In Florida, outside Montevideo, there is a mural of Felipe Seade (…). I have fought during some years for this Seade's mural to be restored in the Liceo of Florida."

Of this artwork we could knew that the first contact with conservation objectives was in 1985, when the technicians of the CCHN of Uruguay ECM visited and examined the mural. They observed that it was a high value heritage but it was in an important deterioration stage. In 1995–1997,

FIGURE 6 Detail of the Assembly Hall of the *Casa de la Cultura* (House of Culture) during the "Gender and violence" workshop in July, 2016. *Source:* Newspaper, the weekly of Colonia, 2016.

Conclusions

and taking profit from the visit of some Mexican restorers to Uruguay who assist to the transfer of some murals of Torres-García to the Saint Bois Hospital, their visit also to Florida was asked to evaluate the artworks there and propose solutions. The experts exposed the difficulties to restore the mural, because the high costs, and so a paneling covered it. Furthermore, a decree authorized the demolition of the Liceo due to its ruinous conditions.

During our visit in April 2011, the UPV team went there to analyze the mural and took painting samples with the objective of studying the chromatic palette used by Seade by comparing the two murals painted by him almost at the same time. Thanks to the pressure of the project technicians, we could remove the paneling that covered it (Figures 7–9), and with the Florida community participation a strong heritage reactivation was developed. It had some immediate consequences of huge transcendence and the most important was the Declaration of Departmental Interest of the Building of the Liceo 2 of Florida (ex-Departmental Liceo), on the 7th June 2011, as it is included in the Document number 181/11: Resolution number, 3639/11, expedient N 2011-86-001-02269:

FIGURE 7 Detail of the artwork "The walk of the village to the high stone" in the Principal Room of the Liceo number 2 of Florida, Uruguay. Figure of 2011, after the remove of the paneling that covered it. *Source:* Graphical record of the R&D Project PUCM, 2011.

FIGURE 8 Detail of the artwork "The walk of the village to the high stone" in the Principal Room of the Liceo number 2 of Florida, Uruguay. Figure of 2011, after the remove of the paneling that covered it. *Source:* Graphical record of the R&D Project PUCM, 2011.

FIGURE 9 Detail of the artwork "The walk of the village to the high stone" in the Principal Room of the Liceo number 2 of Florida, Uruguay. Figure of 2011, after the remove of the paneling that covered it. *Source:* Graphical record of the R&D Project PUCM, 2011.

Conclusions

"The building contains a mural painted by Felipe SEADE (born in Santiago, Chile, in 1912 and died in Montevideo, Uruguay, 1969). This Uruguayan artist of Chilean origin teacher and recognized muralist, painted for the public in contrast to the principle of those who painted for 'the burgesses' saloons.' He painted one in Colonia and other 'The walk of the village to the High Stone' (1939), in the Meeting Room of the Departmental Liceo of Florida."

Thanks to it, the demolition of the building was interrupted and this major artwork of Felipe Seade has been saved.

In the long-term, we have observed how the activation process started in 2011 has been reinforced and consolidated, generating a place for the dialog and compromise of different stakeholders, not only the community and associations, but also in other public and academic fields, where never an artwork has been so social. As a prove of it we enhance the Declaration of National Monument in 2014 by the CCHN, of two murals painted by Jonio Montiel in the town of Tacuarembó, created for the local development of this community. Besides, the Declaration of Cultural Interest in 2016 by the ECM of the Project 'Painting the sidewalks,' an initiative organized by an artistic street movement, private and educational institutions, that have visited some neighborhoods of Montevideo and other locations promoting the integration, the arts, the enjoyment and recreation. Moreover the Public Art Meeting in Colonia del Sacramento organized by the Touristic Association of Colonia and the Municipal Intendancy in 2013, to celebrate the Anniversary of the Declaration of the city as Cultural Heritage of the World and the Day of the Human Rights International Declaration. The 200 meters of the wall of the Rambla of the Municipal Campus was painted by a group of artists, such as Bernardo Cardarelli, Jorge Carbajal, Carlos Duarte, Potoka Gómez, Fernando Fraga, Chino Benítez, Diego Bianki and Daniel Barbeito in collaboration with the community (Figures 10 and 11). Barbeito explains how "Youngsters recognize it, the art comes into their eyes (…) there isn't another way to teach." Moreover, how was the reaction of the community with the mural intervention: "I was very surprised (…) it was like a bestial explosion, I had never seen such a situation…and the people thanking: we spent all the days around and now we are happier (…) every day we discover

FIGURE 10 Meeting of Public Art in Colonia del Sacramento. *Source:* Graphical record of the R&D Project PUCM, 2013.

FIGURE 11 Meeting of Public Art in Colonia del Sacramento. *Source:* Graphical record of the R&D Project PUCM, 2013.

something new" (Informant 78). Finally, the collaboration agreement between the IENBA of the RU and the Restoration Unit of the CCHN of the Uruguay ECM, to start in the academic year, 2015–2016, the progressive incorporation of contents related to the conservation and restoration of mural painting. This is a way of approaching new systems of heritage management to the students of the Fine Arts School of the RU, so that later they could implement sustainable interventions in the field of the Uruguayan mural heritage.

KEYWORDS

- Allegory to work
- Colonia del Sacramento Social Realism
- conservation
- Felipe Seade
- heritage activation
- heritage management
- Miguel Engel Battegazzore
- mural painting
- restoration
- social function
- sustainability
- sustainable intervention

REFERENCES AND BIBLIOGRAPHY

Ainsa, F. (2008). *Espacios de la memoria: Lugares y paisajes de la cultura uruguaya;* Ediciones Trilce: Montevideo, p. 106. ISBN 13: 978-99-7432-484-8.

Alcina Franch, J. (1982). *El fenómeno del arte en el marco de la sociedad y la cultura.* Alianza Editorial: Madrid.

Álvarez, T. (1983). *Catálogo del Museo de Arte Moderno de Buenos Aires.* Buenos Aires.

Benvenuto L. (1981). *Breve historia del Uruguay.* Ediciones Arca: Montevideo.

Caetano, G., Rilla, J. P. (2005). *Historia contemporánea del Uruguay. De la colonia al Mercosur*. 3rd ed., CLAEH/Fin de Siglo: Montevideo, ISBN: 99-7461-429-5.

Escuela Nacional de Bellas Artes. (1986). *Texto de apertura* in *Folleto Exposición Homenaje*. Intendencia de Montevideo. University of the Republic y Escuela Nacional de Bellas Artes: Montevideo.

Espinola, M. (1986). *Catálogo: Felipe Seade Exposición homenaje*. Escuela Nacional de Bellas Artes: Montevideo.

Goldman, S., Handwerg, M. J., Stein P., Faulkner, S., & Pacheco, M. (1996). *Otras rutas hacia Siqueiros*. Instituto Nacional de BBAA: México, ISBN: 96-8299-573-6.

Orsi Meny, Z. (2008). *Liceo departamental de Colonia. Historia y proyección*. Ediciones del Sur: Montevideo, ISBN13: 978-99-7481-492-9.

Peluffo Linari, G. (1980). *Catálogo de la exposición Seade*. Galería Latina: Montevideo.

Peluffo Linari, G. (1992). *Catalogo Realismo social en el arte uruguayo, 1930–1950*. Publicación del Museo municipal de BBAA. Museo Blanes. Ministerio de Educación y Cultura: Montevideo.

Peluffo Linari, G. (2009). *Historia de la pintura en el Uruguay*. In: *Representaciones de la modernidad, 1930–1960*. 6th ed. De la banda oriental: Uruguay, Vol. 2. ISBN: 99-7410-053-4.

Rivero, S., & Carro, L. (2002). *La construcción de la identidad: 1912–2002*. Ediciones Revista U. Liceo de Colonia: Colonia del Sacramento.

Santamarina-Campos, V., Carabal-Montagud, M. A., & De-Miguel-Molina, M. (2013). *Design and implementation of inclusive cultural policies: contemporary uruguayan muralism as sustainable assets activation*. In Tourism & Creative industry. Workshop Proceedings; UPV, Servicio de Publicaciones.

Santamarina, V. Carabal, M. A. De Miguel, M., & Martínez, E. M. (2015). Social agents and Contemporary Uruguayan muralism. New trends of research and Heritage Management Plan. Sánchez, M. Shank, W. y Fuster, L. (Eds) *Conservation Issues in Modern and Contemporary Murals*. Cambridge Scholars Publishing: United Kingdom, pp. 406–430.

Santamarina, V., & Carabal, M. A. (2013). *Informe Final del proyecto Función social del muralismo uruguayo del siglo XX como vehículo y modelo de activación patrimonial sustentable. Descentralización, identidad y memoria*. Ministerio de Asuntos Exteriores y de Cooperación.

Santamarina, V., & Carabal, M. A. (2014). *Informe Final del proyecto Función social del muralismo uruguayo del siglo XX como vehículo y modelo de activación patrimonial sustentable*. Universitat Politècnica de Valéncia.

Santamarina, V., & Carabal, M. A. (2016). *Informe finaldel proyecto Diseño e implementación de políticas culturales inclusivas: el muralismo uruguayo contemporáneo como herramienta de activación patrimonial sustentable*. Ministerio de Economía y Competitividad, Dirección General de Investigación Científica y Técnica.

Santamarina, V., Carabal, M. A., De Miguel, M., & Martínez, M. L. (2015). Societal and environmental sustainable tourism development. New ways of activation, delivery- and difussion of the Contemporary Uruguayan muralism. M. Shank, W. & Fuster, L. (Eds.) *Conservation Issues in Modern and Contemporary Murals*. Cambridge Scholars Publishing: United Kingdom, pp. 489–512.

Sullivan, E. J. (1996). *Arte latinoamericano del siglo XX.* Ed. Nerea S.A,.: Madrid, ISBN: 84-895-6904-5.

This Wednesday a workshop on "Gender and violence" was held (July 21, 2016). Newspaper, the weekly of Colonia. Recovered from http://www.colonianoticias.com.uy/.

INTERVIEWS

- Informant 1. Didier Calvar. Profile: Lecturer of Arts History, Faculty of Humanities and Education Science (RU) and Professor of the University ORT, Montevideo. Date of Interview: 28–9–2010.
- Informant 3. Norberto Baliño. Profile: Associate Professor 1r. Period of Studies of the NIBA, RU. Coordinator of the "Academic Group for the study and analysis of the contemporary local and regional esthetics." Date of Interview: 12–10–2010.
- Informant 4. Ángel Kalenberg. Profile: Director of the Journal *Artes y Letras* in 1963. Member of the Fine Arts National Commission, 1967–69. Director of the Museum of Visual Arts, 1969–2007. Author of several books about Uruguayan art. Date of Interview: 12–10–2010.
- Informant 14. Javier Alonso. Profile: Lecturer in the NIBA of Montevideo. Emergent artist of Montevideo (figurative style). Date of Interview: 12–10–2010.
- Informant 24. Miguel Angel Battegazzore. Profile: Artist and lecturer. Date of Interview: 2–4–2011.
- Informant 29. Mari Miranda. Profile: Ex director Restoring Workshop CCHN-ECM. Date of Interview: 6–4–2011.
- Informant 30. Silvestre Peciar. Profile: Lecturer of Fine Arts/Sculpture and painting. Date of Interview: 7–4–2011.
- Informant 32. Carolina and Juan Felipe Seade. Profile: Artists of recognized prestige in Uruguay. Descendants of muralist Felipe Seade. Date of Interview: 14–4–2011.
- Informant 37. Nenusa Carmen Peralta. Profile: Local community Colonia del Sacramento. Date of Interview: 19–4–2011.
- Informant 51. Carlos Deganello. Profile: Director of the Culture Department IMC. Date of Interview: 26–4–2011.
- Informant 60. Juan Flo. Profile: Full Professor of Aesthetics. Humanities Faculty. 11–06–2013.
- Informant 74. Gabriel Peluffo. Profile: Ex Director Fine Arts Local Museum Juan Blanes. 28–06–2013.
- Informant 78. Daniel Barbeito. Plastic artist of Colonia del Sacramento. 31–12–2013.

INDEX

A

acrylic
　emulsion, 232
　micro-emulsion, 233
Action-research methodology, 114
activation model, 213
advocacy, 32, 264
Afro-American slaves, 117
agricultural lands, 83
air conditioning mechanisms, 279
airbrush
　color application, 232
　watercolor, 242
Allegory to work, 8–10, 12, 14, 15, 50, 62, 66, 69–71, 76, 80, 81, 88, 90, 91, 108, 110, 127–130, 140, 141, 160, 164, 178, 183, 185, 191–193, 196, 200, 212, 213, 223–226, 228, 242, 252, 273, 281, 284, 288, 294, 303, 304, 307, 313
ambient temperature, 272, 273, 276
　deterioration process, 272
　relative humidity, 272
Americanism themes, 55
Analysis/evaluation of,
　mural deterioration risk, 277
　building, 279
　mural painting, 278
　space: hall, 279
　secondary source, 12
analytical test, 87
anthropologist, 43, 97, 98
anthropology, 14, 98, 103
antisocial behavior, 259
aqueous-alcoholic mixture, 231
architectural
　projects, 35
　structure, 272

Art
　Deco expression, 28
　exhibitions, 69
　market institutions, 37
Artistic
　contextualization, 198, 199
　development, 66
　expressions, 43
　language, 56, 76
　movement, 50, 80, 223, 302
　production, 55, 62, 76, 80, 88
　street movement, 311
　techniques, 302
　testimony, 90
artwork penetration capacity, 142
asymmetrical confrontation, 98
authoritarianism, 259
autobiographies, 12
avant-garde art movements, 32, 38
awareness campaigns, 42

B

Bangor, 98–101, 103
　Young Newton, 100
Beautification of city, 288
benchmarking method, 289, 290
bibliographic documentary, 50, 51, 81
biennial (modern museum), 37
Bingham's medal/right, 100
Bogside murals, 102, 258, 265

C

Canadian independence, 259
Candombe, 115
capillarity, 278
carved scrawl, 88
Cataloguing model design, 197
　inventory sheet, 197, 198
　technical documentation sheets, 198, 199

Cathedral Quarter, 265
Catholic
   families, 100
   neighborhoods, 261
centenary celebration, 55
chemical
   analyzes, 168
   mineralogical characterization, 16
chromatic
   coordinates, 165
   data, 164, 167, 178
   palette, 309
   register, 167
   reintegration, 232, 244, 245
   scanning, 165
   variation, 164, 179
chromatism, 176
chrome orange, 176, 185, 188, 191, 192
City branding, 248, 262
cityscapes, 259
civic
   life, 257
   participation, 118
classical antiquity, 32
clay minerals, 188, 191, 192
cleaning
   methodologies, 231
   mode, 280
   process, 17, 152, 160, 231, 233
   service, 279, 281
collective identity, 52, 197, 213, 252, 277
Colonia del Sacramento
   social realism, 313
   world heritage site, 133
Colonial
   heritage, 119
   identity, 127
   muralism, 110
colorimetric, 15, 17, 109, 130, 164–168, 176, 179, 196, 198, 213
   analysis, 176
   characterization, 16
   measurement, 16, 17, 168, 196
   monitoring, 15, 109, 130
   record, 199, 201, 202
   studies, 164, 179
   values, 167
Colorimetry, 130
communal, 258, 259, 265, 266
   consensus, 265
   moral consensus, 260
communicating vessels, 46
community
   consensus, 259, 261
   development, 299
   heritage, 303
   mural movement, 260
   murals, 102, 264
   participation, 109, 309
Conservation
   field, 131
   methodologies, 131
consistency, 242
constituent materials, 198, 273, 278
constructive universalism, 10, 303
constructivism, 2, 32
consumerism, 43
contact video-microscopy, 16
contemporary
   art, 37
   cities, 262
   muralism, 10, 12, 13, 18, 131
   wall paintings, 206
conventional radiation techniques, 142
Cooperative, 42
   gymkhana, 112
   interactive competition, 115
   plural development, 118
cornerstone, 252
craftsmanship, 86
cultural
   assets, 8
   cachet, 263
   center, 284, 298
   development, 83
      policies, 10
   heritage, 1, 5, 8, 10, 12, 13, 15, 26, 27, 45, 49, 50, 65, 79, 105, 106, 108, 109, 112, 114, 118, 128–130, 139, 140, 163, 181, 195, 211, 225, 226,

262, 263, 267, 271, 294, 298, 301, 307, 311
house, 9, 111, 274, 276, 286, 288, 289, 294–299, 304, 305, 307
   program, 293
muralism heritage, 288
natural heritage, 112, 114, 122, 129
properties, 106, 119
richness, 263
rights, 118
tourism, 7, 252, 299

D

Data
   collection, 226
   processing, 16
Decentralization, 24, 25, 132, 196, 213
decorative function, 259
Definitive material identification, 152
degradation products, 182
democratic, 53, 108, 258
democratization construction, 108
demolition, 309, 311
deontological code, 127
Depression-era murals, 260
deterioration process, 17, 272
devastation, 54, 262
dictatorship, 42, 53, 86
didactic
   intention, 57
   nature, 55
diffusion sheet, 205, 206
digital photographic documentation, 16, 17
Direct intervention, 17
   projects, 226
dissemination, 25–27, 46, 130, 206, 213, 281, 303
diverse paint layers, 229
documentary
   films, 12
   references, 89
documentation, 25, 50, 51, 62, 66, 67, 80, 90, 91, 125, 127, 142, 196, 197, 201–206

domination, 51, 53, 54, 62
Dry
   physicochemical cleaning tests, 229
   point compasses, 222
   painting technique, 214
durability, 86, 232

E

Economic
   benefits, 290, 293
   communicative dimension, 122
   development, 53, 107, 108, 122, 125, 127, 290, 299
   politic element, 122
   political power, 97
educational levels, 45
effective cultural events, 43
egalitarian connections, 25
egg-encaustic technique, 86
electrical installation, 141
electromagnetic radiation, 143, 160
elemental
   compositions, 183
   determination, 182
   semiquantitative analysis, 184
elite cultural consumers, 266
emblematic mural, 285
encaustic, 38, 86, 87, 214
enshrinement, 101
environmental
   conditions, 141, 272, 273, 278–280
   data, 140, 199
   sustainable development, 8
ephemeral, 258, 263, 295
   political statements, 258
epigrams, 30
epistemic conception, 32
epitaphs, 30
equalitarian tendencies, 2
equity/integration, 43
erection, 97
erosions, 88, 213, 214, 218, 242
esthetic, 2, 4, 55, 56, 95, 101, 199, 213, 260, 266, 302
   adaptation, 266

charge, 237
plastic formations, 56
significance, 4
ethical commitment, 29
ethnicity, 98
ethnographic, 98, 103, 295
   research, 8, 10, 305, 308
   study, 12
ethno-national
   claims, 261
   living space, 99
exaltation, 303
exhibition spaces, 294
experimentation period, 2
expert testimonies, 81
extensive quotation, 44
extortion, 100
extrajudicial activities, 101
extrinsic nature, 278

F

Façades (informant 40), 107
Facebook account of cultural center, 296
Felipe Seade, 67
   biography, 69
   work, 69–76
financial investment, 293
fissures, 98, 215
fluorescence characteristic, 160
forge alliances, 54
formalism, 31
formative process, 40
framework of collaboration, 226
fresco technique, 73
functionality, 278, 280
fundamental rights, 66

G

gallery art, 257, 261
gastronomic heritage, 114, 115
genital embellishment, 102
gentrification process, 107
geometric
   abstraction, 38
   art, 30

German fleet, 101
globalization, 7, 8
glocalization, 8, 108
Gothic romantic art mural, 102
government training projects, 293
graffiti, 46, 100, 102, 103, 231, 232, 259, 261, 264, 277, 278, 288
graphic
   art, 28
   representation, 168
graphical texture, 232
graphite, 87, 218, 219
grassroots solidarity, 260
gray monotony, 263
gypsum, 185, 188, 192, 232, 233, 273

H

Hampton Court, 95, 96, 102, 103
hegemony, 43
heritage
   activation, 8, 9, 18, 109, 132, 196, 307, 313
   artifacts, 258, 263, 264
   deactivation, 9, 10
   exploitation, 122
   investment, 284
   management, 4, 118, 122, 128, 252, 313
   policies, 106
   resources, 294
   restitution, 106
   sacking, 116
   sustainability, 118
   sustainable responsibility, 125
   values, 108, 131
heritagization, 8, 132, 133
heterogeneity, 231
historical
   events, 51, 212, 237
   neighborhood, 107, 112, 115, 119
   quarter, 291, 295
   research, 62, 140
historic-artistic value, 12
history paintings, 260
holistic training, 25

Index 321

hospitality facilities, 288
House of culture, 62, 70, 81, 82, 141, 226, 308
human drama, 29, 68, 303
humanist realism work, 56, 62, 80
humid subtropical climate, 276
hygroscopicity, 278

I

iconic image of British soldiers, 100
iconographic
　aspects, 80
　description, 199, 303
ideal citizenry, 259
identitarian
　art, 2, 56
　symbols, 12
ideological
　conflicts, 62
　dispute, 46
　expression, 260
　individualities, 302
　nuances, 50, 56
　retaliations, 88
　social conflicts, 53
　struggle, 53
illusionist chromatic reintegration, 8
imagined community, 258
immaterial heritage, 114–116
immigrant groups, 54
impeccable management, 298
impregnation, 231, 233
incidence angle, 144
incision marks, 87
incontrovertible images, 99
Information digitalization, 15
Infrared
　photography, 149, 156, 161
　ultraviolet radiation, 130
inorganic material, 231
inscriptions, 88, 144, 160, 218, 219, 221
institutional frames, 261
institutionalization, 129
instrument calibration, 165
Instrumentation, 142, 163, 164, 184

intangible heritage, 285
Intendancy, 108, 287, 303, 311
intercommunal relationships, 258
interculturalism, 10
interdisciplinary team, 197, 200
Internal
　paint layers, 17
　political structure, 53
international
　agencies research projects, 293
　art conceptions, 2
　languages, 56
intervention, 8–15, 17, 80, 91, 106, 109, 110, 127–130, 140, 196, 212, 214, 216, 219, 222, 224, 226, 228–233, 237, 242, 249, 252, 272, 284, 288, 294, 304, 306, 311
　campaigns, 226
　management, 14
　process, 8, 9, 80, 110, 140, 224, 249, 304
　proposal, 231
intimidation, 100
intracommunal tensions, 262
inventory sheet, 197, 198, 206
inventorying, 15, 109, 129
Irish culture, 265
iron oxides, 169, 176, 192

J

Japanese paper, 230, 231, 233–236

L

laser distance-metric record device, 16
lead
　chromates, 169
　white, 188, 191, 192
legitimacy, 260, 261
legitimate
　heritage, 132
　implication, 109
　response, 261
legitimization, 263
liberal/authoritarian tendencies, 53
light radiation, 196

lightfatnes, 237
lineage/prestigious heritage, 54
Link-Oxford-Isis X-ray microanalysis system, 184
literary art, 33
lithopone, 168, 185, 186, 188, 191, 192
livestock farming, 54
local
   government scheme, 261
   identity, 112, 298, 299
   national media, 243
localization, 15, 152
loss of identity, 223
loyalism, 101
Luminist roots, 28
luxmetric, 16
lyceum, 82, 86, 90

M

Macro
   photography, 142, 144
   photos, 17
maintenance logbook, 281
management process, 106
maritime market, 117
marketing places, 299
masculine/masterly, 95
matèriel remnant, 263
mean colorimetric values, 166
mechanical stability, 231
mechanization, 117
mercantilist degradation, 107
metallurgical work, 83
metamerism, 156
methodology, 9, 11, 14, 109, 114, 118, 164, 213, 229
   participatory action research, 14, 109, 114, 118
Mexican
   muralism, 302, 303
   muralist, 29, 55, 62, 76, 80, 302, 303
   revolution, 1, 55, 259
microphotography, 144
microscale coating, 183
military mural, 101

mimetic retouching reintegration, 237
minium, 169, 192
mis-interpretation, 101
model country, 31
modernity, 24, 32, 53
monographs, 12, 51, 67, 81
monumental heritage, 114
mortar, 16, 97, 216
mosaic, 34, 35, 38, 40
mulatta, 303
multianalytical research, 182
multifunctional environmental controller, 141
mundane landscapes, 262
Municipality, 89, 228
Mural
   art, 34, 258, 259, 290, 299
   assets, 252
   interpretations, 101
   intervention, 9, 110
   painting campaigns, 40
   painting, 24, 28, 40, 42, 81, 272
   tradition, 259
muralism, 8, 10, 12–14, 288, 308
muralist production, 2, 50, 73, 303
murals, 1, 2, 4, 7–9, 12–14, 24–26, 29, 34, 38, 45, 46, 57, 59, 66, 69, 73, 95, 99, 101, 102, 127, 141, 196, 197, 216, 257–267, 284, 288–291, 293, 295, 299, 305, 308, 309, 311
museographic program, 11
museological
   itinerary, 290
   proposal, 284
mutilated/distorted reality, 33
mutilation, 226

N

National
   borders, 42
   flag creation law, 73
   heritage, 228
   historical monument, 7
   institutional level, 25
   painters, 56

Index

party, 52
recession, 223
nationalism, 2, 56
nationalist
   identity standards, 55
nation or solidarity-building, 258
neighborhood-level organizations, 264
nonconformist character, 2, 56
nondescript urban landscapes, 263
Non-governmental organizations (NGOs), 11, 290
noninvasive analysis method, 140, 161, 182
Non-visible radiation photographs, 149
   infrared photography, 156–160
   ultraviolet fluorescence photography, 149–155
novelty, 37

O

ochre, 87, 89, 101, 169, 176, 184, 192, 215
open-air museum, 107
optical microscopy (OM), 182, 191, 193
optimal
   intervention, 213
   preservation, 228
organic
   binder, 86, 214
   synthesis, 11
organizational model, 281
organoleptic
   analysis, 218
   physicochemical analyzes, 199
   study, 140, 196, 213
original
   painting, 87, 151, 154, 226, 230, 233, 237
   pictorial layer, 214, 216
outdoor paintings, 9
over-interpretation, 101

P

Painting room, 307
panorama, 132, 226
paramilitary
   groups, 261
   mural, 101, 261
participatory
   action methodology, 118
   action research (PAR), 10, 14, 18, 105, 106, 109, 132
   collective values, 118, 122
   constructive dialog, 112
   group dynamics, 114, 119, 123
   interactive dialog, 116
   investigation, 122
   social tools, 114
Patriarchs, 70
patriotic celebration procession, 73
pedagogical
   educational experiences, 26
   program, 26
   stance, 44
perimeter zones, 218
periodical publication, 30
personnel administration, 281
photo index reference, 198
photochemical degradation processes, 273
photographed area, 144
photographic
   analysis, 109, 119
   record, 140–142, 196, 198
   register, 160
   techniques, 141, 143, 152
   video-graphic record, 15
photography, 15, 17, 29, 39, 130, 139–143, 150, 160, 161, 213, 215–217, 219, 266
physical
   chemical resistance, 214
   identification, 15
physicochemical, 198
   analysis, 152, 160
   record, 199
   study, 196
pictorial
   consolidation, 231
   inpainting, 216

layer, 214–216, 219, 222, 223, 231, 232
surface, 140–143, 168, 233, 237
technique, 143, 222
picturesque places, 288
pigmented polychromic samples, 185, 192
pigments, 86, 87, 89, 151, 156, 160, 182, 184, 192, 193, 213, 273
plaster, 86, 89, 214–216, 232, 273, 278
plaster/vinyl synthetic resin, 216
Plastiglas, 35
pluralistic sector, 38
poaching license, 97
politic activities, 127
political
   cultural program, 55
   murals, 29, 264
   opportunity, 55
   party affiliations, 38
   social movement, 10
   struggle, 46
polyester resin, 183
polyvinyl acetate, 87
popular
   art, 55, 62
   culture, 46, 110, 118
   sales, 42
positivism, 33
post-revolutionary government, 259
power switch box, 102
pre-Columbian culture roots, 56
pregnant woman, 83, 86
preliminary restorations, 198
pre-renaissance art technique, 86, 214
prerogatives, 73
preventive conservation, 17, 18, 206, 272, 273, 280, 282, 298
   actions, 272
   plan, 271, 280
primitive art, 32
private
   businesses, 264
   commissions, 258
   economic interests, 127
   educational institutions, 311
   resources, 265
   transport, 291
professional
   education, 249
   intrusiveness, 5
   license, 97
   profiles, 13
   visual examination, 164
preventive conservation plan proposal, 280
   building, 281
   mural painting, 280
   space: hall, 280, 281
protein binder, 86
protein-based tempera mixture, 214
Protestant
   group, 99
   neighborhoods, 261
Prussian blue pigments, 168, 188, 192
pseudo-military signifiers, 99
public
   art, 46, 258, 259, 262, 267
   policy strategy, 284, 298
   private archives, 12, 50, 66, 81
   sphere, 258

Q

quartz, 185, 188, 192

R

radical confrontation, 37
radicalization, 31
rational knowledge, 32
reactionary policies, 31
reactivation, 132, 309
recognition, 46, 50, 212
Record data, 198
recuperation, 14
Red reflectography, 17
redundancies, 69
reflectance, 164, 165, 176
reflection spectrometry, 165
reflective attitude, 83
refunctionalization, 108
regimented bank, 100

regional human landscape, 32
Reimaging communities, 261
relative humidity (RH), 140, 141, 199, 213, 272, 273, 276, 279, 280
rendition, 100
replastering, 89
reports/expert testimony, 67
Republican
   murals, 261
   paramilitarism, 261
restoration, 5–9, 11, 13, 17, 25, 89, 126, 141, 164, 182, 198, 206, 224, 226, 228, 232, 242, 248–252, 263, 274, 277, 278, 280, 305, 308, 313
restorative techniques, 226
reversible process, 229
Revolución de los, 52
roaming deer, 97
Romper room, 264
roof apex, 100
royal park, 97
rural population, 68, 80, 303

S

sabotage, 266
safeguard measures, 197
sandpaper, 237
saponified wax emulsion, 86
saturation point, 273
savage battles, 100
scalpel, 230, 231, 237, 238
scanning
   document capture, 51, 67, 81
   electron microscopy, 182, 191, 193
scientific cataloguing, 11, 17, 18
sectarian
   landscapes, 263
   politics, 263
selfconsumption, 54
semiotic imagery, 101
semiquantitative determinations, 16
sensibilization, 10, 14, 18
sensitization, 108–110, 114, 128, 132, 133
   community program, 128, 133

project, 110
   training program, 108, 109, 132
sgraffitto signatures, 213
shorthand staccato signatures, 102
sienna, 87, 237
Silver River's natural assets, 288
site-specific nature/quality, 258, 262, 266
social
   archetype, 67, 80, 303
   artistic context, 50
   assemblies, 52
   atomization, 51
   awareness, 26, 50
   conflicts, 55
   construction, 46
   criticism, 32
   documentary commitment, 73
   economic balance, 106
   function, 8, 10, 11, 13, 117, 295, 302, 313
   mentor, 302
   participation, 108
   political forces, 98
   realism, 2–4, 29–33, 38, 50, 54, 55, 62, 66, 67, 69, 76, 117, 212, 223, 260, 284, 302
   redemption, 29
   relationships, 54
   sensibilization, 10, 18
   structure, 97, 125
   symbolism, 289
societal
   harmony, 262
   problems, 263
Socio-cultural changes, 52
sociological perspectives, 266
sociopolitical events, 212
sovereignty, 73
Spanish Civil War, 29
spatula, 89, 237
spectrophotometer, 164–166
spectrum, 142, 165, 186–190, 192, 260
Specular component excluded (SCE), 164, 167, 172

Specular component included (SCI), 164, 167, 168, 174, 177, 178
stability, 52, 232, 237
stakeholders, 8, 11, 25, 106, 197, 311
   academics, 11
   local community, 11
   NGOs, 11
   public institutions, 11
standard deviation, 166, 167, 178
state
   buildings, 263
   oppression, 261
stenciling, 46
strategic marketing process, 289
Stratigraphic study, 16
structural instability, 213, 218
stucco, 184, 216, 218, 231, 237–239, 241
sustainability, 112, 114, 118, 122, 125, 133, 313
sustainable
   activation of heritage, 24, 25
   cultural management, 109
   development, 109, 122, 123, 128, 132, 252
   heritage, 8, 118, 128, 132, 196, 213
   heritagization, 118
   intervention, 106, 129, 313
   management, 8, 26, 50, 114, 281
symbolic
   cultural capital, 260
   social value, 224, 281
symptomatic, 263
synergies, 10, 11, 108
systematic implementation, 199
systematization, 26

T

Tango dance, 115
tapestry, 34, 35
Tartan street gangs, 100
Technical
   analysis/materials, 199
   documentation sheets, 198
   knowledge, 9, 13
   material experimentation, 69
   pictorial execution, 140
technological/cultural development, 90
television aerials, 100
tempera technique, 87
temple method, 86
terror tourism, 263
Test
   evaluation, 229
   protocol, 229
thermodynamic transformations, 272
thermohygrometric room factors, 273
Titanic Belfast marketing, 264
tonalities, 90, 212, 222
topography, 144
tortas fritas, 115
tourism, 1, 8, 44, 49, 65, 79, 105, 107, 108, 110, 122, 125, 127, 129, 132, 257, 258, 262, 267, 283–290, 294, 296, 298, 299
   attraction, 107
tourist
   board, 263, 265
   commercial interests, 108
   cultural attractor, 288
   culture demand, 106
   destination, 293
   itinerary, 289
   observatory, 106
   promotion, 288
trading, 54
tradition/relevance, 43
traditional
   art circuits, 38
   circuits, 38
   language, 62
   societies, 32
   society, 54
Training program, 15, 106
transcendence, 309
tratteggio technique, 232

U

Ulster
   Defence Association (UDA), 100

Index

freedom fighters (UFF), 99–102
ultramarine, 168, 192
ultraviolet
    fluorescence photography, 149
    light, 152
umber, 185, 188, 191, 192
unification, 73
unqualified practice, 127, 132
urban/regional policy-makers, 258
Uruguayan
    art, 4, 14, 27, 31–33, 52
    artistic heritage, 249
    artistic panorama, 10
    contemporary mural, 132
    cultural expressions, 128
    cultural heritage, 206
    economy, 294
    flag, 115
    heritage, 11, 132
    history, 55, 57, 62, 223
    independence, 52, 70
    lifestyle, 223
    maps, 115
    mural national heritage, 243
    muralism, 8, 12, 13, 18, 24, 25, 284
    nationality, 303
    social realism, 56, 62, 76, 80, 91
    society, 52, 54, 55, 66, 83, 90, 212
utilitarian official architecture, 263

V

vandalism, 88, 144, 218, 295
vertical illumination, 280
video-endoscopy, 15
vinyl binder, 216
violent imagery, 261

visible
    invisible radiation, 130
    light photography, 142
        general/detailed photographs, 142, 143
        macro/microphotography, 144–149
        photography with oblique light, 144
    radiation, 17, 141, 161
    spectrophotometric, 16
visual
    arts, 24, 27, 28, 32
    elements, 73
    test, 216
volumetric sensors, 281
volunteer programs, 294

W

Wall
    paintings, 76, 141, 182
    to-wall, 97, 103
water management, 54
Western art, 27
wooden shutters, 274
woodwork, 274
work ethic, 69
World heritage site, 284

X

X-ray microanalysis, 193

Z

zinc white, 186, 191, 192

PGSTL 11/20/2017